Post-Marxism
and
the Middle East

Edited by
Faleh A. Jabar

POST-MARXISM
AND
THE MIDDLE EAST

Saqi Books

British Library Cataloguing-in-Publication Data
A catalogue record for this book is available from the British Library

ISBN 0 86356 961 7 (hb)

This edition first published 1997

In-house editor: Jana Gough

Saqi Books
26 Westbourne Grove
London W2 5RH

Contents

1. Introduction

Faleh A. Jabar

On the eve, during and after the collapse of the Soviet Union, the various strands of Marxism worldwide have faced the gravest crisis in their history. The chain of developments unleashed by Gorbachev's *perestroika*, *glasnost* and 'new political thinking' culminated in the disintegration of what had hitherto been known in Marxist jargon as the socialist camp or the world of existing socialism. Some of the events in this process were dramatic: the execution of the Romanian dictator Ceauşescu, the collapse of the Berlin Wall and the removal of communist-led regimes through popular protest. In the end, the genie boomeranged against its very initiator, Gorbachev himself, who was ousted from office twice: first, by his own party and hard-line generals (the failed coup attempt from 19 to 21 August 1991) and then by the new liberals emerging from within the party (Yeltsin, on 25 December 1991).

These historical events changed the world. They marked the end of the Cold War era, paved the way for a globalized market economy and unleashed a third wave of nationalism. As part of the backlash came what a liberal review called 'the Decline of the Left'.[1] Indeed, the demise of the Soviet Union, which represented the climax of this process, meant the collapse of socialism as an attractive model and the apparent bankruptcy of Marxism itself as an intellectual tool to analyse world and national processes. It should be remembered that, for some developing countries, existing socialism had provided moral support, inspiration and material backing. For the Arab radicals, there was the additional loss of a superpower ally on whose military, economic and political patronage they could count.

The theoretical and moral loss sustained by the left was very similar throughout the world, but the responses differed. Compared to West European leftists' quest for new theoretical venues and practical solutions, Marxism in the Arab world was far less creative or productive. It is true that West European responses had started earlier on: Eurocommunism was one; identity politics, as distinct from class politics, was another; radical democracy was a third; and a global civil society was another. Needless to say, Marxism in the West was invigorated by the challenge posed by the progress in social and philosophical thought. The apparent failure of the Soviet model was another factor. The relative autonomy of research and the freer flow of information in a pluralistic, open society (in which differences prevailed) enhanced the quest.

By contrast, Marxists in the Arab world responded only after the demise of the Soviet Union. The event has left a sense of desperation and *angst* among the new generation of Arab Marxist activists, leaders and intellectuals. The previous experiences of this generation had been traumatic. Unlike the old guard, who had bathed in the sun of Soviet and other socialist successes (the triumph against Nazi Germany in 1945, the victory of the Chinese communists in 1949, the phenomenal rise of Indo-China in 1954 and the Cuban revolution in 1959), the orphans of the Gorbachev era had experienced successive defeats at the hands of the rising nationalists (Nasser of Egypt, Boumedienne of Algeria, Saddam Hussein of Iraq and Numeiri of Sudan, to name but a few). The zeal, confidence and vitality of this generation had been eroded by years of persecution, and the vacuum they had left was frequently occupied by the rising new current of Islamic fundamentalism. In retrospect, the end of existing socialism was merely the dramatic climax to a long, arduous chain reaction. But for this generation it was an abrupt rupture. Finding themselves exposed, a painful search for identity followed.

A mood of scepticism prevailed—both in the fruitful sense of a critical scrutinizing of theoretical and practical issues, and in the traumatic sense of suffering from the 'unbearable lightness of being', in Kundera's words. Essential questions were raised: How and why was socialism, presumably a higher stage in the schematic development of social formations, so technologically backward and industrially underproductive? Why had the state not withered away under socialism as promised in theory; or why had it grown into an omnipotent and omnipresent Leviathan? Why was the working-class state so unrepresentative of the working class proper? Why had the capitalist class not only survived in the West but held firm, although it was divisively represented by various political parties? Why had the working class in Eastern Europe, by contrast (represented by a single, unified, monolithic party) lost power? If the Marxist schema of world history is flawed, what is the actuality and potentiality of the world system, if the latter term has any meaning at all? Is there any teleological end in history? What is the real image of the world system today? Is the concept of imperialism still valid? What role, if any, may the market economy play in future development? What in fact *is* development? Has planning any role?

The old set of theoretical concepts, which had hitherto been accepted almost uncritically, was questioned anew. The classical formulae had explained the past, the present and the future, defined stages of development in the idiom of socioeconomic formations and pure class struggle, fixed the various roles of social classes at every stage, and provided the organizational instruments needed to effect change and interpret the universe (nature, society and thought, the Hegelian-Marxian trinity)—all this implied a world that was known, predicted and even controlled in advance. Even providence could not have organized world history in such a lucid way. This world, however, collapsed.

The veterans of Marxism in the Arab region pronounced their final word. For example, the oldest communist leader in the Mashriq, Khaled Bekdash, did so a year or so before his death in 1995. In his memoirs[2] he stated his philosophical will: the world is wrong. He insisted that the international working class would stage a come-back and would ultimately prevail. The new generation had a different response, however. They re-examined Soviet-interpreted classical tenets with a sceptical, free-thinking approach. A sort of Manheimian de-hypnotism started. Radical Arab nationalists also began to rethink their positions.

The Marxists who have come out of this process are very different from what they had been before it started. Various trends are now in the making. This book attempts to describe and trace the theoretical issues and endeavours which have influenced and shaped this rethinking. The chapters are structured around several major, interconnected themes: an examination of the theoretical, political and organizational responses evident so far among the Marxists in the Arab world. Needless to say, changes in this field are far from final; an analysis of abstract, theoretical issues which have a pivotal importance in the Marxist conception and are shared in different national settings; an examination of globalization; and an analysis of the demise of the Soviet Union itself on the one hand, and how this was seen by the major Arab ruling elites on the other.

Most chapters have an explicit or implicit comparative outlook that reveals to what extent Marxism in the Arab world has common inherited features with, or divergent perspectives from, its European counterpart.

The book resulted from a seminar organized at the School of Oriental and African Studies, University of London, in June 1995. The contributors are well-known academics, practising politicians or both: they are all respected figures in academic and Marxist circles. Five contributors come from the Middle East.

Part One

The Demise of Marxism, and the Arab World

2. *Marxism and the Arab World*

Fred Halliday

Perhaps I can begin this chapter with a personal reminiscence: nearly thirty years ago, when I was a student at London's School of Asian and African Studies, we had a Marxist discussion forum. Among its various activities, the SOAS Marxist Group sought to develop a Marxist analysis of the Middle East. Quite a number of students from the Arab world participated in that forum—some of them were veterans or members of Arab communist parties and some belonged to the Arab nationalist movement. They included Palestinians, Persians, Kurds and Turks. At that time we thought we knew what the 'correct' position was on the Middle East: there was imperialism, there was zionism, there was Arab reaction, there was capitalist oppression and what we had to do was apply a series of general concepts. It is worth recalling against whom the argument was directed: there were three targets, three points of reference in terms of which this Marxist discussion—as it affected people here in the West, rather than people in the Middle East—was defined.

The first was what is very broadly termed 'orientalism', i.e. conventional, ahistorical analysis. (The term 'orientalism' is much abused these days to cover almost anything about the Middle East, including much that is sensible.) It was an attempt to critique an approach to the Middle East, and to Arab society, according to which the latter was unchanging: this approach denied the role of social factors, including class, laid excessive emphasis on the importance of Islam in defining Arab society, and so on. Since that time we have had a huge literature on orientalism: Edward Said[1] is not the first to write about this, nor is he, in my view, the best. But the critique of this orthodox academic approach, the critique in the name of history, in the name of social and materialist analysis, and in the name of some possibility of emancipation, was certainly one starting-point.

There was a second starting-point, however: a critique of the predominant social science of the period—modernization theory—and the idea that the Middle East, like other parts of the developing world, could develop along a series of stages towards something called modern society. The debate on imperialism, in particular, and the application of concepts of imperialism to the Middle East, seemed to be a way of countering modernization theory, above all because by talking about imperialism one is talking about the obstacles to modernization, about impediments to economic and political development, and one is also providing a very different history of where Middle Eastern societies have come from. They have not come from the undifferentiated 'Islamic' past or the 'Ottoman' past; they have come from a particular pattern of political and economic domination arising in the late nineteenth and early twentieth centuries. The way in which imperialism was introduced into the discussion was therefore a critique of modernization theory.

There was, however, a third point of reference, which originated more in the region itself—this was the Marxist critique of Arab nationalism, and in particular the critique of Nasserism. As far as a non-Arab Marxist audience of the mid-1960s was concerned, the starting-point for much debate about the Arab world was the discussion about Arab nationalism and, in particular, the debate about the Egyptian revolution which was by then some ten years old. On the one hand, there was the emergence of a defence of the Egyptian revolution, broadly framed in the Soviet Marxist terms of 'non-capitalist' development or the national democratic revolution: this reflected the alliance between Nasser on the one hand, and the Egyptian communists on the other, in the Arab Socialist Union. Against this was the emergence of an Egyptian Marxist critique, whether in the work of Samir Amin or in that of Anouar Abdel-Malek, who identified a state capitalist new class, or in the much more radical approach which emerged after the 1967 war of the authors who write jointly under the name Mahmoud Hussein.[2]

Some of the best work on the Arab world was produced in these years, in the Arabic language and in an Arab context, but there has also been in the Arab world, as elsewhere, a tendency to repeat slogans or particular terms of analysis. When I was with the guerrillas in Oman in early 1970, we would meet in the evening after the day's patrolling and shout slogans such as, 'Down with all the kings, amirs, sheikhs, sultans and imams in the Arabian peninsula.' Then they would shout, '*Taskut al-tahrifiyya*' [Down with revisionism]. One day I asked them, 'Who are the *muharrifin* [revisionists]?'

They replied, 'We don't know who these people are. We're against them but we don't know who they are.'

At the same time, part of the critique of the Nasserist regime before 1967 (and even more so afterwards) was that this showed the bankruptcy of the petty bourgeois regimes and that there was a 'crisis' of such regimes. Thus there was a crisis in Egypt, a crisis in Syria, a crisis in Iraq, and so on. As Roger Owen once said, the petty bourgeoisie are the most abused class in modern history, yet perhaps they have achieved more than any other class. The crisis of the petty bourgeois regimes, and of everything else, was inevitable; a new, more radical alternative would come. Of course, in the case of Egypt it did not come: instead of the workers' revolution there was Sadat, another kind of solution to the crisis. In Libya Qaddafi came to power—not a solution to the problem either. Elsewhere there was the long and continuing agony of the Algerian regime and the revolution in South Yemen. What appeared after 1967 to be a positive theoretical and political opening produced something else. There is still a tendency, both within the region and outside, to repeat slogans in a way that does not accord with reality. This is also true of Iran. Much of the literature on Iran, whether by orthodox Stalinists of the Tudeh type or by people in revolt against it such as the Fedayin and the Mujahidin, uses a dogmatic set of categories that still assume there is some kind of 'correct' answer.

Much has happened since that period, both in the Middle East and in the history of Marxism itself. Clearly the certainties of that period are no longer there. Here I should like to examine three broad themes which have emerged in Marxist discussion of the Arab world (*non-Arab* Marxist discussion, it should be stressed) and try to show how those ideas, and the accompanying debate, have developed. It is not a question of an off-the-shelf set of answers to a particular set of historical or immediate questions, but more of defining a zone of debate, so that if Marxism has a relevance, or insofar as it has a relevance to the Arab world, it is through defining a debate as much as through giving any set answer. The crisis of Marxism *vis-à-vis* the Arab world reflects not only a crisis of Marxism in general, but also the evolution of Marxism away from the dogmas of thirty or more years ago. At the same time, it reflects shifts in the region.

Let us turn to these three themes. In much Marxist debate about the Middle East and elsewhere, the central issue has been that of the state: this has become more evident as the years have gone by. If the starting-point for my generation was the debate on the Egyptian state, specifically the Nasserist state, this has been extended to critiques of the post-1958 regime in Iraq, or of the Algerian regime, in an attempt to show how a new pattern of social and political power has been established after profound change. It is clear not only that much can be yielded by such an analysis, but that the Middle East is not unique. One of the most important intellectual or emotional impacts of Marxist discussion on the Middle East is to deny the region's uniqueness. Of course, there are features that are specific to any country or any region; but the kind of state that has been formed in the post-colonial Middle East has much in common with countries like Pakistan, or with countries in Africa, or even with certain parts of Latin America. In other words, the debate on the state has not just revealed the social character of the state, or the interests which the state might represent; it has also revealed the location of the Middle Eastern state in a broader international pattern.

The issue of the state also touches, among other things, on the issue of Arab unity. If in the original nationalist problematic, these states were fake, artificial entities which could be removed and welded into one Arab state, and were merely the creatures of imperialism, as was often argued, then Arab unity was not a problem. But in practice, Arab unity *has* been a problem. It has been a problem because these states, however they were created, have a reality. Once ministries have been set up, there are also bureaucrats and drivers, and people with budgets (there are seven different states, four international airports and five armies in the United Arab Emirates). Once the state is established, it acquires a reality and Arab unity becomes harder to achieve. In a sense, the Arab world has lived through the history of Latin America, except that Latin America lived through it 150 years before. The Latin Americans also find it harder to blame imperialism for their own divisions, because imperialism ran away and still they could not unite. Thus the issue of the state has not only allowed a critique of the nationalist regimes but also been a way of recognizing the limits to Arab unity: the map of the Arab world today is basically as it was in 1918. The Syrian/Egyptian union (the United Arab Republic) failed. Nor did 'the unity of tanks' (or 'the unity of rifles' in the case of Iraq and Kuwait) succeed. In the case of Yemen, the North and the South first united politically but later united through war. The reality of the state has undeniably been central to the whole story of Arab nationalism: a broad analysis within a Marxist framework has made an understanding of this possible.

Here Simon Bromley's book, *Rethinking Middle East Politics*, is particularly to be recommended.[3] Bromley sets out to explain the pattern of political and social power in the Middle East within a broad Marxist framework: he sees himself, very clearly, as critiquing two other approaches. One is broadly the ahistorical or orientalist approach: in other words, the Middle East is as it is because of Islam. By contrast, Bromley argues that there are dictatorships in many countries that have nothing to do with Islam;

these dictatorships may be related to the political culture, but not specifically to religion. On the other hand, if Bromley critiques religious explanations, he also critiques the approach associated with much of the new left in Europe and America, which holds that the state in the Middle East is just a creature of imperialism. He tries to develop a more nuanced and sophisticated idea of how imperialism may have created these states, and of how oil revenues may well have kept them in existence, but argues that they are not simply the instruments of imperialism. This is a good example of how the state can be used as a focus for a much broader explanation of the modern history and politics of the Middle East. For all the evils that imperialism has perpetrated, it is hardly necessary to remind Iraqis, for example, of what the modern state is capable of doing *vis-à-vis* its own population.

The second major focus of much of the Marxist and related literature has been the stress on social movements, and in particular the attempt to apply 'class analysis' to Middle Eastern societies. Much of what is produced in the name of class analysis is dogmatic and doctrinaire and explains very little. That has been so both in the Middle East and elsewhere. But this has not prevented the emergence of a body of literature that is much more sensitive, not just to the existence of classes, but to the other factors—national identity, regional identity, faction, religious community—that affect the operation of class. So it is not a case of saying that the Middle East is the history of ideas, or of Islam, or of classes that are preserved in a dogmatic way, but of looking at the contingent, variant ways in which classes have played a role in the modern history of the Middle East. We may take it for granted now, but thirty years ago most of the academic literature refused to talk about class. The widely held view was that class had no role in the Middle East. The question we should now ask is not, 'Is class determinant?' (it is not), but 'What is the role of class, and what are the roles of dominating classes at particular moments in Middle Eastern history?'

The debate on the Egyptian revolution highlighted this issue, but often in a very polemical way. On the one hand, there was the argument that the Egyptian state, the Nasserist revolution, represented the working class and its allies in power. On the other hand, the analyses of Mahmoud Hussein maintained that the workers and peasants, after the riots at Khamshish, the 1967 war, and so on, would overthrow this 'petty bourgeois' regime. Since then, much interesting work on the history and role of the Egyptian working class has been undertaken in both Egypt and the West. Much of it focuses on the history of the Egyptian communist parties (there was never only *one*), but undertaken in a much more sensitive way than earlier research. This was influenced to some extent by the work of social historians in the West like

E. P. Thompson's *The Making of the English Working Class*, but it was at the same time located within a much broader socio-political context: it was an attempt to write, not as Thompson did, the history of the working class as almost a class on its own, but to write a history of the Egyptian working class in the context—domestic and international—of modern Egypt as a whole.[4]

Those factors which rather orthodox historians tended to write about in the 1950s and 1960s—the role of the working class in the struggle against the British in the period up to 1952, and then in the Nasserite regime—have yielded interesting perspectives on Egyptian history. The greatest book produced in the West on the role of class and of social movements in the modern Arab world is undoubtedly Hanna Batatu's work on the Iraqi revolution of 1958.[5] It is an attempt, in a non-dogmatic, creative way, to look at the role of class, tribe and ethnicity in modern Iraqi history. In a sense, it is a monumental contribution to the understanding not just of Middle Eastern or Iraqi society, but of the role of class in modern society as a whole. It is one of the strengths of Batatu's book that it has provoked a vigorous debate among people who disagree with this historical or theoretical approach. Sami Zubaida has written a very important essay showing how the emergence of classes during this period in modern Iraq intersected with other identities of community and of region in a way that Batatu had not sufficiently recognized.[6] But in a sense, Batatu's work provides an extremely rich starting-point for open discussion, one which is of great political relevance for contemporary Iraq.

Similar work has been produced in relation to other societies. Ervand Abrahamian's major reinterpretation of modern Iranian history[7] tries, in a sense, to do for Iran what Batatu did for Iraq, and although in a different idiom, there is the work of Assaf Bayat on the role of the working class in the Iranian revolution.[8] Let us not forget that for all the talk of the role of religion in the Iranian revolution, the people who actually made the revolution were, in a broad sense, members of the urban poor including a very large industrial working class. The irony of Khomeini's victory was that it came about not through people mouthing '*Allah Akbar*' all the time, but from a very old-fashioned form of struggle. It was a three-month *political general strike* that destroyed the Shah. It was not armed insurrection; it was not the action of guerrillas; it was not a military coup; it was not people praying—it was people demonstrating and organizing a political general strike. The role of that strike in the Iranian revolution, which is well recognized in the work of Bayat and others, is worth remembering. In conclusion, the last twenty or thirty years of Marxist writing on the Middle East represents a very important body of literature, and an increasingly self-critical and creative one insofar as it moves away from dogmatic conceptions of class and examines issues of culture and of social movements, including women's movements, both in the Middle East and elsewhere.

A third issue, and perhaps the most controversial of all, is that of imperialism. The conventional approach of thirty years ago was that because of imperialism, and because of the Middle East's insertion into the world capitalist market, the region was incapable of developing economically. Again, it should be stressed that this argument was not specific to the Middle East, but was a general argument (the dependency theory argument) about the Third World. The most forceful critique of the dependency theory approach came from Bill Warren of SOAS, who had done his fieldwork in an Arab country, Sudan.[9]

Warren was a communist who had worked very closely with the Sudanese Communist Party and maintained close contacts with it throughout his life. He knew many of those who died in the massacre of 1971. Warren's study of Sudan and of the role of the Sudanese working class (a class as important as that in any Middle Eastern country) but also his scepticism, born out of his Sudanese experience, about the possibility of alliances with the nationalist military, were important points of stimulation for his work as a whole. The other country he had worked in—again a Third World country with a large working class and one where 'Islamic' politics has come to play a major role—was Nigeria. Warren's central argument was that we should return to the classic Marxist position, the position that Marx himself held, namely that capitalism does not retard but develops the Third World. Yes, we live in a world which has hierarchies, inequalities and social conflict, but we should study the incorporation of the world into capitalism, and the development of industry in the Third World, just as much as the ways in which imperialism constrains development.

Warren's work has many implications for the Middle East. The first is that imperialism cannot be blamed for everything in the Middle East: the inability of Middle Eastern societies to develop, or the difficulties of industrialization, land reform and education, cannot all be ascribed to imperialism. The question to be asked is, what is the relationship between the insertion of these countries into the world market and the pattern of internal development?

Warren's work has received confirmation, or partial confirmation, from two quite different processes which have subsequently taken place, even if they do not provide a conclusive answer. One is the success of capitalist development in many areas of the Third World, but not in the Middle East. But if not in the Middle East, why not? Why have Middle Eastern countries not gone down the path of Singapore and Thailand, or Taiwan? It cannot just be imperialism, because imperialism is as strong in these countries as it is in the Middle East. It cannot be lack of capital, since the region is not short of funds, thanks to oil.

The other (more negative) factor that is relevant to Warren's argument is the record of those countries that have broken away from imperialism, or have tried to do so. They have not had a very successful economic or political record, whether in Algeria, South Yemen, Syria or Iraq. So the mere removal of the imperialist connection does not solve development problems. Warren's theoretical and political argument was a very important critique of the simplistic application of concepts of imperialism. Such concepts are still around: today many of them take the form of a critique of cultural imperialism—everything bad is a result of foreign values, everything is ethnocentrism. This is just a replay in the realm of cultural studies of the simplistic dependency theory argument of the 1960s.

The implication for the Middle East is that, whether the region is viewed from a historical or a contemporary perspective, its insertion into the world market, and into the world capitalist system, is essential to any understanding of what has happened. But this insertion cannot explain everything, and the very different economic records of the Middle East compared to other Third World countries also need taking into consideration.

Why is there virtually no direct foreign investment in the Middle East? And why is there no investment in manufacturing, with the exception of Turkey and Tunisia? Why are the levels of industrial exports to developed countries, which are perhaps the clearest criteria of economic development, so low? Why does the level of manufactured goods exported to developed countries from Syria, Iraq, Iran and Egypt equal that from Panama, Zimbabwe and Haiti? The latter countries have much lower populations and, it might be assumed, much greater disadvantages in the international market.

Not everything can be ascribed to imperialism. I can think of twenty occasions in the last few years when somebody has tried to persuade me that Saddam Hussein was simply an agent of the British. At the time of the 1975 Algiers Agreement between Iraq and Iran, I remember Iraqi opposition members saying, 'It's clear that Saddam's just an agent. Otherwise how could he have signed the Algiers Agreement?' Again, when Saddam Hussein invaded Iran in 1980, he was said to be an agent of imperialism. The fact that he had his own reasons for invading Iran was forgotten. There were many explanations, of increasing intricacy, to explain why Saddam's war with the Americans over Kuwait in 1990–91 was really part of the same imperialist conspiracy. There *is* such a thing as imperialism, and there *are* conspiracies: it is important to identify them. But not everything can be explained in this way. If we have moved away from this simplistic image, whether at the level of political or of economic explanation, it is all to the good.

Let us now turn to another, perhaps even more sensitive issue—the national question. If a historian of ideas were to ask when Marxists in the West first started discussing the Middle East, other than what Marx himself wrote, the answer would be largely connected with the issue of zionism. There was a period, particularly from the 1940s to the 1960s, when virtually the whole of the Western left had a basically pro-zionist position: zionism was a progressive social force, the Arab states were feudal and reactionary, and the Palestinians had no right to their own state. It was a very one-sided and inaccurate picture. After 1967 we had almost the opposite: Israel was now simply a tool of imperialism, the Arab masses were the vanguard of Third World revolution, Jordan would be the second Vietnam, and so on. The injustices suffered by the Palestinians were acknowledged, but there was no recognition of the right of the Israeli people to their own state. In the middle were those who tried to adopt neither position. These were people who, particularly in the late 1960s and early 1970s, tried to identify a position on the Palestinian question (still within a broad Marxist framework) which was neither a simplistic apologia for zionism, nor uncritical support for Palestinian nationalism. The most famous intellectuals to take this position were Maxime Rodinson and Isaac Deutscher. Both were veterans of the communist movement but by that time were independent Marxists.

Rodinson's and Deutscher's views may sound uncontroversial now, but they were not tame at the time. They maintained that there was a Palestinian nation with a right to its own state, and an Israeli nation with a right to its own state, and that policies should be developed to take account of both positions. Rodinson and Deutscher were hated by those people who were sympathetic to Israel because they supported the right of the Palestinians to their own state. However, they were also denounced by the majority of the metropolitan left and by most people in the Middle East because, while denouncing Israel's oppression of the Palestinians, they, as internationalists, acknowledged a clear right of the Israelis to their own state. Deutscher's famous *New Left Review* interview on the 1967 war, which still reads very well, was reproduced in the Arab world, but the translation simply omitted the parts about Israel's right to a state.[10]

The national issue, and the inability to come up with a common position on that issue, has been a persistent issue of division. Needless to say, it is not just in the Arab-Israeli context that the national question arises: it is also of great relevance for Iraq and Iran. Interestingly, prior to the Iranian revolution of 1979, there was a considerable interest in and literature on the national question because Iran is a country in which, it is said, the Persians are the largest minority. Probably over half the population do not have Persian as their first language. Curiously, the Iranian revolution itself did not provoke an explosion of the national question. There were revolts among the Arabs in the south and the Kurds in the north, but not among the Azerbaijanis (who comprise over 20% of the Iranian population), where people had also expected it most. The unresolved nature of Marxist analysis of the national question has persisted, and the over-expectation in some areas of Iranian Azerbaijanis is but one example. At the same time, the refusal to recognize this issue by others, which has happened on both sides of the Arab-Israeli question, has been a recurrent theme in this debate.

In conclusion, let us turn to two broader points. First, compared to three decades ago, we are now faced with a wholly new situation with the rise of the Islamist movements. Sadly, the greatest success of Marxism in the Middle East may have been to provide the Islamists with much of their political vocabulary. Eighty per cent of Khomeini's terminology was stolen from the Tudeh Party and the left—'republic' and 'revolution', for example, were words he had never used before. Khomeini's most important political slogan—*Marg bar liberalizm* [Death to liberalism]—was taken straight from the Tudeh. Abrahamian's *Khomeinism*[11] and Zubaida's book on Islam and the state[12] both reveal that many leftist concepts—even that of May Day—have provided the Islamists with a vocabulary and a set of themes (of which a broad, manipulative, anti-imperialism is the most obvious) with which to articulate their threadbare ideology. But at the same time, the Islamist movements, not just because of their shift of ideology but because of their reality and their strength, present a major political challenge. They also present an analytical challenge: some of the best work produced on contemporary Arab society, and on contemporary social movements in the Middle East, has been produced by people writing in broad Marxist or post-Marxist frameworks with regard to these very movements which are the most anti-Marxist in their outlook, either explicitly or by implication.

The second point that needs making is that at a purely academic level, the predominant language of critique, of discourse, of an alternative approach, is the one derived from Edward Said's critique of orientalism. I am in considerable agreement with parts of that critique; Said has played an important political role on some questions, above all in putting the Palestinian issue on the agenda in the United States, and in clarifying the Salman Rushdie issue, for which he deserves great credit. However, the terms in which he posed the argument in *Orientalism*, and in the school which he has generated, are extremely confusing and confused. This is so not least because it implies that this is the only critique of external domination, the only critique of 'essentializing' literature, that can be produced. So we have a new confusionism, a new set of critiques in the broad (and, in its own way, 'orientalist') school that Said has generated. Its roots lie in the origins of this kind of postmodernist discourse within French intellectual life itself and a misconceived critique of dogmatic Marxism. In some respects, the Marxists bear responsibility for this because of their doctrinaire approach on many issues. There is, however, another set of debates which will keep all those who are interested in the Middle East busy for a long time to come.

3. *The Demise of the Soviet Union and Eastern Europe*

Susan Saunders Vosper

The tragedy of the Soviet Union and its satellites was that by the time its ruling and influential elites reached some consensus as to the desperate need for reform in the mid-1980s it was already too late. When Khrushchev had attempted an earlier and similar reform, there had been considerable confidence in the future of the Soviet model. Khrushchev could boast that the Soviet Union would overtake the United States in food production by 1980 and with its developed welfare system would empirically prove to be superior to the capitalist system.[1] If it had industrialized in ten years under Stalin, then the assumption that it could adjust its top-heavy, over-centralized and producer-goods-oriented economy to a more decentralized, consumer-goods model within twenty years seemed reasonable.

By the 1970s, however, the chronic failings of the economy—stagnation, inefficiency, massive wastage, an inability to apply new techniques, the black market, and corruption—going hand in hand with alienation, cynicism and loss of legitimacy, led Brezhnev himself at the 1981 Party Congress to describe the situation as entailing a 'collapse in ethical standards, spiralling divorce, galloping alcoholism, rising crime, lack of motivation among workers, bureaucratic indifference, frustrated consumer demand as well as youth alienation'.[2] Although he did not mention it, it was clear that the perception of the party–state bureaucracy as a privileged elite penetrated by corruption at the highest levels (including Brezhnev's own son-in-law) had something to do with the emerging cynicism and lack of incentive. The confidence of the elites, especially among professionals, was severely damaged.[3]

This damage to confidence was especially significant given the assumptions of the ideology. Although Marxism-Leninism might have been an impoverished version of the ideas of both Marx and Lenin, it did reflect the founders' belief in the need to release the progressive forces of technology and science in order to build a high level of industrial wealth as the basis of socialism and communism. The Soviet economic model seemed to be failing the productivist assumptions of the ideology. Without the material basis, it had become clear that welfare spending could not be maintained let alone increased. The Soviet Union could no longer compete in the arms race with the West nor sustain the global role it had espoused without a significant transformation of its economic base. No matter how badly flawed the political aspects of Stalinism had been, at least the economic model had appeared impressive, especially to the Third World. Socialists outside the Soviet Union in the immediate post-Stalin decades had recognized the need for superstructural transformation but assumed the substructure to be reasonably sound. That everything now needed rethinking —both substructure and superstructure—provoked intense critical questioning of the ideological base. This ideological base had, moreover, become vulnerable. Used as an ideology of state, it had lost its critical capacity for internal analysis at an early stage in the 1920s. Throughout the forced industrialization phase of the 1930s and the Second World War, the ideology had served as an essential tool of popular mobilization and legitimization.

By the post-Stalin period, however, the ideology appeared to be waning[4] and was increasingly recognized as no longer instrumental in solving practical problems. Professionals now looked to the West for ideas, only paying lip-service to Marxism-Leninism. Moreover, a great gulf emerged between the content of the ideology and the reality on the ground. As an established ideology of state, it was almost inevitable that Soviet youth would eventually reject it. Hence when the crisis hit, Marxism-Leninism offered no analysis, no way forward. It had become blind: atheoretical and non-critical. More worryingly, it had even ceased to be an effective legitimizing agent. The Soviet populace had accepted socialism, but displayed an increasing contempt for the party apparatus and its credo. Despite elite disaffection, the Soviet model of party–state required some continued allegiance to Marxism-Leninism without which it had no claim to legitimacy.

Gorbachev, the Intellectuals and Reform

The Gorbachev attempt at transforming the conservative bureaucratic structures was very much an attempt at reform from above—indeed, there seemed no other way in which the Soviet Union could have been changed. It represented the tradition of the enlightened bureaucrat initiating reforms in order to save and preserve the 'great power' status of the nation, or in this case socialism and Soviet power. It followed the pattern of Witte's (the nineteenth-century finance minister under Nicholas III) industrializing in order not to lose wars and Stalin's industrializing to survive Western imperialism.[5] The consensus among the intellectual cadres of the 1980s, who had been young students in Khrushchev's time, was that there was no alternative to a complete transformation. It was not simply that by the late 1970s the economy had hit zero growth, but that the long-term prospects for the future, as outlined by Aganbegyan, were bleak unless science and technology could be sufficiently developed to exploit raw material resources that were inaccessible to the existing methods and techniques.[6]

The Soviets were acutely aware that in many areas of technology they were nearly two generations behind many Western nations. They had been aware from the late Stalinist period of the defects in the command structure of the economy and the need to transform it when a shift towards consumer goods was required. The old siege model of the economy had been suitable for war and large-scale producer goods but could not cope with the variety and quality required of more developed economies. But attempts at reform under Khrushchev and Kosygin had failed, either abandoned rapidly due to unforeseen and massive dislocations or simply submerged and ignored by the entrenched corporate management.[7] By the 1980s the radicals around Gorbachev not only recognized the urgency of the need to transform, but predicted the sheer intransigence of the bureaucratic forces that would need to be shifted as well as the many entrenched social patterns of behaviour that were inimical to initiative and efficiency.

The critique of the Gorbachev intelligentsia had moreover covered more than the purely economic field. Sociologists such as Zaslavskaia had convinced Gorbachev that no economic reconstruction would be successful without political and social change.[8] Given past experience, this seemed incontrovertible. The Chinese in the late 1970s were also discussing the importance of democratization to accompany economic reforms.[9] Dissident intellectuals created by the Khrushchev liberalization, as well as professional elites, had long been campaigning for openness and democratization. Whether this was necessary for economic transformation or not, it was what they wanted. There was no doubt that Western liberal ideology had made a substantial impact on the thinking of professional elites. Marxism-Leninism had been progressively confined to its specialized department of the Central Committee. Despite Burlatsky's efforts to combine it with Western liberalism, it failed to adapt, which is not surprising given the importance of its unifying and legitimizing function.[10]

In one key area, however, that of foreign affairs (arguably the only remaining area where Marxist analysis was applicable), change appeared mandatory. The success of internal economic transformation demanded a scaling down of weaponry, involving a massive reduction in the military budget as well as building links into Western markets, making Western technology accessible. Khrushchev had pioneered this softening up to the West and Gorbachev, influenced by such writers as Shakhnazarov, resumed the policy with determination.[11] The rationale seemed flawless. In the global village of the twentieth century, no one wins a nuclear war, hence peaceful coexistence is an imperative. But Gorbachev went further and wanted cooperation to maintain the peace as well as cooperation and help on environmental, economic and social issues. To gain this, the party was able to agree on a fundamental ideological change which negated its Leninist base. Class analysis, the concept of revolution and the use of force were rejected as the basis of analysis for international relations and foreign policy. In other words, international relations had to be de-ideologized.[12] This went beyond Khrushchev's idea of peaceful coexistence, which had been recognized as a necessity and a form of class struggle. Khrushchev's elite had thought that the Soviet system would prove the superiority of its ideology and social system by peaceful competition. By Gorbachev's time, the elite had ceased to believe their system was superior at all. Hence the use of a discourse that transcended class, recognized the priority of human values and denied any major difference between various systems which might bring them into conflict. This implied a withdrawal from any attempts to promote revolution, especially in the Third World. Indeed, it entailed a withdrawal from involvement in external conflicts and ultimately pulling out of Afghanistan (an act demanded by the United States as proof that the Soviet Union meant what it said).

Although Marxism-Leninism had been waning for decades, this new abandoning of its crucial content had a significant impact, especially in the context of Gorbachev's policy of *glasnost*, or openness: this meant opening up all areas, hitherto secret, to public discussion and debate.[13] Some of the worst flaws and excesses of the Stalinist period were aired—forced collectivization, the elimination of the old Bolsheviks, and so on. Khrushchev had gone only so far, but Gorbachev's *perestroika* (restructuring) went further, undermining confidence in the system and leading, for the first time, to a critical examination of the state's history. Marxism-Leninism had functioned as an official state ideology which had controlled all interpretations of Marx, Lenin and the revolution, and the history of the Soviet Communist Party (CPSU) and the state. The legitimacy of both the CPSU and the state depended upon it. To undermine it would have serious repercussions. As an outraged rejection of Stalinism was followed by an examination of its historical origins, first Lenin, then the October revolution and finally Marx came under critical scrutiny. The Soviet Union thus began to question its identity and its base. It is interesting that only party conservatives such as Ligachev truly understood the monumental danger to the regime.[14]

The radical pro-*perestroika* elite led by Gorbachev clearly thought that the main problem lay with an unwilling, recalcitrant *nomenklatura* bureaucracy and, for some time, they assumed a bedrock stability of party and state. In his first work on *perestroika*, Gorbachev continued to speak in Leninist terms—as if a 'correct' interpretation were still in force.[15] There was doubtless a need to justify developments using such language, but it was clear to the elites that there was no Leninism left. Gorbachev's pragmatism was revealed when he candidly admitted on television that if the economic reforms did not work, he would simply try something else. Any theoretical conception of a 'correct' line had disappeared. Nevertheless, Gorbachev himself was a socialist and he genuinely believed in the party's mission to perfect a socialist state even if elements of the ideology itself seemed problematic. Moreover, he felt that both party and state could be transformed from within and from above to achieve the goal. The programme of *perestroika*, 'new thinking' and *glasnost* had an intellectual coherence which made it appealing, but it assumed *ceteris paribus* and an essential stability and consensus that were illusory. The stability of party and state was, in fact, immediately challenged when the open and political aspects of *perestroika* were first introduced. That the Soviet Union was an imperial regime whose national components were not entirely satisfied with the imperial connection seems initially to have been ignored.

The Logic and the Consequences of Perestroika

It is not surprising, however, that the logic of *perestroika* and the sheer need to do something mesmerized a good section of the elite into uncritical acceptance of the *perestroika* programme. This logic postulated that the 'new thinking' in foreign affairs would establish a relationship with the West which would enable the Soviets to reduce military expenditure drastically, switching investment to science, new technology and consumer goods; the economic programme would construct a more decentralized, market-oriented system with financial incentives for workers and managements. Trade with the West and aid would boost new technological development and investment. Legitimacy would be fostered by new methods of democratization, reform of the party and transformation of the Soviets. *Glasnost*, which was essential for both political and economic accountability, would reduce corruption and ensure a more open, meritocratic selection of cadres and management. In the field of ideology, cynicism would be replaced by a closer relationship of words and deeds.[16]

All this appeared misleadingly familiar. An earlier version had been tried by Khrushchev and abandoned by the party when it led to outbursts in Poland and Hungary and to economic dislocations at home which had angered the planners.[17] This time, however, it was clear that the Soviets could dispense with Eastern Europe as a *cordon sanitaire*. Modern weaponry made the East European countries less essential for security. Preferably they would follow the *perestroika* movement voluntarily, but if not, the loss of Eastern Europe, although unwelcome, was insignificant compared with what was at stake at home. Arguably, Hungary, with the 'new economic mechanism', had already proceeded along the path of *perestroika*, as indeed would Czechoslovakia have done had it been allowed to in 1966–68.[18] Once again, however, the semi-imperialist relationship of the Soviet Union to Eastern Europe was underestimated. What might have been an acceptable programme of transformation in the 1960s was by 1989 too late in Eastern Europe. Popular rejection of Moscow's domination, the contempt for quislings, a widespread cynicism and the loss of belief in Soviet ideology meant that Dubček in 1989, although given a nostalgic welcome, was yesterday's man.

Given the unforeseen and catastrophic consequences of *perestroika* for the Soviet Communist Party and the state, it is worth trying to assess why things went so badly wrong. At first, the international policy appeared successful—disarmament treaties were negotiated and old conflicts patched up; Gorbachev was acclaimed as the universal peacekeeper. The Third World lost out on aid and support, the military grumbled at home that too much had been given up for too little, but Gorbachev achieved what he had set out to do. The domestic transformation was in trouble, however. As outlined above, *glasnost* and the ideological transformation had undermined the legitimacy of both party and state at a crucial stage. Had the new economic reforms of 1987 had some degree of success, the situation might have been salvaged, but they began to founder on the same rocks as all previous attempts at reform (especially those under Kosygin). All the well-intentioned economic legislation tended to be merely enabling legislation.

Persuading Soviet firms to introduce *perestroika* was quite another matter. Not only were procedures and habits well entrenched, both on the part of management and of workers, but the effect of the reforms was to partially dismantle the planned system without instituting a viable market structure as a substitute. Worry about the effects of lifting price controls, while fully understandable, led to continued price irrationality and there were no clear economic indicators for market response. The handful of more successful cooperative ventures were disliked since few people could afford their high prices. Profit accounting in monopoly supply conditions often led firms to produce less in response to higher prices, rather than more, or switch from cheaper to more expensive lines of goods where profits were easier to show. Many firms continued to look to the state for orders and relied too heavily on state credits. Often it was difficult to do otherwise. The net effect of this dislocation of the old planned system (which had worked to some extent, even if badly) was to make things worse: production went down, bottlenecks got worse, chaos reigned, prices rose and shortages increased. Inter-republic and inter-area trade and exchange decreased, making areas resentful of their interdependence.[19]

These, perhaps predictable, failures of the early transition phase were blamed on the conservatism of a recalcitrant apparatus, fuelling democratic cries for tough measures against the bureaucracy as well as a proliferation of plans for speedier reform and a more decisive change to a market-based system. Some people began to doubt the feasibility of a third way between a market and a planned economy and others that the Soviet system was reformable. After 1989 many were influenced by the application of 'shock therapy' in Eastern Europe. Hopes that the West would ease the transition pains with generous aid fuelled support for a deeper, more incisive marketization. Decentralization of the economy grew as planned indices from above were reduced and the party was no longer allowed or able to interfere with economic management.

In 1989, when Gorbachev introduced the political reforms of *perestroika*, ostensibly to bolster and aid economic change and to foster legitimacy, the dye was in many ways cast which led to the destruction of the CPSU and eventually the Soviet state.[20] In addition to the pluralism and openness of *glasnost*, Gorbachev instituted democratic reforms of the Soviets, creating an alternative form of legitimacy to the party. A very real element of freedom entered the election process of 1989. The result was a blow to the collective ego of the party, many of whose representatives were rejected.[21] Gorbachev had not anticipated such a degree of unpopularity nor had he fully assessed the likely consequences. Worse still, nationalists swept the board in Lithuania and the first free Soviet Congress rang with complaints from national areas and clear assertions of the need for more autonomy.[22]

Gorbachev had little understanding of or sympathy for nationalism: he simply assumed that once the economy improved, nationalism would disappear. The new democratic Soviet was clearly meant to serve as an alternative vehicle to the party for implementing *perestroika* and legitimizing his position. He intended to avoid the fate of Khrushchev, who had been removed by the party elite. Following this strategy, the party was reformed, its bureaucratic element reduced, its offices opened to election and free discussion allowed. The secrecy of the *nomenklatura* processes were to be abandoned in favour of more open selection on the basis of merit. Gorbachev himself moved speedily to associate himself with the new Soviet, becoming its chairman and, a year later, bolstering his authority by transforming the chairmanship into an executive presidency. In place of the party, this new forum was intended to convey a new legitimacy. It did indeed give Gorbachev another channel through which to operate, making him appear more democratic, though in practice it was not necessarily easier to implement change through the new Soviet.

The upshot of this transference of power, as well as the party reforms, was that the party was decisively weakened and began to lose its effective hold over the Union and its authority. The politburo ceased to be the channel through which Gorbachev would operate. Party institutions were also to be more clearly separated from state institutions and were instructed not to interfere with the practical operation of the economy. Gorbachev consequently undermined the stability of his own base. Had he been able to get himself directly elected as president this problem might have been overcome, but by the time he was ready to make this move he was so unpopular that rejection at a free election would have been inevitable.

The Collapse of Party Unity, State Power and Imperialism

Hungary was the first East European country to take advantage of Moscow's loosening grip by declaring a multi-party state in 1988. Encouraged by the events of 1989 in the Soviet Union, and urged on to *perestroika* themselves by Gorbachev, the East European states one by one moved to democratization. There was an initial resistance to this, especially on the part of the communist elites in East Germany and Czechoslovakia, aware that the rug was about to be pulled out from under their feet. However, the Soviet Union made it clear that unpopular communist parties would no longer receive support, and once free elections were called, communist party monopolies were doomed and in most areas the party faced defeat. Had Moscow allowed these parties to transform and make themselves more popular at an earlier date, their fate might have been different.

The defeat at this time was, however, predictable given the rejection of foreign control and what was regarded as the imposition of an alien system upon them.[23] Most areas thought they would be economically better off leaning towards the West and Europe; few were able to weigh up the real benefits of trade within the one-time Soviet bloc and the cheap fuel from the Soviet Union. The sensation of independence was intoxicating, optimism was high and most problems were attributed to Soviet imperialism. The naivety of this approach only dawned on the East Europeans as they attempted market liberalization, causing plummeting production and soaring inflation. The chance, however, for a close relationship between Moscow and the ex-Soviet bloc states was lost. This might have been possible for some countries, if not all, if democratization had been accepted earlier. The effect of the imposition of the Soviet model upon them, and Moscow's domination, was to drive them towards Europe and the West.

Events in Eastern Europe impacted back on the Soviet Union itself. In addition, the democratic new Soviet proved unexpectedly and increasingly difficult to control, while at the same time the party itself began to split in 1990 under the impact of free discussion. The Democrats, following Boris Yeltsin, wished to push *perestroika* faster, while the Conservatives under Ligachev wished to slow it down, leaving Gorbachev and his allies in an uncomfortable centrist position. Not unreasonably, the Conservatives pointed out that the Democrats appeared not to believe in the communist ideology any more and should therefore leave the party, which they ostentatiously did following the Party Conference of July 1990.

But the party was not only split on attitudes to *perestroika*; it was also split on the national question. In 1989 the Estonian Communist Party was the first to claim its independence of Moscow. Subsequently more and more communist parties followed the Estonian lead in an effort to make themselves popular with their electorates. Once relatively free elections became the route to authority and power, they could not afford to ignore the popular appeal of nationalism. As it was, nationalist parties were free to operate against them, and toeing a Moscow line was a sure recipe for defeat. The CPSU therefore lost its historic monolithic unity, its centralist logic and, in 1990, with the repeal of clause 6 of the Soviet constitution, its leading and guiding position in the Soviet state. Henceforth, it was to be one party among others. As Ron Hill has described it, it was death by a thousand cuts.[24]

The Soviet state, following the tsarist heritage, had from the beginning been an imperial power. Between 1917 and 1922 the Bolsheviks had fought to retain national areas often against the wishes of the nationalist elites.[25] They had promised national self-determination but failed to see it through. They had undoubtedly built up a concept of Soviet citizenship and their nationality policies had not all been unenlightened. The vast economic area of the empire was inherently rational. Much damage had been done in the Stalinist period, however, when in the cause of spreading industrial and rational progress, ethnic Russians, Ukrainians and Belorussians had moved into non-Slav areas, taking superior positions and seldom learning the local languages. Russians held key positions as second secretaries in non-Russian areas and native elites were seldom transferred to important posts in Moscow.[26] Some areas, like Uzbekistan, felt they had been ruined by the cotton monoculture imposed from above, others that they were the dumping ground for polluting industries, and many that Moscow's hegemony was an illegal imposition from the beginning. In short, they all had a case against the centre—some wanted out, some wanted help, others wanted more autonomy and respect.

The party had functioned as the kingpin holding the vast, sprawling empire together by its authoritarian monopoly power over all appointments. As it disintegrated, it lost its grip over the bureaucratic apparatus, which began to decentralize. Although Gorbachev and his followers were in favour of economic decentralization, they deplored what they saw as the irrelevance of nationalist separatism. Consequently, the reaction to demands for sovereignty was unsympathetic. There was no speedy analysis to distinguish those areas demanding separatism from those that were content with a loosened, genuinely federal constitution. Indeed, the immediate reaction was to fight nationalism (thus stiffening national minority opposition), often using force and seemingly backtracking on the rights supposedly guaranteed by *perestroika*.[27] The net effect was to exacerbate the problem, encouraging an escalation of opposition to the centre from one republic to another.

The Soviet Union could clearly have survived the loss of some of the smaller republics—the Baltics, the Transcaucasus and Moldavia—which were also the keenest to enjoy sovereignty. But a lack of subtlety in dealing with them, together with a steadily worsening economic crisis, encouraged other larger republics like the Ukraine to pull away from the centre, their national leaders gaining popularity in the process. There is no doubt that Gorbachev took too long to formulate a new constitutional relationship between the republics. By the time he was ready to make concessions, the situation had already moved on and those concessions seemed too late and unacceptable. He was, in addition, hindered by Yeltsin and the Russian Democrats, who, having left the party in 1990, adopted a strategy aimed at destroying the central party–state apparatus. The Democrats believed that a progressive, liberal economic policy could not be implemented through the All-Union, totalitarian, conservative apparatus and that it would have to be removed. Consequently, Yeltsin backed the Baltics and other republics demanding sovereignty and declared the Russian Soviet Federated Socialist Republic (RSFSR) to be sovereign too.

Unlike Gorbachev, Yeltsin had transformed his presidency into an elected one, giving him the authority and power to attack Gorbachev and the party–state central apparatus. It must be remembered that the RSFSR comprised three-quarters of the territory of the Soviet Union. What had, in effect, happened was that an alternative structure of power and control through the Russian Federation, led by Yeltsin, had challenged the power and authority of the All-Union structure. Given the collapse of the economy, the centrifugal tendencies of the republics and the increasing disillusionment with *perestroika*, it was easy to become popular by attacking those held responsible for the economic crisis and by promising that all would be righted once they were removed. The declaration of Russian sovereignty, which entailed a rejection of the superiority of All-Union laws, was crucial to the collapse of the Union. When a territory the size of the RSFSR declared sovereignty, there was no point in others remaining in the Union, and subsequently the Ukraine, Belorus and Soviet Asia left, despite this being totally against the interests of the latter.[28] The refusal to obey central laws led to a refusal to pay taxes, so that the centre was progressively starved of resources.

By mid-1991 the crisis had deepened. In an effort to maintain the Union and stabilize the economy Gorbachev had surrounded himself with conservative forces, yet at the same time he had been forced to recognize the reality on the ground. Thus he conceded the prospect of a decentralized, almost confederal state as envisaged in a draft treaty to be signed on 20 August 1991. By this stage, it appeared to be the only form of union acceptable to the republics. It was, however, anathema to a sizeable section of the top leadership, notably in the Security Council, whose members planned the failed coup of 19 August to prevent the signing of the treaty. This bungled, illegal move illustrated the polarization of forces for and against the new conception of the Union, but also provided a unique opportunity for Yeltsin to rally the Democrats against what appeared to be a return to the old order. The coup failed for three main reasons: the conspirators failed to take account of the new conditions and real change which had transformed the system; the army and police were divided; and the conspirators failed to follow the first rules of a coup, such as cutting off communications.[29] That Yeltsin won, however, obscured the genuine polarization of the population on the two issues of the Union and economic reform. The consequences of the coup were, in effect, the opposite of its intended goals. Yeltsin was able to use the illegal move to discredit the entire Union apparatus, particularly the Communist Party, and demand the resignation of Gorbachev as General Secretary and the abolition of the All-Union party apparatus. The centre subsequently collapsed, lacking both the authority and the resources to maintain itself. It became fairly clear that Yeltsin's Russian Federation was considering resurrecting a new Union, but by this time the republics were suspicious and wary of a revitalized Russian central structure.

The collapse of the Union could perhaps have been avoided had there been an early agreement about a federal system. However, concessions to nationalism had always been resisted in the party, which helps to explain Gorbachev's inability to respond effectively. The collapse was also an unexpected consequence of the attempt to transform the Soviet model. How far this model could be transformed without turning it into something radically different was also questionable. It rested on the combination of a tight, centralized monopoly power at both the economic and the political level.[30] To transform one level would necessarily impact on the other. The Chinese were currently transforming at the economic level and resisting political transformation but the pressures were evident. Whether the Soviet Union could have followed a similar pattern is debatable. Transforming Russian agriculture was even more difficult than transforming its industrial structure, which was difficult enough. There had also been the previous failed attempts, pointing to the need for some form of political transformation. The dramatic nature, however, of the measures of democratization chosen clearly hindered rather than assisted the proposed limited form of economic transformation, bringing the model to an abrupt and total end. Attempts to transform everything at once clearly endanger the stability and order upon which viable economic and legal orders are based.

As the model collapsed and the party lost authority, large numbers of the one-time party elites were quick to abandon the ideology. Indeed, even Alexander Yakovlev, a top party ideologist, had by 1991 concluded that not just Stalin and Lenin were to blame but Marxism itself. In his *The Fate of Marxism in Russia*, he utilizes many philosophical Western sources to demonstrate the totalitarian nature and inevitable outcome of Marxism, very much in the genre of the God that failed.[31] This is just one illustration of the degree of penetration of Western thinking in the Soviet Union. It is clearly a typical overreaction in which all the features of normal, correct and desirable development are seen as coming from the Western liberal experience and all the flaws of the Soviet model can be traced to a single indictable source.

Reflections on the Soviet Model and Marxism

Despite such oversimplification, it is worth reflecting on the genesis of the not inconsiderable flaws in the Soviet model as well as some of the positive features which were initially submerged beneath the deluge of criticism. The worst features are clearly traceable to what has been termed the second revolution, when industrialization and collectivization from above at breakneck speed created the top-heavy, highly centralized economy and police state. Although led by Stalin, the policy was popular in the party, at least in the initial stages. Despite Bukharin's opposition to it, based on his fears of its harmful consequences, it seemed in keeping with the industrializing ethos of Marxism. The manner in which it was accomplished exacerbated the dictatorial consequences, especially for the peasantry which was, in effect, re-feudalized. The will and the ability of the Bolshevik Party to impose itself in such a way on the bulk of the population must also be traced back to decisions made under Lenin during the revolutionary period from 1917 to 1924. The results of the 1918 free elections to the Constituent Assembly, as well as Lenin's own assessment in 1921 that they had lost the broad masses, made it amply clear that the regime had started on an illegitimate basis which even the concessions of the New Economic Policy (NEP) failed substantially to transform.[32] This in turn led to a system of socialization from above, erecting a cult of Lenin and turning Leninism into a didactic, authoritarian ideology to justify the party's monopoly of power.[33] Critical Marxism withered under the need to cement unity and control; it disappeared almost entirely under Stalin, never to recover.

This deleterious development is usually explained by the lack of industrial development in 1917. Although partly the problem, this is insufficient explanation. The Soviet Union was more industrialized in 1917 than is often recognized. It was, in effect, caught in a transition stage of early development with its archaic social and political structures under the strain of structural dislocation and then war. Marxist analysis was uniquely applicable but massively problematic, as indeed it would have been elsewhere.[34] There was a greater likelihood of a revolution at a time of transition to a new form than when that new form had fully materialized. Indeed, the problem for Russia was that the revolution which was expected to come in the advanced industrial states never came. The analysis in Lenin's *Imperialism* which justified the holding exercise of short-term dictatorship failed to reflect reality and the Soviet Union was left stranded. At no point was this analysis ever openly reassessed, but the consequences of socialism in one country clearly followed.

In attempting to implement Marxist ideas, the young Soviet Union was disadvantaged given its relative lack of development, but many of the problems it faced might well have occurred elsewhere. Marxism gave a detailed analysis of capitalism but had little or nothing to say about the construction of socialism. Moreover, there was scant treatment of political forms, given the general idea of the withering away of the state. Indeed, the Soviet state grew like Topsy with no theory to justify it other than Stalin's assertion that it would have to build itself up in order to wither away. Earlier theoretical conceptions of state and law in the 1920s, while philosophically interesting, were of no practical help or application.[35] Although Polan's analysis of the defects of Lenin's *State and Revolution* (with its indirect assault on Marx) overstates the causal relationships between Marx, Lenin and Stalinism, it does with some validity point to the possible consequences of the total scorn for many liberal political ideas such as the separation of powers, the rule of law, parliamentary representation and pluralist forms of civil society—built up as the result of hundreds of years of political learning and bitter experience of coercive power.[36] The culture of Bolshevism, based as it was on Russian revolutionary traditions, seized on this rejection of liberal ideas with considerable emphasis, undermining any inclination to question the unchecked nature of the monopoly of power.

It would have been useful to remember Lord Acton's liberal dictum that all power tends to corrupt and absolute power corrupts absolutely.[37] For Bolsheviks it was all too close to Anarchist and Socialist Revolutionary petty bourgeois mentality. Even the concept of legality smacked of bourgeois thought for many early Bolshevik theorists. Although these can be identified as theoretical problems which needed to be addressed, it is doubtful whether in 1917 they had any major impact on Soviet development. Herein lies a problem concerning the relationship of theory to practice. As Polan indicates, Lenin's *State and Revolution* disappeared into historical oblivion, the contents scarcely referred to until the Khrushchev period. The major explanation of the authoritarian model lay elsewhere: in the events of 1917–21, when all opposition was outlawed and factions were banned in the party itself.[38] In the midst of civil war it was highly unlikely that any liberal or democratic model would emerge even had the ideology paid due attention to it. In fact, the early Soviets were extremely representative and to a large degree democratic and Lenin's *State and Revolution* would have supported such a democratic style.

The real problem was that the early Soviet model emerged from conditions of militarization engendered by the First World War, and then civil war, leading to the language of communism becoming punctuated by military metaphors.[39] These conditions led, on the one hand, to centralized, coercive power with scant regard for human rights, legality and democratic participation and, on the other, to a collapsed economy which needed to mobilize support for rebuilding. Consequently, any early inroads made into autocracy after 1905 were undermined in 1918–22, confirming much of the analysis of the legal Marxists before 1903.[40] But it is worth noting that the relatively free period of the 1920s—at least to 1928—was maintained on the basis of Lenin's NEP. Bukharin fully understood the need to continue this policy if any sort of free civil society was to emerge and it is not surprising that the Gorbachev elite initially attempted a return to this model. However, in the 1920s this had been seen as a step backwards to be superseded by some improved, more socialist economic form in the future, whereas for Gorbachev it *was* the future.[41] Even in this period, however, Leninism had emerged as an authoritative interpretation of Marx to be taught in schools, the party and the army, and the political structure was highly authoritarian. Marxism as a critical form of thought was no longer to be applied at the political level and by the 1930s, with the elimination of the capitalist classes, it appeared internally irrelevant. New states clearly need legitimizing ideologies which cannot, by definition, be critical. The use of Marxism in this way certainly undermined its future use as anything but a credo of state, and the regime's chronic lack of legitimacy made its transformation into an authoritarian dogma a functional necessity.

Many Marxists have rejected the Soviet model as neither Marxist nor socialist, either criticizing its early coercive base and blaming Lenin or viewing Stalinism as the key to deformation. Thus its collapse and demise are welcomed as a possible beginning of something more in line with the true spirit of Marxism. But many of Marx's key ideas concerning the future should now be recognized as problematic—especially the withering away of the state. If it is conceded that a state is necessary, then the type of state desired and its institutional base and relationship with society become important developmental concepts. Clearly, the model of the Soviet state was flawed in a multitude of ways—it was imperialist, massively over-centralized and hierarchical, with a model of socialism that was more related to the industrializing, technological and authoritarian model of Saint-Simon than to Marx. This was partly due to its attempt to build up the productive forces in haste, but also to its tsarist past. If there is one lesson to be learned from the Soviet experience, it is that very substantial elements of past societies live into the new. There may be grounds for optimism here if one believes that the Soviet Union did in fact achieve some socialist goals. There is evidence that, at the social level, it provided a more egalitarian structure than in most capitalist societies. If there was an elite, it was a relatively poor one in comparison with the West.[42] Great strides were made in access to education, health and life opportunities, especially for women. Despite discontent with the leadership and the inadequacies of much consumer and welfare provision, the bulk of the population supported socialist values. A huge socialization project had been effected and the economy had been modernized, albeit precipitously. The challenge was to find an efficient economic base to deliver agreed socialist goals as well as a responsive political and social structure which encouraged participation. It was also evident that, in the absence of any spiritual incentives, a disgruntled, apathetic materialism had taken root. In the chaos and continuing corruption of the post-communist era, there is a remarkable quest for something above and beyond the material—this request demands a response.

Despite the rejection of the entire model as a mistake and the subsequent initial worship of the market, the population of the ex-Soviet bloc have a clear nostalgia for the better features of their past socialist history which will not easily be erased. As the reality of the West and pure capitalist forms become transparent, disillusion sets in and the past is reassessed. Yet the major problem is finding some acceptable economic base which is not capitalist. The socialist project has been undermined to the extent that there is no clear alternative. It will take time for ex-communist countries to find some balance between market and plan, but it is heartening that most are not prepared to contemplate vast masses of unemployed, whether for practical or ethical reasons. But these states have now seen the need to plug into the world market and their development will, of necessity, be influenced by it. The drift to total Westernization—due initially in the Soviet Union to pessimism about the transformability of the communist system, and in Eastern Europe to a rejection of Moscow's domination and a reassertion of a European identity—has now been halted. In Moscow the Atlanticists are on the wane and the Eurasians to the fore.[43] Optimism for the future is not necessarily warranted, but there are at least clear signs that the strengths and weaknesses of different systems are being progressively recognized. There will be no return to the old order, either economic or political. New communists are different from the old, but already the continuities are in evidence and new forms will clearly emerge, taking in large elements of the past, some of which are positive in socialist terms and others not.

The major damage caused by the Soviet model was to the socialist ethic, by the building up of privileged, dominant *nomenklatura* elites, but the circumstances of its demise have undermined world belief in the viability of an alternative to Western liberal capitalism. At both the economic and the political level, much thought is now needed to reformulate new routes to instrumentalizing old and widely accepted socialist values. It is now clear that the Soviet siege model, cut off from international communications, was only a short-term model which had many defects that made it difficult to transform. It does not follow that it achieved nothing, nor that new forms will repeat the same mistakes, but there is no doubt that the way forward will be complex: simplistic aproaches, at both the theoretical and the practical level, will need to be abandoned. If Marxism is to be not simply a philosophical exercise but is intended to change the world, then the key area of the relationship of theory to practice must take precedence. The history of the Soviet Union demonstrates many such problems that were not anticipated by Marx, but now have to be addressed.

4. *Can Marx Survive the Collapse of Communism or 'Real Socialism'?*

Maurice Godelier

Principal Theoretical Elements of Marx's Vision of Society

New Ideas and Overall Perspective

Several ideas are basic to Marx's thinking. The first is that the appearance of new forms of society is linked to the development, at certain epochs and among certain human groups, of new 'material and intellectual' capacities for acting on nature in order to draw from it the material means of their existence. In time these developments would call into question the reproduction of forms of work, forms of property and forms of wealth—in short, the social relations within which the processes of production had taken place up to then.

In common with many writers of his day, Marx considered that the way in which the process of production is organized within a society, the way in which the individuals and groups which compose the society appropriate the conditions of this process (territory, natural resources, human labour-power), as well as its results (the products of human labour), play an essential role in the functioning of this society and its evolution. In his view—and this is another key idea—the development of new capacities for acting upon nature has led to the appearance of societies that are no longer based on inequalities linked to sex, age or kinship as in primitive societies, but on inequalities associated with the existence of dominant castes or classes and that of the state.

In short, it was in the combined interaction of two kinds of contradictions —the first, born of the long-term incompatibility between the development of new productive capacities and the reproduction of earlier social relations of production, and the second, born of social inequalities and contradictions contained from the outset in the texture of relations of production and which develop with the latter—that Marx saw the principal reason for the appearance of new forms of society, the 'prime mover' of human history and of the evolution of humanity.

These were powerful ideas which broke with the previous ways of writing history which, for the most part, attached primary importance either to politics (but politics reduced to the actions of the dominant caste or classes or, indeed, solely to the 'historic deeds' of the great and powerful) or to religion which, through its great doctrines and its ability to convince and persuade, seemed to hold the key to the history of many societies, notably in the Orient.

Without denying the role of these forces, Marx thought that they were combined with other, more powerful forces—those of material and economic realities to which they seemed to him to be, broadly speaking, closely related. And it is precisely because material realities and economic relations are to do with the physical survival of people and their subsistence, just as much as the production of material riches, the exercise of power and the practice of religion, that they have a greater impact on the functioning of societies, and their reproduction or disappearance, in short, on the history and evolution of humanity.

Clearly, Marx was indebted to ideas developed in Europe by thinkers who mainly came from the bourgeoisie of those nations in which new forms of wealth (linked to trade and commercial production) had developed in varying degrees since the sixteenth century. This is the context in which the mercantilists and physiocrats, Quesnay and Ricardo, gave shape to a new science whose object was the production and distribution of wealth—the science of political economy.

But the extent of Marx's break with his predecessors and contemporaries is also clear. He neither glorified the civilizing role of trade and industry, nor bewailed the demise of the former European feudal order of personal relations and values. This break followed logically from Marx's idea that some form of exploitation of man by man, whether involving direct or indirect appropriation of another's labour, or even his person, lay behind all inequalities of power and wealth. We do not find in him an idealized, one-sided view of the effects of the development of productive forces. Marx's audacious breakthrough lies in this dual (analytical and critical) broadening of ideas, which at first sight seemed to be valid above all for Western societies and for the epoch of their birth.

There was an analytical extension in the sense that it was no longer simply the emergence of capitalism in the West, and its expansion worldwide, that was to be explained in terms of the primacy of material and economic forces, but the whole of human history.

This general materialist view of history implied a theoretical critique of other ways of seeing history. But the critical extension consisted in more than this. For in postulating that behind inequalities of power and wealth we must discover various mechanisms of exploitation—in affirming that the exploitation of man by man has played and continues to play an essential role in the evolution of humanity—Marx casts general critical doubt on all philosophical or religious systems of ideas and values which legitimate the ruling social order while remaining silent about its forms of exploitation or minimizing their importance. He was for the same reasons equally critical of the notion of progress dear to the thinkers of the Enlightenment—in the nineteenth century, this culminated in the complacent vision of the West as the apotheosis of civilization, the end point of all the progress that humanity had achieved since its origins in primitive 'savagery'. Marx repeatedly demonstrated the unilateral, partisan character of the notion of progress because, in his view, the progress of productive forces, far from having contributed to the elimination of social inequalities, had engendered and fostered them.

Such were the ideas that were to establish Marx as the source of a critique of ideas and ideologies that was almost certainly more radical in its impact on the human sciences than anything that had preceded him. Not until Freud do we have a comparable advance in the critical interpretation of the representations and fantastical forms of consciousness projected by human beings. But one should never forget Marx's passionate declaration of his intent not merely to interpret the 'world' in a different manner, but also to transform it. In other words his ideas are not confined to theory, but made him the spokesman for all the oppressed, an ally of their struggles, and specifically those of the proletarians and the working classes who were subordinated to the new dominating class of the time, the industrial bourgeoisie.

This is why Marx, once he had, together with Engels, elaborated his basic ideas in *The German Ideology*, devoted the rest of his life and resources to a reinterpretation, not of all of past history (though he continued to study it), but of the bourgeois society of his day, its origins, its function and its specific mode of production of wealth and exchange. This was the capitalist mode, which was already, after the appearance of machinery and the development of large-scale industry, dominating a great part of the world economy.

But Marx's scientific work aimed not only to reveal the secret of the origins of capitalist profits but also of the accumulation of capital—he believed he was doing this by demonstrating that the workers' wages were not, contrary to the economists' theories, the price for their work but merely equivalent to a part of the commercial value created in the course of their labour in the service of capital.

Marx hoped for more: to analyse the development of capital, its overall movement as well as its local forms, its internal and external contradictions. He wanted to reveal the conditions and forces which would eventually bring about the disappearance of bourgeois society and the capitalist mode of production, and their replacement by a mode of production and a superior way of life that would not rest upon human exploitation and its accompanying forms of domination and oppression.

Marx discerned signs of the capitalist system's tendency towards dissolution in the appearance of workers' cooperatives in the second half of the nineteenth century. These he considered as points of rupture (*Durchbrechungspunkt*) of the capitalist form of production, as a local abolition of its form, even if such cooperatives were still subordinate to the logic of profit. He believed he could see here a glimpse of a logic that would supplant the profit motive.

Other indications suggested to Marx that capitalism was already entering (at least in places where it was most developed) a period of transition towards another mode of production. The appearance of cartels and trusts, the growing number of limited companies, the concentration of financial resources and so on, seemed to demonstrate that large-scale modern production was limited by the framework of capitalist private ownership on the basis of which it had developed. Marx saw the development of these institutions as indicating various attempts to overcome the limits imposed by this form of ownership without abolishing the form itself. He thus detected a number of transitional forms (*Ubergangsform*, *Durchgangsform*) leading to another mode or organization of production and society. It was a mode which this time would rest on social ownership of the means of production and on concerted action by associated workers, sharing the products of their work between themselves and throughout the whole of society. But to reach this stage, something more than the evolution of the capitalist economy was required. The classes exploited by capitalism had to engage in a political revolution led by the industrial proletariat, on the basis of its practical, everyday experience of organization and struggle.

Marx placed great faith in his scientific work. He hoped that his findings would suggest a feasible strategy which would make the revolutionary struggles of the proletariat and exploited masses more effective and achieve success faster than anything promised by the anarchists (who looked to the immediate destruction of the bourgeois state and the state as such) and more certain than by following the programme of the utopian socialists (who sought the immediate realization of the aspirations and egalitarian dreams of the masses).

Although Marx tried to keep to a scientific discourse, he could not resist the temptation to speak in a utopian vein. Here and there in *Capital* or in *The Critique of the Gotha Programme*, he sketches out a distant future—a golden age in which class differences and the state would have disappeared, where employment would cease to be necessary, and where everyone would receive according to his needs; in short, an age where humanity would finally take its first steps towards freedom. As in every theory which exceeds the bounds of experience, historical materialism was transformed into an expansive fiction which told us most about the dreams and desires of its author—Liberty, Equality and Fraternity.

Such, in essence, was the nature of the design and development of Marx's argument. We shall note, equally briefly, its limitations.

Limitations

We shall not spend time on the utopian dimension of Marx's thought and his vision of a classless and stateless society where human relations would finally become transparent. His concepts had meaning and we shall not deny their importance, but we prefer to come back to his central intuition: the core idea that human beings, contrary to other animals, have the capacity to transform their social relations, to act on their history, as they are the only ones capable of consciously transforming their natural surroundings. From this perspective, the diverse forms of society throughout history would correspond to different moments and levels of development of their material or intellectual capacities, and their effects on nature.

Expressed in this manner, the idea presented itself with the universal force of a synthetic judgement applicable to the entire movement of history, from the stone age to the nuclear age. But the idea tends to become blurred as soon as it is used analytically to explore a specific society, at a given moment of history.

What are we to make of this notion of determination by material forces and the economy? To what types of linked relations and mechanisms is Marx referring? Reading his methodological texts, and particularly the Preface and Introduction to the *Contribution to the Critique of Political Economy*, it is apparent that Marx saw the mechanism of this determination as the combined action of two types of relations: those expressed through the metaphor of the relationship between a building and its foundations; and those expressed in terms of the notion of correspondence or non-correspondence between the diverse points of a whole.

Let us examine the metaphor. Marx uses the German terms *Grundlagen* and *Uberbau*, which are usually translated as 'infrastructure' and 'superstructure', though the literal meanings are 'foundations of a building' and 'the building constructed upon it'. Certainly, in order to build a house one has to start with the foundations, and the durability of the building will depend on the strength of those foundations. Marx's metaphor tries to show us certain types of relations: the relations of dependency that exist in a world where some realities become the condition for the possible existence of others. It does not refer to linear and mechanistic relations of cause and effect.

If one wanted to play with this metaphor, one would say that a house is not built in order to live on its foundations. It is built for certain needs which dictate their own forms of spaced enclosure. One must therefore conclude that as far as the use of a building is concerned, what counts is the 'superstructure' and not the 'infrastructure'.

Leaving this imagery aside, let us ask which elements of society Marx is referring to when he speaks of his *Grundlagen/Uberbau*: what lies behind these two concepts? Briefly speaking, the material and economic 'foundations' of a society would include two sets of distinct but inseparable elements, the productive forces on the one hand, and the social relations on the other, within which the process of production is organized. As for the building that is constructed on those foundations, it is composed of everything else in society: kinship relations, political and religious interactions, whether distinct or not, ideas and the arts, and so on. This description may give the impression that these relations exist in a disordered manner, in the midst of a society, but for Marx, a society is an organic entity which supposes the existence of a certain functional order between the parties that compose it.

For Marx, this order engendered the relations (whether close or distant) that the various non-economic institutions, in virtue of this basic function, maintained with the social and material process of production. He saw politics, in the broad sense of the sovereignty exercised by a given society over its territory and above all over its people (which includes but goes beyond its government), as the domain of those institutions and practices that are most closely linked to the material and social conditions of production. A society's laws and customs are also very closely linked to, though not confined within, the sphere of production.

The question of religion is a complex one. While recognizing the link between the development of religious institutions and representations and the evolution of human interactions with nature, and of forms of power,

Marx was not looking for a direct link between the major religions (Christianity, Buddhism and Islam) and given forms of production. As for art, he went so far as to declare that, 'As far as art is concerned, we know that the flourishing of art at certain epochs was not in any way related to the general development of society, nor consequently to its material foundations.' Everything occurred as though the more attenuated the relations of correspondence between all these social elements and with the social and material mode of production, the less direct were their lines of connection with the process of production. This brings us on to an examination of the second set of relations: the action of the material and economic basis on the organization and evolution of societies. These are relations that Marx calls of 'correspondence' (*Entsprechung*).

The notion of correspondence contains, first, the idea that social relations must be or should (up to a point) be compatible in order for them to coexist in the same society, at the heart of a new totality which Marx calls a 'social formation'. But among all the internal transformations which allow distinct social relationships to become increasingly compatible, those which, arising *within* a specific set of relations, most favour *the development of other* relationships coexisting with them, constitute transformations which allow the first relations to enter into correspondence with the other ones. The setting up of these correspondences cannot therefore be a matter of pure chance, and Marx even speaks of the existence of real 'laws of correspondence' that it is the task of social science to discover. Besides, there would be no such science were these laws not thought to exist.

It goes without saying that Marx was not unaware that transformations, for various reasons, could appear in the midst of a society without a direct link to changes from within the productive and production forces. But Marx assumes that among all the transformations that take place (and this is a 'postulate') and have an impact on the consequent results, only those arising from significant transformations of the productive forces have the capacity to modify completely the overall structure of society. And we have seen why. These transformations will act upon the relations of ownership, upon the material (and therefore social) differences between groups, upon the forms of wealth and power which could in the long term bring important changes in the religious or philosophical representations of nature and of society, and so on. In other words, these transformations are a source of constraints which weigh upon other elements of society, and cause them to assume a form which more closely corresponds to the conditions of development of new productive forces and new social relations of production.

Basically, Marx's idea is that there is continuous change *within* society, but that such changes, for the most part, do not amount to a change *of* society. They contribute, on the contrary, to maintaining the same overall structure of a society, ensuring its perpetuation. By contrast, certain changes help to eliminate an old form of society and replace it with another, and these constitute the elements of a process of transition from one social system to another. For Marx, the changes which bring about a transformation of society are not arbitrary, but only occur at certain epochs as part of a chain relation that has its origin in productive forces and the relations of production.

Marx does not believe that the arts or artistic and religious practices or doctrines have the power to change society. Christianity, for example—born in an eastern province of the Roman empire from a mutation of Judaism—did not bring about the eradication of slavery. Nor was it the reason for the emergence of feudal systems seven or eight centuries later or the forms of capitalism sixteen centuries later.

These, then, in brief, are the principal theoretical elements in Marx's vision of society which he saw as giving a 'scientific' character to the thesis of the determining role of material and economic relations. We shall now examine the limitations and weaknesses of his theories and see if they have bequeathed anything to the science of our time.

First (and this is now obvious despite being long contested by most Marxists), the distinction between 'infrastructure' and 'superstructure' needs, if it is to make any sense, to be interpreted as a distinction between functions rather than institutions. To speak of relations of production as existing separately from other social, kinship or sovereign interactions has an application only in exceptional historical situations.

The form of capitalist production is one of these exceptions because production is organized essentially on the basis of private ownership of the means of production and of money, and via the sale of the labour-power of individuals who are free from any religious, family or other obligation to work for others. They are forced to do so only because of material constraints. This was not the case within the framework of feudal production and society, and Marx was aware of it as much as anyone. The fact that the relations of capitalist production exist apart from other social relations is an exception, which has nonetheless had great importance for the development of social sciences. It has allowed Western thought to acknowledge more clearly the role of material and economic forces in the functioning of societies than at times when the production was organized from within social relations which at the same time assumed other functions—relations of kinship as in classless tribal societies, or politico-religious relations as in ancient oriental theocracies.

But if the 'infrastructure/superstructure' distinction retains meaning in so far as it is understood to refer to distinct social functions, it immediately gives rise to a problem. When, for example, kinship relations in tribal societies function also from within, as production relations, and therefore as both 'infrastructure' and 'superstructure', one needs to know why. Marx then refers us to the nature of the productive forces and their level of development, that is to say to the productivity of social labour. But as we shall see later, this explains neither the nature nor the internal structure of these kinship relations.

The important question is therefore to ascertain whether, as Marx postulates, the material and economic conditions of social life are really the sole conditions of the existence of other social relations, and function as the general conditions of social life. Here 'general' means not simply in the sense of being essential to the basic physical survival of individuals or even to the material development of humanity, but in the sense of being the condition for the emergence of other aspects of social life, of other social relations, of which they are, in a certain manner, the source.

Let us take the example of kinship relations. These are the social relations which arise among groups and individuals as a result of the application of three sorts of rules, those of alliance, affiliation and residence. The rules of alliance determine whom an individual, man or woman, can marry in society, and the rules of affiliation define to whom the children born from this union belong. This affiliation could be patrilineal, matrilineal, bi-lineal or non-lineal, and thus constitutive of many distinct 'systems' of kinship. It goes without saying that there are numerous links between the functions of kinship relations and the forms of wealth and power existing in society, but in no way does the kinship 'system' present itself as the superstructure of a 'mode' of production; and kinship relations can in no way be reduced to one of the superstructures of particular sets of social relations of production. Social anthropology has still not discovered a direct causal relationship between a mode of production and a mode of affiliation and alliance. In fact, if kinship relations do not depend directly for their appearance upon a mode of production, it is because they have their own functions and possess (the paradox is only apparent) an independent material base: the biological relations between the sexes and between the generations, the material conditions of the reproduction of offspring, which the rules of affiliation and alliance endow with meaning and social customs.

As far as religions are concerned, we have just seen that they cannot be explained solely, or even directly, by the transformation of modes of production and of power which evolve within a certain period of history. Christianity clearly owes a large part of its success to its association with the

Roman empire, then to feudal and lastly to bourgeois power. Over two millennia, it evolved, was threatened by sects and heresies and came finally, with the development of bourgeois society, to split into two branches, namely Catholicism and Protestantism. In no way does it owe its existence to these diverse mode of production; only its evolution. In fact, as with other religions, Christianity is first of all a code and symbols which, in virtue of their abstraction, are capable of integrating situations that are completely different from those with which it was associated at its origins—in other words, that of the situation of the Jewish people during the last centuries before the birth of Christ. An essential aspect of this code, which distinguishes it from some other great religions and puts it in consonance with those particular forms of economic and political evolution which encourage a sense of individual worth and importance, is the assertion that there is only one God who governs the universe.

Thus, Marx's central hypothesis that the material and social forms of production are the general foundations of social life has not been confirmed. Yet it retains a more limited, if nevertheless impressive, capacity to explain the functioning and evolution of societies. It has therefore not lost all its significance. As experience has shown, there is a realm of reality in which Marx's hypothesis has always made sense. It is that of the existence of close relations between the forms of production of human means of subsistence and wealth, and the forms of power exercised by some groups over others, in which, of course, the forms of thought, ideas and doctrines legitimizing or contesting these arrangements will always be implicated.

Production and power create dual realities and forces, nourishing one another and developing together, even in their very oppositions. In order to explain the close links between these two realities and their mutual and reciprocal development, neither the base/superstructure metaphor nor the notion of correspondence suffices. Let us take the example of India's caste system. It is not enough to discover the correspondence between the forms of power of the superior castes and the organization of production, nor of the distribution of the means of subsistence and that of the redistribution of wealth. One has to explain why the supreme power, the ultimate power in this society, belongs to the caste of those who accomplish and perform sacrifices and rituals—the Brahmans, who are in control and possess the monopoly of the (in our view) imaginary means of reproduction of the universe and of society. It is this which establishes their right to the labour, products and services of the peasants and other lower castes. That almost suffices to explain why power and production in ancient Indian civilization were organized in accordance with 'corresponding' forms. But it does not explain the Brahmans' monopoly over the sacred that these forms presuppose.

In our view, nevertheless, it is this coupling of the forms of production and the forms of power which lies at the source of these forces that are most capable of bringing about change not only within society but also of the form of society itself.

A final question: in this duality of production–power, what role do the productive forces play? Do we find the ultimate point of departure for those which usher in new forms of society? Some of Marx's formulations certainly give us to believe so: 'The Handmill gives you feudal society with its lords; the Steam-mill, society with its industrial capitalists.'[1]

Curt and polemical remarks such as this jibe at Proudhon (though Marx gave vent to many others that were equally scathing) provided rich pickings both for Marx's unswerving partisans and for his bitterest opponents. But does this represent Marx's last thought on the subject, the central thesis of his materialism? To claim so would be to deny or neglect all those writings of Marx in which he insists that the forces of production do not exist separately from social relations, which organize production, and that they are in no sense capable of self-development. The productive forces develop or stagnate as a result of extrinsic compulsions or restrictions, which have their source in the specific social relations of production, and which are themselves caught up in other social relations. These productive forces cannot be the primary or final cause of the movement of history, because a reality whose major conditions of development are extrinsic to it cannot figure as the final cause. There does not exist, within society, a primary institution from which others are born. There is no final cause either, nor a unique point of origin in the movement of societies. The problem is indeed to understand how and why human labour and productivity can be altered, and how and why new productive capacities are created. The answers are not in the productive forces as such, even if the nature of the existing productive forces sheds light on the obstacles which need to be overcome in order to create new productive forces.

Moreover, it is thus that Marx analyses the role of productive forces in the transition from the feudal to the capitalist mode of production. As we shall see, what was new initially was the capitalist mode of production, and not the forces of production which were harnessed by it and subsumed at that point in merely formal fashion within the new relations of production.

In Marx's view, the transition to capitalism is completed only when this situation has been overcome, and when the old productive forces—a past inheritance—have been replaced by new forms, created precisely by the development of the new relations of production. Such a process is the reverse of that described in the above quotation by Marx.

In short, Marx's work is not a seamless whole, nor is it presented as such.

It is not to be taken as the Bible or as a sacred text of religious revelation. Marx certainly would not have wanted it to be regarded in this light. But used in a critical manner and in the light of scientific and social discoveries in our time, his work is of major importance as he was the first to reveal forces and mechanisms which had previously been only vaguely understood.

Marx is certainly not what he is loudly claimed to be today, a sterile accident in Western ideology, burdened by a theory long buried. It is not, nevertheless, the insistence on the importance of the economy and the role of the state in social development that lie behind the current neglect of Marx's work. Doubts and rejections arose because of the practical consequences when others tried to realize Marx's cherished aspiration to move to a 'socialist' society and mode of production, but instead ended up imposing a communist dictatorship upon their own people, together with a bureaucratic economy, inefficiency and many hardships. History has not taken the path predicted by Marx: socialism was not born where he expected—in the most advanced capitalist countries—but in countries from which the mode of capitalist production and bourgeois society were absent or played only a minor role. Countries such as Russia and China were submerged under the weight of the decomposition of their internal social structures. What was being destroyed was not capitalism but ancient forms of production and power which were the old foundations of the Russian and Chinese states. Paradoxically, however, it is this recent history which (although it appears to contradict and confound Marx in every respect) has been used to confirm, or at least demonstrate the interest of, a crucial aspect of Marx's theory: his analysis of the transition process.

A Short Assessment of Marx's Analysis of the Processes of Transition in Western Europe from the Birth and Development of Capitalist Forms of Production and Exchange

Before beginning this assessment, it would seem necessary to remind ourselves of Marx's self-imposed limits within his work. He wanted above all to discover the economic laws of movement in bourgeois societies during the development and various phases of evolution of exchange and capitalist production. He therefore postponed his analysis of the transformations of family structures (their evolution within the bourgeoisie, the working class and the peasantry), of political regimes (republics or constitutional monarchies) and of systems of thoughts and values (the rise of Protestantism, the development of rational philosophies, and so on) which marked the various phases of development of capitalist production forms in bourgeois societies. Although he comments frequently on these issues, he does not treat them in detail.

Periodization of the Processes of Transition from Feudal to Capitalist Forms of Production

Taking his cue from Lyell, the founder of the science of geology, who had denied that there were clear divisions between geological epochs, Marx rejected the idea that one could make a sharp distinction between the various socio-economic phases through which society passes. From this perspective, the fundamental point was that political or social revolutions (such as the French and Russian revolutions) cannot constitute the starting-point of a transition towards a new economy or a new social formation. These were exceptional moments in history, in the sense that they served to accelerate processes already initiated by empowering those social classes which had a vested interest in achieving as rapid and comprehensive a change as possible.

As for the appearance and development of capitalist forms of production, Marx distinguishes three stages which he sees as allowing a broad periodization of these processes. He dates he first period (which he calls the 'prelude' or the 'premises') from the last quarter of the fifteenth to the end of the sixteenth century. The second period is that of the youth and development of the capitalist mode of production, together with the establishment of a world market economy and the expansion of manufacture and industries. Lastly, from the end of the eighteenth to the second half of the nineteenth century, manufacture slowly gave way to mechanization and the industrial revolution. The latter was responsible for profound changes in agricultural and urban production in the West and for introducing great upheavals and strains in the relations between the city and the countryside.

This periodization could only be very approximate in Marx's view, for he saw no sharp divisions between, on the one hand, a historical period in which a mode of production remained dominant together with its corresponding forms of social organization and processes of thinking, and, on the other hand, a period wherein this mode of production was waning, and had been relegated to a secondary role in the reproduction of society and become subordinate to the expansion of a dominant new mode of production.

Let us go back to the first stage—the birth, the 'prelude' or the 'premises'—and essential moments in history. Marx's hypothesis is that when new sporadic and spontaneous social forms of production appear, they do so only when an economic system begins to break down. These new social forms flourish on the basis of existing technical knowledge, know-how and inherited processes of work, up to the point at which, in order to continue their development, they have to destroy their starting-point and replace it with new techniques and more adequate means of production, and these latter are the product of their own development. This is what Marx calls the transition from the formal subsumption of old labour process within new relations of production to the real subsumption of a new labour process within those relations.

The Methodological Priority of the Analysis of the Structure of New Social Relations over the Analysis of their Genesis

Marx's problem was to identify what was novel about these ways of organizing production and exchanges, and to understand the capitalist structures which had appeared to arise spontaneously, at various places in Europe, from the beginning of the sixteenth century onwards. In terms of 'methodology', the analysis of the process of transition must first reveal the structure of the relations of the new production before reconstituting the genesis and the evolution. We may surmise that from the time of his *Grundrisse*, Marx adhered to the following definition of the capitalist mode of production: a method of production and exchange that has its origin and conditions of reproduction in the coming together of four elements, each of which refers us to a distinct set of social relations:

1. It is, historically, the most developed form of commodity production.
2. It rests on private ownership of the means of production and money.
3. These means of production and money function as capital, that is to say, they are used to produce an added value to the initial investment for the process of production, a value which corresponds to the various forms of capitalist profit.
4. This capital enhancement of value is realized by putting to work and exploiting waged workers who, although free in person, have no means of production or subsistence and are thus obliged to sell the use of their labour-power to those who possess those means.

It is immediately apparent that none of these four elements has come into being in modern times. Producing merchandise, making money with money, using paid workers, and creating the means of production on the basis of private ownership, are all social interactions found at different epochs in diverse societies. The specific character and capitalist manner of production reside in the combination of these elements. And each time this combination happened, a capitalist method of production was realized locally: the capitalist form of production.

To analyse, then, the genesis of capitalist relations is not to provide the genealogical history of the forms of commodity production, of wages, and so on, in every society and during each period in which they occur. It is to analyse their development at the heart of the evolution of the feudal mode of production in Western Europe and the circumstances and reasons which brought them into combination at a certain moment in history. To undertake such an analysis is to take account of what the classical economists referred to as 'the process of primitive accumulation of capital'. This a process which led certain countries of Europe (at the forefront of which were England and Holland) to the concentration, at one social pole, of monetary wealth, and of the means of production and subsistence, and to the creation, at the other pole, of a mass of individuals freed from personal ties of bondage of the feudal type, but at the same time separated from the means of production and subsistence essential to their survival.

Back to the Origins: The Regressive Method

Consequently, the investigation into the processes of transition proceeds in a 'backwards and regressive' manner because, in the past, one had to identify the reasons for the decomposition of the old feudal relations of agricultural production, industry and commerce and for the partial extinction of these relations within this regressive method; one tries to discover the reasons and the forces which brought about the decomposition of the old system, while conserving and re-combining a number of these elements. For Marx, as for Braudel[2] a century later, these forces were engendered by the expansion of commerce and commodity production, which began at the start of the fifteenth century on the basis and within the framework of feudal relations which themselves had been profoundly altered by the great crisis of the fourteenth century.

Initiated before the discovery of America, this expansion proceeded apace after the opening up of the New World and was further accelerated by the progressive expansion of a world economy. It changed artisans into merchants, and forced the merchants to organize with a view to controlling artisan production; it forced everyone to gainsay the rules and regulations of the corporations and guilds to which they belonged. In other words, they had to go beyond the limits laid down by the feudal organizations of production and exchange, which were forcing the development of commerce and mercantile production upon them. Within these processes, the ancient forms of artisan and agricultural production and the ancient forms of commerce broke down and began to disintegrate. Certain elements disappeared, while others were preserved and combined together. Marx shows us, in his unfinished Chapter 6 of *Capital*, how he analysed the transition of the corporate artisan workshops to the capitalist workshops. Since his findings are particularly interesting, we shall now give a brief summary of the most important points.

In the corporate workshops, the master, his colleagues and his apprentices are all free to do as they please; and so are the capitalist and his workers. The master–artisan is the owner of the raw materials and some of the instruments or tools, while another part is owned by his colleagues.

The master–artisan is the master since he both controls his trade and participates directly in production. The colleagues and the apprentices are tied to him because of personal relations, forming an extended family as they eat their meals together, and receive half their wages in kind and the rest in money. As for the master, he, like the capitalist, is the owner of the product of labour, both his own and that of his colleagues, but he is also a merchant as he buys and sells goods. His aim is both to grow rich and to preserve his social status as master of his trade. He practises his trade within a corporation that controls the quality and quantity of goods produced by him; in other words, the master–artisan and his colleagues produce goods as though they were reproducing, at the same time, their social structures of production, the corporations and guilds to which they belong.

What elements of ancient corporative organization were abolished in the formation processes of capitalist relations of production? Payment in kind for workers was eliminated and, when the size of the company allowed it, so too was the master's direct participation in the work process. The master was then able to spend most of his time in the management of the process, as well as in the mercantile duties of buying and selling. In terms of history and society, and in order to eliminate certain elements of a social structure, it is not possible to do without social struggles, tensions, conflicts, and ideological or philosophical battles, in other words, without specifically directed socio-cultural changes. The formation of capitalist relations is not simply a matter of 'economic' phenomena. It implies a whole set-up of social struggles, conflicts of interests and ideas. But (and this point is very important theoretically) not every social and cultural change belongs to the category of processes of transition. All those changes are excluded which serve to reproduce the old system of production and social organization by adapting it to internal or external shifts in its evolution, in other words, all changes designed to preserve the system.

The Three Phases in the Birth of New Social Relations of Production

New social relations of production therefore come into being at the end of a process of disintegration: certain elements belonging to the old mode disappear, while others are preserved, but recombine to initiate a new development. Everything happens as though the three aspects of this process (division, elimination and conservation) were releasing a new historical potential for advancing transformations and developments that had already begun.

Moreover, after the 'regressive' phase, the analysis must proceed to a 'progressive' engagement with the secular development of the new relations of production from their beginnings through to their full flowering.

From the Birth to the Fruitful Expansion of New Relations of Production: The Progressive Method

The regressive method becomes progressive. The analysis follows the course of history and its development through time and space of a new form of production. Hence Marx outlines in *Capital* the progressive conquest (or destruction) by capitalism of various traditional branches of industrial and agricultural production, and national and international commerce. He also describes the possible creation of new branches of production and forms of commerce that owe nothing to the past. Marx draws on England for most of his examples of these transformations, as it was the most advanced industrial capitalist country in the nineteenth century. Marx explains his procedure clearly. His goal, in these chapters, is not to write England's history, nor even that of the development of capitalism there. His approach is that of an economic theorist who wishes, through analysis of chosen examples, to discover the material conditions and economic mechanisms that allowed these developments to take place.

Marx concludes that capitalism has gone through two periods or stages. For a long time (roughly speaking, from the end of the eighteenth century to the birth of mechanization and large-scale industry), production, while being reorganized on the basis of capitalist relations, continued to rest largely on the material base, procedures and inherited knowledge of pre-capitalist forms of production. But with mechanization—which appeared in the framework of manufacture—large-scale industries became possible and production continued to develop ever more vigorously, but this time upon a material base and with the help of new productive forces which were created by the development of capitalism itself. Far from being completed in the nineteenth century, this process began again each time a branch of economic activity came under the control of capital.

In order to show the difference between these two stages in the relations between the social and the material conditions of production, Marx has recourse to a somewhat hermetic juridico-philosophical vocabulary, in which he speaks of the transition from a stage of 'formal subsumption' of the labour process within the new relations of capitalism to a stage wherein they were 'really' subsumed. (He also speaks more simply about subordination, or *Unterordnung*, whether formal or real.) But—and this is the main point of his theoretical conception concerning the genesis and development of the economic and social systems—in Marx's eyes, it is this transition from 'formal' to 'real' subsumption which bears witness to the fact that the transition from pre-capitalist modes of production (of unaltered form—feudalism, slavery, primitive communism) to the capitalist mode has been achieved. And this transition can be achieved in one or more branches of industry without it taking place throughout the economy of a country as a whole. In order for that to be accomplished—and Braudel agrees with Marx on this point—a country needs to be in the forefront of international commerce. In other words, it should occupy an important place in the centre of the international division of labour within the new world economic order which had first begun to function in the sixteenth century. It was in the countries of the centre that the transition to the mode of modern capitalist production was most completely and rapidly achieved, rather than in societies on the periphery of the new system. Marx therefore distinguished between the forms of transition obtaining in countries where the capitalist mode originated and those obtaining in countries which were gradually subordinated to one or more of these centres of capitalism.

Transition from Formal to Real Subsumption in the Countries of the Centre

According to Marx, the subsumption of different labour processes under the capitalist forms of production did not profoundly disrupt existing forms of technical and material knowledge, nor the material base of production inherited from feudal production. However, a fundamental modification was rapidly taking place in the social organization of production: work itself was becoming more intense and continuous, and the labour force was increasingly exploited through cuts in holidays and longer working hours. In other words, 'formal subsumption' leads to an absolute increase in the surplus value appropriated by the capitalist. The ultimate evolution of capitalism towards the creation of a new material base of its own leads, in turn, to a general upheaval in the conditions of work and productivity of labour.

For Marx, the transition from industrial artisan forms of production to manufacture had opened up the way to the introduction of machinery and large-scale industry, via inventions and transformations which occurred within manufacture itself. Manufacture had already created piece-workers who specialized in only one task while the technical basis of work and manual labour was retained. Mechanization, by contrast, had profoundly altered the conditions of production. Little by little, machines had replaced the manual worker, first as instruments for work and then as sources of motive power, and had done so by the increasingly systematic application of scientific knowledge to the processes of manufacture. These processes were themselves subsequently analysed in terms of the laws of chemistry and physics, that is to say, without any reference to the human body and its possibilities. With mechanization and the industrial revolution, capitalism created the modern conditions of production which came increasingly to rely on mechanized systems operated by the collective worker. Direct producers became the complements, the extensions and even the appendages of a system of machines, and of machines that create machines.

The 'transition' from pre-capitalist forms of production in Europe ended with the industrial revolution. It began in England, followed by France, Holland and Germany, in short, in those countries which were at the centre of the global capitalist system. But these societies were thereafter divided into central and peripheral zones: into, on the one hand, industrial and new urban zones, and, on the other hand, rural zones providing the urban communities with the labour workforce needed for the factories, including some of the new urban population. In the course of these processes in the countries of the centre and in their industrial heartland, the exploitation of the waged workforce changed its nature and form. During the first stages of capitalism, while it was still based on old methods of manufacture, the increase in profits came from more intensive and longer working hours, and the shortening or elimination of holidays. Marx referred to this source as 'absolute' surplus value. It is typical of all forms of 'formal subsumption' of labour under capitalism. But with the disruption of the processes and means of production, the productivity of social labour increased enormously, lowering the relative value of the reproduction costs of the workforce. 'Relative' surplus value became the principal source of profits and the mark of societies in which the 'subsumption' of work under capitalism had become 'real'.

With the industrial revolution, capitalist methods of production were able to conquer, disrupt or gradually eliminate all the old forms of industrial and agricultural production. It thereupon created new ones while at the same time changing the systems of transportation. From that moment on, the contradictions intensified between the industrial and rural zones. Under competition from industrial products, local peasant and rural crafts collapsed, and for the first time in history agriculture began to exist away from the industries which sustained it and were necessary to it. This led to a doubly contradictory development: on the one hand, older forms of production were destroyed or weakened under the impact of capitalist competition, which undermined their material base; on the other (as can be seen in the examples of share-cropping, tenant farming and direct holdings that exist today) capitalism reproduced them upon a material base provided by itself, and, by virtue of the power it exercised over the whole of commodity production, made them dependent upon it.

Marx could have stopped his analysis at this point, i.e. with the forms of capitalism that existed in his day—in certain European countries where capitalism already seemed to have reached maturity, and to be flourishing in the midst of pre-capitalist forms of production which were either already under its sway or doomed to disappear. But for Marx, history did not stop there. The facts seemed to suggest that another transition was already taking place during the second half of the nineteenth century, to the extent that, within the global capitalist system, the development of large-scale industry and mass production had started to come into conflict with the ownership of the means of production, commodities, money and capital. Marx saw the appearance of workers' cooperatives as testifying to this no less than the increasing numbers of capitalist forms or advanced monopolies. Europe (at least, the Europe of the capitalist countries) was, from then on, in a transitional phase leading to a 'reconversion of capital into the property of the associated producers, into directly social property'.[3] But this reconversion could not come about through a purely economic transformation. It required major social and political struggles, through which the exploited classes would seize power. It demanded a revolution, or revolutions.

We shall not pursue further the analysis of Marx's ideas on the process of transition towards a new form of production and a new society, except to observe that the shift to 'the mode of production of the associated workers' did not take place, as he had hoped and anticipated, in capital's heartlands, but on the periphery of Europe, in Russia.

It is true that towards the end of his life, Marx foresaw this possibility, but only as an exception.[4] Nonetheless, this exception became the rule, as was the case with the other breakpoints which, half a century later after the Second World War, were the events which took place even further away from the centre, in China, Vietnam, Mozambique and Cuba.

Return to the 'Progressive Method': Following History in all its Phases

West European economic history over the past four centuries is not reducible to the stages of development of industrial capitalist production, even if this development became the dominant aspect of this history. Other factors and forms of production were no less a product of the evolution of the feudal system, such as the small mercantile, artisan and agricultural forms of production, which were likewise released from communal or corporative constraints. These forms have developed or disappeared over time and those which have survived alongside capitalism are subordinate to it. In short, it is only when history is followed in all its different stages that the historian is able to explain how and why the capitalist form of production, which was initially just one of several social forms, finally became the dominant form of production and exchange.

We shall take only one example, that of the forms of organization, ownership and production in agriculture which succeeded the feudal forms. The evolution of feudal relations of production under the expansion of the market and the monetary economy had initially spurred the landowners, the aristocracy and the bourgeoisie gradually to substitute money revenues for other forms of feudal revenue in countries linked to the world market. The rent relations gradually ceased to be personal and became contractual. This evolution took a number of different forms. It gave birth to diverse forms of 'share-cropping' and non-capitalist farming or, if peasants were able to buy back the lands or obtain them through agricultural reforms, it gave rise to peasants who owned their own lands and cultivated them themselves. It is this last form that Marx called 'the smallholding mode of production'.

But in England, and in certain regions of France and Germany, this evolution led to the emergence of capitalist farmers: that is to say, it ushered in a form of production in which the land remains the property of an absentee landlord and is worked by a farmer who himself owns the instruments of production and capital, and who no longer employs subservient peasants but paid agricultural workers. The land has become, under this relation of production, a purely material and economic reality and its ownership is denuded of all the political and ideological attributes which were characteristic of pre-capitalist forms of land ownership. Even as the twentieth century draws to a close, these diverse forms of agricultural production still coexist in Europe.

The Centre, the Centres and the Two Peripheries

There is only one factor missing in these analyses: that of the forms of production which were developed in the peripheral countries surrounding the zone of the creation and expansion of capitalism. In fact, there are two peripheries: that of the European countries which traded with England, France and Holland; and that of the non-European countries that were slowly colonized by or otherwise subordinated to Europe's own interests. Here too, a careful analysis of Marx's texts shows us that, contrary to the interpretation of Wallerstein, Samir Amin and others, Marx did not believe that a peripheral capitalism had developed from the beginning in the capitalist peripheries.

In Eastern Europe, in Eastern Prussia, in Poland and in Hungary, the development of agricultural production (destined for export to the cities and to the populations in the capitalist centres of Western Europe) brought with it the institution and development of a new form of serfdom. This is the so-called problem of 'second serfdom' as outlined by German historians in the nineteenth century. By contrast, in the Danube provinces, as Marx had already noted from his research on this region, the aftermath of the Ottoman empire's defeat by France and England led to the monopolization of a part of the territories belonging to the Wallachian community and others by the local aristocracies, and to the emergence, for the first time, of a form of individual serfdom.

In the second periphery, things turned out very differently depending on whether the countries were transformed into colonies or only forced beneath the yoke of European economic and political pressure. In Mexico and Peru, the old forms of social production and organization were to be destroyed and replaced by an economy of mines and plantations exploited for Europe's profit and for European colonial interests, with forced and imposed labour and other means of individual and collective servitude, as well as an obligation to pay state contributions and taxes. The indigenous local labour was radically transformed with the overthrow of their elites, the imposition of Christianity and the exploitation of most of their lands. But elsewhere, in the south of the United States for example, when the local Indian populations disappeared or refused to work on the plantations, an uprooted labour force had to be imported from Africa, thereby reinstating slave modes of production. 'Second serfdom' in the eastern part of Europe, 'first serfdom' in Romania, a plantation economy based on slavery in North America and on collective and individual 'pseudo-feudal' forms of servitude in South America and in Mexico—these are all examples of the structures which developed in the various peripheries of the world capitalist system during the first centuries of its creation and expansion. It was not until another epoch, another time and the emergence of other conditions that the basic forms of capitalist production really appeared.

Overall View of Marx's Theoretical Analysis of the Transition Process Fruitful Hypotheses, Methods and Models. Our examination of the way in which Marx theorized the process of transition from one dominant socio-economic system to another reveals the importance of his method, which combines regressive and progressive movements, economic theory and historical researches, and micro-/macro-sociological analysis.

For Marx, the process of transition is one aspect of a wider process of decomposition of a hitherto dominant socio-economic system. This process of decomposition destroys certain elements of the old relations of production and preserves others. Thereafter a process of transition begins when the elements are combined in a new and original manner. These ideas were elaborated above all in Marx's attempt (pursued over many years) to explain the birth and various phases of development of the capitalist mode of production and exchange, which finally asserted itself in the middle of the nineteenth century in parts of Europe and elsewhere. As an explanation of the genesis of capitalism, it is up to historians and economists to compare this model with what we know today about the origins of capitalism. But it seems to us that this model has a more general impact and could help to analyse other historical or contemporary processes of transition.

There are several very interesting hypotheses which help to explain not only the birth but the development of a new economic system. Above all, there is the idea that an economic system develops only by destroying the material and technical bases upon which it originally relied, and which it inherited from the previous dominant system; the idea that this destruction proceeds correspondingly with the extent to which the new relations of production are capable of creating a new material base, new forces of material and intellectual production—in short, the idea of a transition from a stage of formal subsumption of an old technical base, under new relations of production, to the real subsumption under those relations of a new base which they helped to create.

But this same process of creating a new base (of a kind that guarantees the self-development of a new system) also helps to explain the conditions under which a new system of production comes to prevail over other forms of production which continue to coexist side by side with it, and which slowly and eventually become subordinate to it, so that they survive only on the technical bases provided by it and within the limits that it imposes upon them.

We should note that this perspective is not that of the development of new productive forces that give birth to new social forms of production, but that of the arrival and development of new social forms of production which bring forward the development of new productive forces. In general, productive, material and intellectual forces are not developed for their own sake, but in a precise historical context and for social reasons, whatever their nature may be.

Equally important is the idea that a process of transition is a phenomenon that is both micro- and macro-sociological; it is composed of a multitude of spontaneous births, of local developments, many of them fleeting but which operate together in aggregate to bring about new global structures which then enter into conflict with the reproduction of global structures of the dominant system. It is important to note that Marx, when analysing the genesis of capitalism, accentuated the initially spontaneous and sporadic, and then ever more massive and concentrated, character of the development of the new relations of capitalist production. This is why he thought the mode of production of associated workers (which he predicted would succeed the mode of capitalist production) would develop in areas where its premises had already appeared spontaneously under the guise of workers' cooperatives, and where its material conditions—the modern, gigantic and socialized productive forces—already existed.

He accepted that other 'births' (but this time 'voluntary' ones, 'imposed' by a revolution and allowing a society to inaugurate 'a foreshortened process of development') were possible, particularly in Russia. However, he saw them as exceptions which could only last if the workers were subsequently able to seize control of production and of society in the advanced capitalist countries, in the countries of the centre.

For—and this idea of Marx has today become a commonplace—a socio-economic system develops out of one or several centres in the direction of one or several peripheries which encompass other socio-economic systems which more or less rapidly, more or less violently, are destined to disappear or to have to transform themselves in order to continue to exist within the limits and under forms imposed by their subordination to the logic of the dominant system and to the interests of the countries where this system prevails.

Gaps and Problems. Alongside these fertile theses and useful instruments of analysis, however, there are also serious gaps and formidable problems in Marx's argument.

One could, for example, conclude, contrary to Marx, that if France was the 'classic' site for bourgeois revolution, it was mainly because capitalism was 'less' developed than in England; and that the French bourgeoisie, in order to reach its goals, had to collaborate politically, and 'provisionally', with the peasant and artisan classes which then 'radicalized' its struggle. This led, after the sales of national and church properties, to a growth in numbers of peasant owners and direct producers, which in turn came to erode the process of industrialization and urbanism. A further point is that, to note but one aspect of the revolution in modern society, there is no analysis in Marx of the evolution of peasant and working-class families.

Another area that is still unresolved in Marx's writings is that of the key role of the state in the processes of transition. It is to Marx's credit that he emphasized the importance in these processes of the creation of national banks, state systems of taxation, forms of political protection, colonial policy, wars and conquests, employment legislation, assistance to manufacturers, and so on. But he did not take his analysis further (although he had planned to do so in another volume of *Capital*, which was never written). Today, more than in Marx's lifetime, the state intervenes continuously in the evolution of economic structures, whether through credit systems or price fixing, and, in underdeveloped countries, through various development plans linked to agricultural reform.

The most pressing questions raised by Marx's theory are not to do with errors or gaps in his interpretation of the genesis of capitalism in Western Europe. They arise, rather, as a consequence of the course taken by world history since Marx's death: notably the arrival, following the Bolshevik revolution of 1917, of 'socialist' forms of production and society—forms which arose not in the centre but in the peripheries of the capitalist system, and were the upshot of victorious revolution (Russia, China and Cuba) or followed on the superpower division of global influence (the countries of Eastern Europe) which have either almost wholly disappeared or are in ruins.

In fact, when these revolutions took place, they coincided with struggles for national independence (as in China, Angola and Vietnam) against occupying foreign forces (China) or colonial powers (Vietnam, Angola). In these struggles, the revolutionaries often showed themselves to be the most resolute and the most capable when confronted by other movements assisted by the local dominant classes. But apart from these particular historic circumstances, and these specific political and military struggles against foreign powers and their local allies, in none of these societies—all very different in size, history and traditions—did 'the material conditions of existence of new and superior relations of production blossom forth', which, for Marx, was an essential condition for the transition to the 'mode of production of the associated workers'.

Instead of the free, voluntary association of workers, we have seen the imposed collectivization of ownership and production. Instead of the progressive socialization of the processes of production, imposed by the development of the productive forces combined into an ever more complex division of labour, we have seen the nationalization of the means of production. Instead of democratic processes in self-managed production, we have seen a general bureaucratization of the instruments of production. Instead of a political and cultural democracy, at the service of the people and richer than the bourgeois democracy of advanced capitalism, we have seen the dictatorship of a party against its own people, and the imposition of the will of an elite of party bosses, the inevitable consequence of which has been the institution and generalization of terror. Instead of building a material base which would demonstrate socialism's superiority over capitalism, the socialist countries have managed, even with untold sacrifices, to build a material base that still leaves them far behind the most advanced capitalist countries.

In short, the transition to socialism in countries where capitalism either did not exist or was very underdeveloped has plunged, if not Marx's own thought, certainly the various Marxisms of those laying claim to it, into a profound crisis at both the theoretical and the practical level. A theoretical crisis has arisen because we have so far been provided with no convincing 'Marxist' analysis of these events. In the wake of a failed transition, in which all our revolutionary forces and hopes have been dashed, shall we be witnesses to a transition without revolution—a transition sustained solely by the virtues of a prudent pragmatism, yet doggedly committed to serving the interests of the currently most threatened peoples of the world? Are we to pass from the heat of the age of revolutions into a cooler period of historical evolutions whose outcome seems more promising?

5. *From Marxism to Liberal Nationalism: A Transformation in Palestinian Marxism*

Mahir Sharif

In the aftermath of the collapse of the Soviet Union, the Palestinian Communist Party (PCP) was renamed and is now called the Palestinian People's [Sha'b] Party (PPP). What is the significance of this change? Is it an attempt to form an authentic or domestic form of Marxism, to develop it independently after the decline of the schematic, ready-made plans for social development with their mechanistic standardized frameworks? Or is it simply a renunciation of Marxism altogether, i.e. a complete rupture with all the traditions that Marxism had created and accumulated on Palestinian soil?

The Second Congress of the PCP in late October 1991 (which took the decision to change the party's name) asserted that the new 'People's Party' was a 'continuation of the revolutionary heritage of the struggles waged by Palestinian communists over decades of action'. Yet there is not one explicit mention of Marxism in the programme, which presents a new approach to the Palestinian reality in conjunction with Arab and world conditions. This approach reveals a discontinuity with traditional communist thinking. Hence the two questions raised above are valid and even necessary. In this chapter, I shall attempt to answer them on the basis of a critical survey of the major events in the history of the Palestinian communist movement in Palestine. The survey will focus on how the Palestinian communists approached Marxism while being part of the international communist movement with a leading centre that has, until recently, played the role of ideological authority. This central authority defined the frameworks of thinking and forms of party patterns. It created a centre/periphery relationship within the international communist movement, resulting in both negative and (at times) positive consequences. The chapter does not attempt a reformulation of history but rather a rereading.

How Marxism Emerged in the Mashreq

It is perhaps relevant to remind ourselves of the origins of the term 'Marxism'. Marx's supporters never labelled themselves Marxists during his lifetime. The term was introduced by the Bakhuninists, the followers of the nineteenth-century Russian anarchist, in their polemic against Marx and his disciples. When the latter called the former Bahkuninists, they retorted by calling their rivals Marxists. The term was thus used in a derogatory manner. It was not until Marx's death in 1883 that the label came to have a positive meaning in the sense of signifying a particular trend which is distinguished from other political and ideological currents within the leftist movement. As the *Critical Dictionary of Marxism* points out, Marx had strong reservations about this term lest 'Marxists' would distort his thesis and turn themselves into a closed caste, thereby destroying the attempts to lend socialism a scientific basis.[1] On various occasions, Engels stressed Marx's rejection of the idea of himself as a 'Marxist', though the spread of the term finally prompted even Engels himself to endorse it. Since then, 'Marxist' has come to denote anyone who adopts not only the thesis formulated by Marx and Engels but also the many additions incorporated into it. Hence it has become extremely difficult to define what the word Marxist really signifies. Among the many additions by Kautsky, Rosa Luxemburg and others, that of Lenin occupied a special and even a central role in the wake of the First World War and the triumph of the October revolution in Russia.

Although Lenin's Marxist methodology helped him analyse the situation in Russia at the time, it developed into a bridge over which Marxism would travel to the Orient, the Mashreq (i.e. the Arab East) included. Before the October revolution and the establishment of the Comintern (the Communist International), the Mashreq's interest in Marxist thought was limited to a handful of intellectuals who were acquainted with Marx's works through their contacts with the West, their command of Western languages or their knowledge of Western intellectual trends. The first references to Marx in an Arab publication date back to 1890: he was referred to as a political-economic scientist or prominent social philosopher in the West. The first serious attempt to review the socialist ideas of Marx was made in 1915 by the Egyptian writer Hasanin al-Mansouri in his *History of Socialist Systems*.[2] It was not until the 1930s that some of Marx's works were translated into Arabic. The Syrian Khaled Bekdash translated the *Communist Party*

Manifesto in 1933; it was the first Marxian text to appear in Arabic. In 1947 the first translation (of Volume I) of *Das Kapital* was printed in Cairo; it was translated by the Egyptian economist Rashid al-Barrawi from the German original.

The pioneers of the communist movement in the Mashreq became acquainted with Marxism through Lenin's writings. Yousif Ibrahim Yazbik, one of the founders of the Communist Party in Syria and Lebanon (established in the autumn of 1924) recalled in an interview with the *Dirasat Arabiya* quarterly review in August 1971 how he had only recently read a text by Marx or Engels, and that Lenin's *What is to be Done?* was the first text he had read in 1926. Lenin's works were translated into Arabic in the 1920s. His *State and Revolution* appeared in Egypt and was translated by Ahmad Rif'at.[3]

The reason why Lenin's contributions attracted radical revolutionaries in the colonized and semi-colonized countries to Marxism becomes clearer when we recall that Lenin was, in their eyes, the leader of a socialist revolution which had declared a complete rupture with the imperialist policy of the colonial exploitation of these countries. He was the leader who highlighted the fact of the world's division into oppressive and oppressed nations; he also pioneered the idea of the alliance of socialism with the national liberation movements. But those radicals who started to form communist parties in the colonized and semi-colonized countries, the Mashreq included, were soon on the horns of a dilemma when, after Lenin's death, Marxism was turned by Stalin into the petrified dogma known as Marxism-Leninism. All parties affiliated to the Comintern were obliged to adhere to this official dogma, although Lenin himself had warned against the blind copying of Bolshevik experience, especially in the backward and colonized regions. According to Lenin, Marxists should conceive of the living reality of today rather than commit themselves to the theory of yesterday which could, at best, only reveal the most general truths. As the Soviet Communist Party assumed overall ideological and political authority, the communists could never develop the Marxist system into a flexible methodology which might help them understand the realities and differing conditions of their own countries. They were deprived of any opportunity to develop their own free and independent analysis. This applies equally to the communists in the Mashreq.

A Narrow and Irrelevant Class Approach

At its inception in March 1919, the Comintern was both an alliance between communist parties the world over and an international party led and directed by one centre. After Lenin's death, the movement lost this first feature and was transformed into a single, centrally led and directed movement. Lenin himself contributed to this change. The twenty-one conditions set for membership of the Comintern, drafted at Lenin's initiative during the Second Congress (summer 1920), state among other things:

- The daily propaganda and agitation waged by every party should have a communist character and be consistent with the programme and decisions of the Comintern.
- The affiliated parties should be organized in accordance with the principle of democratic centralism. [It is interesting to note how these organizational 'principles' of centralism and iron discipline were declared necessary in that period of escalating world tension.]
- All decisions taken by the Comintern and its Executive Committee are compulsory for all affiliated member parties.
- All parties wishing to join the Comintern should rename themselves as: the Communist Party—branch of the Third International. [The renaming, of course, was far from a mere formality and assumed great political significance.][4]

The Palestinian Communist Party was thus only a branch of the Third International. Moreover, it was created among Jewish immigrants and by Jewish revolutionaries who were far removed from the Palestinian reality. Their outlook was determined by the experience of class struggle and civil war in their (mostly European) countries of origin. Their experience produced a narrow class approach to any analysis of the Palestinian reality, focusing on the social problem, i.e. the emancipation of the working class, and relegating the national liberation of the people as a whole to a secondary position. Those Jewish revolutionaries failed to understand the importance of the Comintern's call to 'Arabize' the party in Palestine: without Arabization, the Comintern thought, 'there would be no future for the whole communist movement in this country'. Among the impediments to such a transformation was the leadership's view that the PCP was but one 'contingent' in the great international army led by the general staff in Moscow, waging a battle against the world bourgeoisie on the road to the final victory of international socialist revolution. To them, Soviet power in Russia was only one step in this direction.

Both the Arab nationalist movement and the Jewish zionist movement were considered reactionary, the former seen as representing the interests of the Arab bourgeoisie and landlords, the latter the interests of the Jewish bourgeoisie, against both of whom the PCP was opposed. The party was supposed to represent the Jewish and Arab workers, who should march in brotherly unity, hand in hand in a common struggle against their class enemies. Thus the party's political discourse was directed to the working class and their allies, the peasants, and was couched in the language of class struggle. When the party mouthpiece *Ilal Amam* [Forward] published its first edition in March 1929, it defined its character in the following terms:

> Our paper, *Ilal Amam*, is at present the only paper to focus on the defence of the interests of the working class and the peasants, who are oppressed by the capitalist and landlord classes irrespective of their nationality on the one hand, and oppressed by British colonialism on the other . . .
>
> *Ilal Amam*, O workers and peasants, is your paper; it is the mirror which will reflect your life, the lamp to illuminate the path for your emancipation from your oppressors and exploiters.

In the 1930s the PCP took steps to Arabize the party and tackle the colonial question in Palestine, stressing the need to widen the participation of the Arab workers in the struggle for national independence. However, it viewed this participation by the Arab working class in the narrowest sense of the word, not as a contribution to a national struggle that encompassed the people as a whole, but as a form of continued class struggle and a means to achieve the hegemony and interests of the working class.

At the end of 1930, the Seventh Congress of the PCP defined the basic tasks of the party as follows:

> To mobilize workers and peasants in the struggle against British imperialism and its tool, zionism, and in the struggle against the Arab bourgeoisie and its betrayal of the national liberation movement; to encourage by all means the process of an agricultural revolution in Palestine.[5]

A document issued by the PCP in early 1933 reads:

> In the continued, relentless and dedicated struggle for national liberation, the proletariat will explain to the masses, under whatever circumstances, that national independence cannot be achieved without a peasant, agricultural revolution and without the inception of a workers' and peasants' government. The proletariat will not win over the broad workers and peasant masses against the bourgeoisie, imperialists,

> landlords and usurers, and will not attract the poor urban masses and the petty bourgeoisie, unless it mobilizes and organizes in the struggle against imperialism and for national liberation.[6]

The party only managed to go beyond the narrow class approach after the general strike and the great rebellion in Palestine in 1936. Two intertwined factors led to this change of direction: first, the Popular Front policy endorsed by the Comintern in the summer of 1935 and, second, the relative independence that the communist parties began to enjoy in relation to the centre when the Seventh Congress of the Comintern itself radically reduced the central powers of the Executive Committee over the branches, i.e. the affiliated parties.

In a communiqué issued by the PCP in July 1936, there was a new conception that the Arab nationalist movement was a general movement of a whole people which transcended class in the fight against imperialism and zionism. Part of the communiqué reads:

> The general strike of the Arab people has been going on for two months. The worker is on strike, he does not receive his wages; the peasant is on strike, refraining from selling his crops; the merchant is still closing down his shop; the urban employee is declining to work in an office. Thus the imperative of self-defence has united into one fighting front all local classes and strata and all parties against the common enemy. Thus the Arab people are waging a struggle against zionist expansion and British imperialism. The Arab people demand the right of self-determination and a democratic constitution.[7]

The seeds of an independent analysis based on local realities, rather than central directives from the Comintern, flourished in the early 1940s when a new communist movement, the National Liberation League, appeared in Palestine in the autumn of 1943. The organization did not bear a communist name, nor did it have the traditional organizational form of the centrally structured Marxist parties, and for many years it did not even openly declare its adoption of Marxism-Leninism. The League tried to represent the left in the national liberation movement with a wide, flexible organizational structure.

The League came into existence in the wake of two world developments. First, a wide democratic, nationalist and leftist current was taking shape among intellectuals and workers. Second, the rise of nazism and fascism relegated the confrontation between the Soviet Union and the major democratic Western powers to a secondary place and prioritized democracy as an imminent task for which to fight. As a consequence, in the spring of 1943, the Comintern was abolished as a leading centre. Communists throughout the world now had the opportunity to take stock of the particularities of their national settings and act accordingly—at least, this was true of the Palestinian communists, who felt the need to follow a new path, that of openness towards all patriotic Palestinian classes and strata. With the establishment of the National Liberation Leage, they even managed to create a new organization, distinguished in both name and content from the previous one and encompassing the widest national trends.

The League arrived at the conclusion that all popular social classes:

> irrespective of their different economic and social interests, have one, unified national sentiment, since the struggle for national liberation unites them on one level and herein lies the strength of popular power and the meaning of national unity for liberation.[8]

The League's charter defined the current phase as that of national liberation, which united all classes for the following tasks: the withdrawal of foreign troops, the abolition of the British mandate and the establishment of a democratic government which would guarantee the interests of all sections of the population in Palestine without prejudice or discrimination. In this context, the League made a distinction between zionism on the one hand, and the Jewish people in Palestine on the other. Phrased in a traditional Marxist-Leninist idiom, the foregoing position meant that the League, the heir of the PCP, recognized the class approach but declined to lend it an antagonistic character during the national liberation phase. This would pave the way for national unity on the basis of inter-class conciliation, which would create, 'for example, a national solidarity between the worker and the factory owner'.[9] Various calls were made to encourage understanding and mutual support between workers and employers.[10]

In a sense, the formation of the League was a unique attempt to produce an authentic, local form of Marxist critique. Such an innovatory approach was short-lived, however, and in early 1947—and more strongly after the 1948 debacle—there were signs of a retreat to traditional forms of thinking and organization. In the spring of 1951 the League took several decisions among which was the establishment of the Jordanian Communist Party (JCP). The organization and ideology of the League were now denounced as a 'nationalistic deviation', a 'renunciation of internationalism' and a 'negation of the leading role of the Palestinian working class in the national struggle to defeat British colonialism'. The JCP reintroduced the formal official communist discourse, stressing the 'spirit of internationalism, loyalty, love and respect for the Soviet Union, the principal bulwark of world peace . . . and for its great leader Stalin, the master of all communists the world over'.[11]

In the aftermath of the Second World War, a new form of communist internationalism was introduced: the Cominform, which was the Information Bureau of Communist Parties under the conditions of the Cold War. The Cominform was abolished on 17 April 1956, but the tradition of holding international congresses in Moscow for communist parties from all over the world was a substitute for it. With a few exceptions, most of these parties considered the Soviet Communist Party as the source of 'true' Marxism-Leninism, the vanguard of struggle in a world that was split and polarized. The resulting dependency hindered the reemergence of a communist party designed specificially to meet the Palestinian situation. The PCP emerged in February 1982 on the same traditional, formal basis until the Second Congress, held in late October 1991, took the decision to rename the party. The relevant decision states:

> When we selected the communist title for our party, we did so on the basis of a judgement that was embedded in a yielding to the force of tradition without any close and due consideration of the existing reality in our country, the features of our revolutionary movement and the level of its development, or the historical stage through which we are passing.

The re-established PCP shifted its focus from the social to the national aspect of its activities, a drive which paved the way for its further transformation. True, the new direction was still couched in the classical Marxist-Leninist idiom. One aspect was that the PCP could not lead the Palestinian working class unless there was already a Palestinian state, yet it defined itself as a contingent in the international communist movement.[12] The internal analysis of the social forces within Palestinian society was also dogmatic and schematic, speaking of a working class and poor peasants in the same old spirit, although the terms and analysis were inconsistent with the actual social reality.

A Critical Revision Imposed

In the spring of 1985 *perestroika* shook the very foundations of the prevailing modes of thought within the world communist movement. It also highlighted the crisis of the model of so-called 'existing socialism' on various levels. *Perestroika* prioritized human values over the class approach to international relations in an attempt to end the bi-polarity of the world system. New ways of cooperation with capitalism, which had ultimately proved its capacity for self-renewal, were sought. This time the Soviet Communist Party had in practice, not merely in theory, to give up its leading role as the ideological and political authority for world revolutionaries. The communists were relieved of their dependency and set off on a new trajectory of creative thinking. Then came the political earthquake which not only shook 'existing socialism' in Eastern Europe and the Soviet Union itself, but demolished the ideological system and the party-model associated with it. New major questions were raised which required a thorough, critical revision of the ideological, political and organizational pillars that had hitherto been considered sacred.

Shortly before the demise of existing socialism, the Palestinian communists vaguely realized and acknowledged the need for a vast, critical revision. In fact, this need was strongly felt in the wake of the Palestinian *intifada* in December 1987. The *intifada* soon became a battle waged by the people as a whole, in which inter-class, day-to-day cooperation was a matter of course. Workers, peasants, farmers, intellectuals, merchants and industrialists joined hands. The movement acquired a democratic character, especially in the spontaneous forms of solidarity and mutual support among different social groups of the people. Feeling the reality of what may be termed the national interest, the communists concluded that it was necessary to desert the narrow class approach of the past and to approach the widest possible strata. The *intifada* also forced the communists to reconsider their old concept of the 'vanguard party', and the relationship between the organized political vanguard and the people at large. Democratic norms and practices, as regulators of this relationship with the popular masses, were gradually recognized in the course of the *intifada* and the old organizational norms were critically appraised. In fact, the upheaval in Eastern Europe and the Soviet Union gave additional momentum to a process that was already in motion.

The general reconsideration and revision led the Central Committee of the PCP to adopt a new political programme and a new party constitution in January 1990. The draft of both were widely discussed and were finally endorsed at the Second Congress (October 1991) after two years of internal debate. The party was renamed the Palestinian People's Party (PPP) so as to establish a consistency of form, name and content.

Leaving the Class to Meet the People

In the following section I shall refrain from a detailed reading of the new PCP programme, but I shall dwell instead on what I consider the basic changes in the thinking of the Palestinian communists as a result of the domestic and international factors mentioned above. The first and most striking feature was the way in which the structure of political priorities was inverted. The programme analysed, first, the internal situation, second, the Arab condition and, third, changes in the world arena. This reversal rested on a rejection of any schematic model of world development or any imagined historical determinism.

Whether in the phase of the struggle for a Palestinian state or in the phase of building such a state after independence, the PPP stressed the need for inter-class solidarity and mutual cooperation. In the first phase, this solidarity was a sine qua non in facing a colonialist foreign occupation and achieving liberation and independence. In the second, it formed the premises for development on a broad scale. Not only were acute forms of class struggle rejected, but social, inter-class solidarity was proposed as an alternative. Hence the logic of class struggle was dismissed from the mechanics of national liberation.

Although the concept of socialism was not rejected altogether, the content of this concept was reformulated. As determinism and historical schematism were dropped, the need to develop a productive, rational form of capitalism was seen as instrumental in the progress of developing countries. Any future form of socialism would rest upon the coexistence of various modes of ownership, the combination of market and planning and the free choice of the people themselves through political democracy as represented by parliamentary systems, political pluralism, general suffrage and the rule of law.

The PPP no longer claims to be the exclusive representative of a specific social class, the working class, but is now a party open to all patriotic classes of the people. Its leftist character is determined by its aspirations: national independence, democracy, progress, social justice and socialism. To back up its new society-wide drive, the PPP envisages specific programmes for each social class, defending their interests. This also applies to industrial and commercial interests. The PPP has opened up the possibility of political alliances with other forces. It has abdicated its previous claim of being the sole leftist party and recognized other leftist forces. All leftist parties have been urged to form a new leftist organization free from the old ideological discourse.

The new programme has dropped the previous reference to the ideology of the party as Marxism-Leninism or proletarian internationalism. No specific ideology is associated with the new discourse of the PPP. Such an omission may be attributed to the following considerations:

- Although the ideological conflict in the world has not ended, it is likely that the struggle for human liberation will, in the new world context, revolve around basically human values, not around closed, self-sufficient ideological systems.
- It has become unthinkable for science to be incorporated into ideological systems. It is equally unthinkable for nationalist or religious ideologies to be considered as expressions of a definite class outlook. Sharp ideological delineations have lost their ground.
- An open party like the PPP can no longer adopt a specific ideology irrespective of the sensibilities of the various classes to which it appeals.

The new political discourse of the PPP has its implicit point of reference in several intellectual trends: the various sources of world socialist thinking; Arab nationalist thought, notably its progressive and humanistic aspects; the Arab-Islamic heritage; and the Palestinian nationalist tradition. These sources share the common values of freedom, equality, progress and social justice. Such a flexible intellectual framework may appeal to wider strata than in the past. The PPP apparently hopes that such a change will separate science from ideology and reinstate the methodology of analysing reality in its flowing, ever-changing movement in the spirit envisaged earlier by Marx.[13]

The PPP is a qualitatively new leftist party; it has a new identity and organizational structure, and a fresh intellectual frame of mind.[14] Yet it rests on the bulk of the previous traditions accumulated by the Palestinian communists in order to create a particular way of thinking, and a new theory of party-building. In one sense, this is a continuation of the attempts made by the League, but this time the renewal is not anchored in Marxism. Marxism is no longer the sole intellectual source of the party, it is one among many. It is no longer 'the only revolutionary theory', 'the only truth', but one contribution by a great thinker in classical socialist thought. Marx's contribution is related to a specific time and place and has a limited role in the development of sociology, history and political economy. The Palestinian form of Marxism does not consider itself Marxist any more.

6. *The Arab States and the Demise of the Soviet Union**

'Amir Abdullah

The demise of the Soviet Union had a profound impact on the Arab world. Moscow had hitherto been a source of support for radical nationalists in general, and a source of threat for the Western-oriented, so-called moderate Arab states.

Since the early 1950s, the Soviet Union had been a major external factor in the rise of the Arab nationalist, anti-Western movements. It had backed various Arab states in their drive to consolidate their independence and thwart schemes to impose Western political, economic or military hegemony in the region. Arab demands for the closure of military bases, the withdrawal of foreign troops, the regaining of control over national resources and the introduction of radical political change (by means of revolution) had all been backed by the Soviet Union, which found allies within the Arab nationalist (and of course communist) movements during the Cold War era. The Soviet role in major crises such as the 1956 Suez war and the 1967 and 1973 Arab-Israeli wars, or less threatening situations such as the nationalization of Iraqi oil in 1972–73, had been crucial.

* This chapter was written on the basis of the author's interviews, meetings and discussions both with party, state and military leaders in the former Soviet Union and with Arab presidents, ministers and party leaders, including leaders of Arab communist and radical nationalist parties. Part of the material also derives from information gained from attending various UN conferences, Non-Aligned summits and other international and regional gatherings. The author attended these meetings during his service as Iraqi minister of state between 1973 and 1978, representing the Iraqi Communist Party during the so-called 'period of alliance'.

The Soviet Union was the Arab world's major supplier of armaments, military hardware, experts and advisers. It was also a major provider of economic, technical and financial aid. The price of Soviet-made sophisticated military hardware was half that of the Western equivalent: a Soviet MiG-25 cost $8 million, for example, whereas an American F-15 cost $16 million. In addition, the Soviets offered a 33% discount on all Arab military purchases. Interest on credit extended to the Arabs never exceeded 2.5%, according to senior officers in the Soviet general staff and other officials in East Berlin, Prague and Budapest. In fact, easy and soft credits for the Arab countries constituted around one-third of the total foreign loans extended by the Soviet Union, amounting to $138 billion. Paradoxically, the Soviet foreign debt was greater than the loans it granted to the Arab world.

The collapse of the Soviet Union was a source of both joy and fear for the Arab world. It was a source of *Schadenfreude* for all moderate or Western-oriented Arab states, ranging from Saudi Arabia to Egypt. But it was a source of *Angst* for radical nationalist states like Syria, South Yemen and perhaps Libya. The first group celebrated the collapse of the former USSR, expressing relief at the removal of a political, military and ideological foe. The second group felt at a loss and hastened to reorient their course to cope with the uncertainties of the new world.

Below, I shall review in some detail these mixed reactions. I shall take the examples of Iraq, Egypt and Saudi Arabia as representative of the hostile camp, in other words, those Arab states which were anti-Soviet for ideological, political or other reasons. However, in addition to its own history of enmity with the USSR, each of these three countries had enjoyed a period of cooperation (whether long or short, and sometimes of decisive importance) with the Soviet Union. Syria and South Yemen may be seen as representative of the second group of states, which relied heavily on Moscow for military, political and economic support. I shall focus on the military, political, economic, ideological and, at times, personal aspects of Arab-Soviet relations in each case, singling out the main factors that smoothed or poisoned those relations.

Ba'thist Iraq: Double Face and Schadenfreude

Iraq was among the few Arab countries to conclude a treaty of friendship and cooperation with the Soviet Union. Unlike Egypt, Iraq kept the1972 treaty formally in place. But unlike Syria, it embarked on a course which systematically rendered the treaty insignificant, particularly after Saddam Hussein assumed the presidency in 1979. Under Saddam, anti-communism and anti-Sovietism peaked and a pro-Western policy emerged.

It is relevant here to dwell on certain points in the prior history of Iraqi-Soviet relations. Sensing Iraq's internal and regional vulnerability, President Ahmad Hassan al-Bakr had visited Moscow in the early 1970s with a vast military, economic and political shopping list. The Soviet leaders —Brezhnev, premier Kosygin and Marshal Kolikov (later to become supreme commander of the Warsaw Pact forces and chairman of the International Economic Committee of the Communist Party of the Soviet Union, the CPSU)—responded positively. In fact, Iraq's requests were almost all generously met, much to the delight of al-Bakr who, in one session, solemnly denounced certain Arab leaders for their 'unfaithful attitude towards our Soviet friends!' He even praised the alliance with the Iraqi Communist Party (ICP), following Brezhnev's remark that the Soviet Union would increase its cooperation with the Iraqi government to the extent that the latter did likewise with the ICP.

Barely a year after the conclusion of the 1972 treaty, however, the Iraqi government took several measures which revealed a change of direction. This change was not unrelated to the influence exerted by Saddam Hussein. The Soviet, Bulgarian and Czechoslovak cultural centres in Baghdad were shut down and the Iraqi-Soviet cultural agreement was suspended. All Iraqi students were withdrawn from Soviet institutes of higher education and Russian-language courses were stopped at Baghdad University. Soviet journalists and diplomats inside Iraq were humiliated or harassed, including the Soviet ambassador. The Iraqi leader al-Bakr, his deputy Saddam Hussein and the foreign minister all declined to receive the ambassador on the grounds that he was 'arrogant'. During the October 1973 Arab-Israeli war, the Soviet ambassador advised me that he had a letter from Brezhnev to the Iraqi president: the Iraqi foreign minister declined to see him or even to receive the letter. Another humiliating step came when water and electricity supplies to the Soviet embassy were cut off to force the diplomatic corps to leave the area adjacent to the presidential palace.

On the level of trade and economic agreements, representatives from the Soviet Union and other socialist-bloc countries took second place to Western businessmen and the envoys of multinational corporations, as senior officials in Moscow complained privately at the time. These officials cited the cost-effective projects already built in Iraq with Soviet aid such as the Rumaila oilfields, the Basra refinery, and medicine and glass factories in Alexandria (south of Baghdad), in addition to the military equipment complex, the liquid gas plant and other industrial complexes.

The Iraqi change of direction then made itself felt in the military field. Despite Iraq's reliance on Soviet hardware and military/technical know-how, talks between the two countries on building two military air bases at a cost of $1.2 billion were suddenly halted in the mid-1970s. As an illustration of the paradoxes surrounding Iraqi-Soviet relations during this period, the following anecdote may be relevant. During his visits to Moscow in the early 1970s, al-Bakr had urgently requested Brezhnev's help in detecting Iranian military moves by means of reconnaissance and military satellites and asked that Moscow keep Baghdad informed. Yet Iraq subsequently protested when a Soviet reconnaissance jet entered Iraqi airspace while carrying out the requested mission in Baghdad: spying on Iran.

In early 1972, when Iraq was considering nationalizing the foreign oil companies operating inside the country, a possible embargo or international sanctions were feared. Moscow volunteered to finance and build a pipeline running from Kirkuk through Iran to link up with the Soviet lines running towards Europe. After nationalization in June 1972, Moscow dispatched three oil tankers to the Syrian port of Tartus to assist in marketing Iraqi oil, but Iraq dismissed the gesture. Baghdad also ignored the decision of the Council of Mutual Economic Assistance (Comecon, the socialist-bloc common market) to take urgent measures in support of Iraq after the nationalization of oil. Among these measures (which I discussed with the Soviet oil minister in Moscow) was the proposal to establish a joint Soviet-Iraqi tanker company, with payments made in kind (i.e. in crude oil rather than hard currency).

Iraq, however, opted for West European involvement in carrying out strategic oil schemes such as the network of pipelines linking the southern and northern Iraqi oilfields. Other strategic industrial projects such as the iron and steel complex and the phosphate plant, and irrigation projects in Kirkuk, were also entrusted to Western corporations, particularly from France and Japan.

Another contentious issue was regional cooperation or, to put it another way, inter-Arab solidarity. Moscow tried hard to convince Baghdad to ease the tension with Syria and consolidate friendly ties between the two Arab nations. The Soviets urged Iraq to forge close relations with Syria in times of war (against Israel) and of peace (to share the waters of the Euphrates). Iraq simply ignored the call.

Whether implicitly or explicitly, Saddam Hussein was keen to weaken ties with the Soviets, denigrate their reputation and belittle their leaders. His negative view of the USSR derived not only from his anti-communist, Ba'thist-nationalist ideology, but also from his displeasure at what he described as his 'cold reception' during his only visit to Moscow in the 1970s. However, the internal power struggle within Iraq was another important factor. The favours granted by Saddam to certain Western countries, notably France, won him the support of those in the party and the bureaucracy who favoured dealing with the West, and boosted his international position as well. This leaning towards France, Japan, Italy and other Western nations intensified after June 1979, when Saddam Hussein succeeded the ailing and aging President al-Bakr. During the Iraq-Iran war (1980–88), however, pragmatic considerations and regional interests paved the way for closer cooperation with both the major Western powers and the Soviets. But it should be added that during the first two years or so of the war, Moscow suspended arms sales and deliveries to Baghdad, a situation that was only reversed after Iraq withdrew from Iranian soil in 1982.

The internal crises and subsequent demise of the Soviet Union were received with the utmost joy in Baghdad, particularly by Saddam Hussein, who saw this as an ideological triumph for his anti-communist, nationalist, etatist socialism, an ideology that he had inherited from the founder of the Ba'th Party, Michel Aflaq. Another reason for Saddam's *Schadenfreude* was his mistaken illusion that the Arab world would emerge as a third or fourth superpower. In fact from the mid-1970s he had started to preach the doctrine of Arab solidarity—that is, solidarity among all Arabs, irrespective of their ideologies or political systems, against all foreigners. Saddam's war with Iran was an assertion of this drive for leadership of the Arab world. After the Iraq-Iran war ended in 1988, Iraq managed to persuade Jordan, North Yemen and Egypt to join a shaky alliance of convenience designed to encircle, absorb and contain the Gulf Cooperation Council (GCC) states. However, the 'Baghdad bloc' was an aggregation of densely populated countries with sizeable military machines but little economic muscle. Baghdad's aim was simply to trade demographic and military superiority for a larger share of the Gulf's oil revenues. At the heart of this uneven bargain was Baghdad's inflated confidence that Iraq was not only a decisive regional power but could use its might in support of its claim to be the future Arab superpower. The occupation and annexation of Kuwait in 1990–91 was but one symptom of this megalomaniac vision. The imminent collapse of the Soviet Union was not interpreted in Baghdad as a precarious development leading to a more threatening, more US-dominated world but rather as one leading to a world where there was a superpower vacancy for the Arabs, under the leadership of Iraq.

The illusion was soon to be shattered. During the final phase of the US-led air attacks on Iraq in 1991, Baghdad could find no nation prepared to mediate on its behalf other than the much-enfeebled Soviet Union. Gorbachev's last-minute efforts failed to prevent the ground assault on Iraq, however, and the fall of the Soviet Union coincided with the massive destruction within Iraq.

Egypt: A Double Betrayal

The Soviet Union's experience with Egypt is a story of the difficult understanding between Soviet Marxism and radical pan-Arab nationalism or pro-Western local nationalism. It is also a story of the Egyptian nationalists' betrayal of their Soviet ally in exchange for Saudi and US aid. And lastly, it is a story of the further loss of sovereignty and independence by those nationalists just prior to and following the demise of their former patron. These episodes cover a historical period lasting more than four decades, from the early 1950s to the collapse of the USSR in 1991. During that time, Egypt experienced three changes of regime and also changed direction in political, social, economic and international affairs.

The most outstanding episode in Soviet-Egyptian relations is probably the tough position adopted by Moscow against Britain, France and Israel during the 1956 Suez crisis. Both before and after Suez, Moscow helped Nasser challenge and bring to an end the Western monopoly over development aid and military purchases. The Soviet Union supplied Egypt with modern weaponry and allocated sufficient aid for it to embark on various infrastructure projects. The many areas of mutual cooperation helped Egypt break the Western-imposed fetters on its industrialization and general development. In ideological terms, however, Nasser was not at ease in his relations with the Soviet Union and the socialist-bloc countries.

Following the 1958 revolution in Iraq, Egyptian-Iraqi relations deteriorated after a brief interval of cooperation between the anti-Western nationalists who ruled in both countries, i.e. General Qassem in Iraq and Nasser in Egypt. An anti-communist witch-hunt in both Egypt and Syria (the latter was under Nasser's grip during the short-lived United Arab Republic, the union between Egypt and Syria) was then unleashed by the Nasser regime and the ideological campaign against Marxism and the Soviet Union intensified. Many communist leaders died under torture at the hands of the Egyptian security services (among those killed was Faraj Allah al-Helou, vice-general secretary of the Syrian-Lebanese Communist Party). Nasser's aim was to eradicate communism from Egypt despite the fact that the Soviet Union was, strictly speaking, Egypt's patron and the country was reliant on Soviet support in the political, economic and military fields.

Although Nasser later mended his fences with the USSR, his ambiguous relations with Moscow were passed on to his successor, Sadat, who assumed power in 1970, at a moment when Egypt was engaged in a life-or-death struggle with Israel. Moscow had rearmed and retrained the Egyptian army after the debacle of the June 1967 war. Sadat inherited both the reliance on the Soviets and the tendency to curry favour with the West, an ambivalence that characterized many nationalist Arab leaders during the Cold War era.

It was the Soviets who organized the war of attrition against Israel, and it was they who erected a 30-km confrontation line along the Suez Canal over which massive amounts of equipment were deployed, including 3,200 pieces of heavy artillery, surface-to-air missiles, and surveillance and detection equipment. While Moscow was busy shoring up the Egyptian defences, President Sadat was equally busy seeking an excuse to rid Egypt of the Soviets. All Soviet military advisers and experts were finally expelled prior to the October 1973 war on the pretext that they were ineffective and that the USSR was delaying deliveries of modern and sophisticated equipment in sufficient quantities. The military and political consequences were portents of the catastrophic future that lay ahead. Israel crossed the Suez Canal and advanced towards the highway leading to Cairo. The Egyptian Third Army was encircled and isolated in Sinai and, in spite of being equipped with 1,200 tanks, was in danger of being annihilated.

On a subsequent visit to Moscow, I had discussions with senior military commanders and party officials. During the 1973 war with Israel, they stressed, the USSR had flown in more than 1,000 tanks to Syria and Egypt in addition to huge amounts of equipment and ammunition. Soviet warships carrying nuclear warheads had sailed into the waters of the Mediterranean right after Israeli premier Golda Meir's decision to make preparations for the deployment of nuclear warheads. The Soviet leadership had instructed their warships to display their nuclear missiles deliberately on deck so as they would be detected by air reconnaissance—this would convey the message to both Tel Aviv and Washington that a nuclear threat was pending should Israel ever touch its nuclear button against Syria or Egypt. I relayed these details to President al-Bakr at his and Moscow's request.

While I was in Moscow, I also heard how Sadat had summoned the Soviet ambassador, requesting him to contact Brezhnev (it was after midnight, Moscow time) and ask him to mediate with Washington to save the encircled Egyptian Third Army and stop the Israeli advance on Cairo. US Secretary of State Henry Kissinger was invited to Moscow to try to end the hostilities. A letter from the Soviets was dispatched to President Nixon for the same purpose: it warned of a military confrontation between the two superpowers. This was a crucial factor in freezing the situation on the battlefront and facilitating the subsequent Israeli withdrawal. The Third Army, Cairo and perhaps Sadat himself had, for time being, been saved.

The significance of these developments should be read against the background of previous Egyptian anti-Soviet measures. Under Saudi pressure, Sadat had concluded a military deal with France to purchase Mirage jet fighters in the early 1970s. The deal cost $2 billion and was financed by the Saudis. The search for a Western arms deal as a substitute for the cheap, highly sophisticated weaponry purchased with interest-free Soviet military loans (part of which has still not been redeemed) was part of a policy which alienated Moscow and culminated in the abrogation of the Egyptian-Soviet treaty of friendship and cooperation in March 1976.

Under Sadat, there was a degree of continuity in Cairo's attitude towards the Soviet Union: an ideological animosity and antagonism lay beneath the surface, occasionally emerging into the open. It is true that there were phases of cooperation and times when Moscow gave generous military, economic, technical and other forms of assistance. The Aswan High Dam is one example; soft loans, frozen debts and grants were others. Yet the anti-communist ideology influenced Sadat just as it had Nasser and the hostility towards the Arab communist parties, particularly in Egypt, Sudan, Syria and Iraq, was one of the continued hallmarks of Egyptian policy. There was also a dogmatic rejection of Marxist socialism, seen either as a dangerous foe or as a serious rival.

Egypt has now clearly opted for the West. The essence of the bargain is to sell Egypt's strategic services in the Middle East to the US in exchange for aid. Although the crisis and fall of the Soviet regime were received in Cairo with *Schadenfreude*, and a sense of historical revenge, the demise has actually accentuated Egypt's weak position and reduced its main asset: its strategic role in the region.

Saudi Arabia: Paranoia

Saudi Arabia was among the first Arab countries to recognize and establish diplomatic relations with the Soviet Union in the 1930s. A few years later, however, these relations were severed and were never mended. None of the communist or socialist countries in Europe, Asia or Latin America had ever been approached by the Saudis either. With the exception of Kuwait, this had been the position adopted by all the moderate Gulf states.

Saudi Arabia's lack of relations with the USSR and the other socialist-bloc countries covered not only the diplomatic arena, but also the economic, commercial, financial, cultural and social fields. Such an almost total boycott was unique, particularly when compared with the attitude of the advanced capitalist countries, which, after all, were engaged in an ideological confrontation with the socialist camp. The Saudis even declined to establish air links with the USSR. No other country in the Non-Aligned Movement or in the West surpassed Saudi Arabia in its antipathy towards the Soviets. The Saudis allocated vast sums, for example, to prevent communists coming to power in Western Europe, notably in Italy and France, after the Second World War.

Saudi Arabia's vast oil revenues were invested in bonds, shares, deposits or direct investments in the West. Surplus revenues were partly used to grant loans to several developed capitalist nations, or to contribute to the funds of the International Monetary Fund (IMF), the World Bank or the European Credit Fund. Although Saudi Arabia and the other Gulf states sustained financial losses in the 1970s (both because of the fall in the price of oil on world markets and because of the devaluation of the US dollar, which led to the depreciation of part of Saudi Arabia's financial assets and bank deposits held in US dollars), the integration with the capitalist advanced world markets continued as the main policy choice.

It is ironic that while Western financial markets used Gulf oil assets to make loans to the Soviet Union and other socialist countries, Saudi Arabia and the other Gulf states declined to invest in the socialist markets although there were guarantees offered against freezing or appropriation, and guarantees of high interest rates and profits in a centrally controlled command economy. Saudi Arabia and the other Gulf countries (with the exception of Kuwait) declined even to sell their oil to, or to have any oil transactions with, the socialist markets. By contrast, in the early 1970s, Libya and Kuwait planned to build an oil pipeline linking Yugoslavia, Hungary and Czechoslovakia. Another scheme envisaged the construction of an oil refinery in Romania.

It was only when *perestroika* was initiated and the economic situation in the former Soviet Union and socialist bloc began to deteriorate sharply that Riyadh changed direction. Saudi credits were extended to the Gorbachev administration for the first time in the history of Soviet-Saudi relations. Following the disintegration of the USSR, Saudi Arabia has increased its cooperation with the former Soviet republics, particularly those with Muslim populations. The Russian navy has been given leave to sail in Gulf waters and has been granted facilities at Gulf ports. There has also been a move to allow Russian forces to take part in the international task force to police the Gulf. As the Gulf's paranoia of communism withers away, Russian-made weapons and equipment have started to appear for the first time at military exhibitions organized in the Gulf.

Syria: A Sense of Solitude

Unlike the countries mentioned so far, Syria has had a continuous record of good relations with the former Soviet Union. This was not prompted by any doctrinal understanding or conformity, or by any *rapprochement* between the Ba'thist and Marxist forms of socialism. There were other factors and motives, as outlined below.

Since independence, Syria has developed a strong sense of national sovereignty. Unlike Iraq and Egypt, it has never allowed any foreign forces or bases on its soil in the period following the Second World War. It has never taken part in any foreign military blocs or alliances, such as the Baghdad Pact. Nor did it become involved in any Cold War schemes to encircle the Soviet Union. With the exception of the short periods under a military regime and the period of the United Arab Republic, the Syrian Communist Party has remained legal.

Syria's sense of threat, coming from both the north (i.e. Turkey, which annexed Iskenderun province) and the south (Israel), accentuated a strong anti-Western drive and the search for an international patron. The need for a secure source of sophisticated military hardware was another important factor. There was also the need for economic aid to develop the infrastructure and for irrigation and industrial schemes and projects. All these factors led to the strengthening of Syrian-Soviet ties, culminating in the signing of a treaty of friendship and cooperation in the 1970s. Unlike Egypt under Sadat, Syria fought the 1973 war against Israel with the aid of a great number of Soviet military experts, led by a high-ranking officer with the rank of general. (By contrast, there was only one Soviet military attaché in Egypt at the time.)

During the 1973 war, President Hafiz al-Asad invited a team of Soviet experts to attend a meeting of the Defence Council chaired by him. These experts were entrusted with the task of operating the anti-aircraft missiles when Israeli warplanes attacked Damascus. As the situation worsened on the Syrian-Israeli front, with more than 300 Syrian tanks put out of action, Soviet military experts headed for the front line to organize resistance and then a withdrawal (many of them were killed).

Syria's nationalist socialist ideology was at variance with the Marxist conception of socialism. This position was common to all Arab nationalists, but Syria developed a more realistic, less aggressive position than that of Iraq or Egypt. Quite simply, Syria needed the Soviet Union for political, economic and military reasons in the face of the grave Israeli threat on its doorstep. This need was aggravated by Syria's inadequate oil and other mineral resources, its lack of an industrial base and its weak agricultural sector, in addition to its need to maintain and feed a sizeable army. (Syrian defence allocations were relatively high.) Syria's continued relations with the USSR up to the last moments of the latter's existence should therefore come as no surprise.

Needless to say, Syria did its best to gain support from other regional sources such as the Arab Gulf states, Iran after the fall of the Shah, and even the IMF. During the decade that followed the Camp David accords of 1978, Syria received massive Arab financial support, reaching an annual average of $1.8 billion. It also managed to buy oil at greatly reduced prices and obtain soft loans from Iran. These loans amounted to more than $1 billion and remained a delayed credit in the name of the 'strategic alliance' between the two countries. Such benefits were the result of Syria's political stance, namely its support for Iran during the 1980–88 Iraq-Iran war.

With the disintegration and collapse of the former Soviet Union, Syria felt increasingly vulnerable and exposed and its participation in the pro-Kuwait Arab task force in the 1990–91Gulf war did not bring the expected benefits. Syrian and Egyptian forces were subsequently asked to leave the Gulf region whereas part of the Western forces were permanently stationed there under military agreements signed with the US, Britain and France. The Damascus Declaration accord, which Syria had hoped would strengthen its ties with the Gulf states, was rendered meaningless by Kuwait.

In the immediate aftermath of the Gulf war, Syria found itself almost without an international ally or supporter. Perhaps it was this sense of isolation that led the Syrians to attend the 1991 Madrid peace talks and start to investigate the possibility of a settlement with Israel. There was also a change of direction on the domestic level, where pro-market, de-regulative and privatization policies gained momentum under the new circumstances.

South Yemen: The End of an Ideal

The experience of South Yemen (the People's Democratic Republic of Yemen, or PDRY) is unique in many respects. Unlike the ruling nationalist movements in many other Arab countries, the nationalists in South Yemen embraced communist and socialist policies immediately after independence and the withdrawal of British forces in 1969. This culminated in the unification of the various strands of nationalists and communists in one unified configuration, the Yemeni Socialist Party. This unity was based on the adoption of Marxism as the official state ideology and the basis of the country's social system. The new party adopted the Soviet form of Marxism-Leninism, proletarian internationalism and the single-party system.

It is interesting to note that until the mid-1970s the Soviet Union conceived of the South Yemeni party and state as being in line with Chinese Maoist doctrine. This Soviet perception was based on an early, widespread Chinese presence in South Yemen, and the various forms of assistance that

Yemen had received from China. In 1972 the general secretary of the Yemeni Socialist Party, Abdul Fattah Ismail, explained to me that his party was not in the least aligned with China in its struggle against the Soviet Union. It was simply, he explained, that the Chinese had volunteered to build a highway linking Aden to the Hadhramaut and Seyoun and had also made substantial contributions to other projects: Yemen was too poor to reject such generous aid. Ismail urged the Arab communist parties to explain the situation to Moscow and that his party was in line with Soviet positions in terms of theory and practice. This was conveyed in writing to the CPSU.

In December 1975 Ismail and I held lengthy discussions about regional affairs while travelling to Cuba to attend the Cuban Communist Party congress. Ismail expressed his country's need for military equipment, especially warplanes. His wishes were again relayed to officials in Moscow, where I held detailed discussions at CPSU headquarters. The following year, I was advised by the CPSU International Department that they had decided to normalize and improve relations with Aden and they were ready to supply South Yemen with MiG-21 jet fighters. They were also prepared to send a number of military envoys to arrange training for the pilots. Moscow had warned both Saudi Arabia and North Yemen not to engage in threatening behaviour against Aden and asked me to advise the South Yemeni leadership accordingly.

South Yemen subsequently received economic, financial, technical and military assistance from the Soviet Union and the number of Yemeni students in the USSR exceeded that from any other Arab country. Soviet civilian and military experts participated in developing the country. Among the vital sectors that received Soviet help was oil: in oil exploration, the development and expansion of the Aden refinery, pipeline networks and other facilities.

South Yemen adopted the Soviet model of state ownership, central planning and the one-party system. A vast process of nationalization had already turned even fishing boats over to state ownership and state farms were established in the countryside. The education system and the mass media taught and propagated the principles of Marxism-Leninism. A 'Sovietized' atmosphere prevailed in Aden, with its red flags and its posters of Marx, Engels and Lenin, but there was also an air of social equality, with fair and equal educational and professional opportunities for men and women and much greater freedom for women than previously.

The internal divisions created by the 1986 civil war and the beginning of the transformations within the Soviet Union all weakened the role of the Yemeni Socialist Party and party membership declined to under 20,000. In the atmosphere of chaos and frustration caused by the internal power struggle, the Yemeni Marxists turned to a nationalist, outward-looking solution, namely the union with the North.

The collapse of the Soviet Union proved to be the final blow for the guiding creed, party and state in South Yemen. The call to review all their basic tenets, including the name of the party, proved decisive for Yemeni socialists. In the end, the unity with San'a and the North–South war that followed demolished all traces of the 'socialist' heritage in South Yemen. The Yemeni Socialist Party disintegrated and dissolved into small factions. In a sense, the demise of 'actual' socialism in Eastern Europe and the Soviet Union proved fatal for the Yemeni Socialist Party, the only Marxist party to have held power in the Arab world.

Conclusion

Prior to the collapse of the Soviet Union, two major trends were apparent in the behaviour of Arab nationalist regimes towards the USSR. One employed double standards: remaining ideologically hostile to Marxism and the USSR, while nevertheless trying to exploit the relationship with Moscow in order to use this as a bargaining chip with the West (as was the case with Egypt under Sadat and Iraq under the Ba'th). The other trend was one of continued strategic cooperation, with or without ideological conformity, as in the case of Syria and South Yemen. The first group was delighted by the collapse of the Soviet Union but has become more dependent on the United States. The second group, or what is left of it, felt at a loss and is still trying to navigate a cautious course in the chaotic world that has emerged in the aftermath of the end of the Cold War.

In general terms, the Arab popular mood is one of *Angst*. Sober leftists are stressing the need to reconsider the world so as to build new networks of relations with rising powers and make the utmost use of the multiplicity of world centres in the post-Cold War era. 'Fundamentalists', whether leftists or Islamists, are thinking in terms of retrieving a glorious past—the 'socialist camp' and the ancient Islamic empire respectively.

7. *The Arab Communist Parties in Search of an Identity*

Faleh A. Jabar

In as much as the years 1985–91 were destructive for the communist ruling parties in Eastern Europe, they were transformative and/or disruptive for the Arab communist parties in general. The Soviet reforms initiated in 1985 by the Gorbachev team came at a specific, in fact a precarious, moment in the development of the communist movement in the Arab region. With few exceptions, the Arab communists were caught between, on the one hand, the ruling nationalists, who were running into quicksands, and, on the other, the rising challenge of Islamic fundamentalism, which presented itself as an alternative to both.

The nationalist wing had made a U-turn in terms of socio-economic, regional and even international policies. In countries where there was a strong corporate–state economy, often built in the name of a particular form of Arab socialism, there was a fast, downhill move towards economic liberalization (deregulation) and/or privatization (the sell-out of the state sector). The tilt from corporatism to commercialization was coupled with a leaning towards, if not an alliance with, the West.

The Arab communist parties, greatly weakened by decades of state terror, were rising from the ashes in the wake of the modest political liberalization that had taken place in North Africa (Tunisia, Morocco and Algeria) and the Mashreq (Jordan). The Soviet reforms came at a time when many communist parties in the Arab world were reconsidering, from different points of departure, many long-accepted, almost sacred ideological postulates: whether or not to prioritize political democracy over socio-economic transformations (enlarging the state sector, agrarian reforms etc);

the priority of internationalism over nationalism in both ideological and political terms; the right to define their own national course of struggle; the right to resort to armed struggle; the rejection of the concept of socialism as envisaged by Soviet non-capitalist development theory, and so on.

The changes in the Soviet Union can be divided into two phases: first, the *perestroika* reforms; and second, the collapse of the communist regimes in the former German Democratic Republic (GDR), Poland, Czechoslovakia, Hungary and Romania. In order to assess the effects of the changes in the Soviet Union and Eastern Europe on communists in the Arab world, above all in the Mashreq, a brief historical background must be given of the emergence of the Arab communist parties, together with their main ideological and practical concerns during the colonial and post-colonial eras. In the Mashreq, there were communist parties in Palestine, Jordan, Lebanon, Syria, Iraq, Saudi Arabia, Bahrain, Yemen, Egypt and Sudan. This chapter concentrates on the Mashreq, with a few remarks on the Maghreb by way of comparison.

The Colonial Era

The Arab communist movements emerged in the colonial era (the 1920s and 1930s), when the communists, like the nationalists, had to rely on a global external power to help them achieve decolonization. The ex-Soviet Union was the champion of the communists, whereas fascist Germany was the ideal patron for the anti-British and anti-French Arab nationalists of the time.

Most of the leaders and supporters of these parties were drawn from the middle and lower-middle class intelligentsia, a social stratum that was now broad and deep-rooted, expanding in line with the modernization processes that were transforming agrarian societies. With the introduction of modern industrial sectors, a new working class emerged: its struggle was mainly directed against foreign capital, which was present in the oil sector, ports, airports, railways and other enclave sectors. The whole package of political struggle was concentrated on national issues: independence, the removal of foreign military bases, industrialization and agrarian reforms. In this sense, the 'class' struggle was nationalist.

The Soviet Union's victory in the Second World War, and the triumph of the peasantry of China and Indochina under the red flag, gave a boost to the nationalist movement and, by extension, increased the prestige of the Arab communists. The period following the world war was the era of nationalist upsurge in the Arab world, with Nasser in Egypt, Qassem in Iraq and Ben Bella in Algeria. (It should be remembered that this was a global trend, however.)

If the objectives during the colonial era were lucid, namely decolonization in both the political and the economic sense, the goals of the post-colonial period were sometimes ambiguous.

The Post-Colonial Era

The post-colonial era was one of great complexity for many communist parties in the Middle East. What were the next steps? What role could be found for the anti-colonialist nationalists? And what road should the 'revolution' follow: a capitalist path, a move towards socialism, or a third way that involved gradual change?

To grasp the complexities inherent in these questions, we must remember that they were raised within the framework of the Stalinist, five-stage socio-economic schema: primitive communism, slavery, feudalism, capitalism and lastly communism, socialism being the first phase (or a transitory phase) of the latter. However, for the national liberation movements in Third World countries (agrarian societies *par excellence*), there was a slightly different theoretical division of historical stages: the national revolution phase, which is anti-colonialist in nature; then the national-democratic revolution aimed against feudal and semi-feudal remnants. Both these pre- and post-independence phases fall within capitalist socio-economic formations. These two phases, according to the orthodox communist conception, are characterized by the leadership of the 'national bourgeoisie', with the working class playing an important but not the leading role. (Its leading role is reserved for the socialist revolution.)

Yet the Russian Bolshevik revolution was the first anachronism—a working-class revolution supported by the peasantry and aimed at a mixture of tasks: enhancing the small, peasant ownership on the one hand, and nationalizing domestic and foreign capital on the other. The so-called 'popular democratic revolutions' in Eastern Europe after the defeat of Germany, and the national liberation wars in China and Vietnam (and later even in Cuba), where peasant revolutions were led by communists who theoretically represented a working-class perspective, seemed to prove the irregularity of the scheduled stages of revolution. These two different types of experience supported, in the eyes of some leftist Arab leaders, a communist leadership of the so-called 'national democratic phase of the revolution', although it fell outside the realm of the socialist stage and hence involved or implied no leading role for the working class.

The post-Second World War model of 'popular democracy', bypassing capitalism, whether derived from the (East) European version or from the Asian type (China, Vietnam), was, paradoxically enough, not envisaged by most Arab communists. But when difficulties, clashes and rivalries erupted between the anti-colonialist nationalists and the communists, the idea of bypassing the 'limited horizon of the national bourgeoisie' began to be given serious consideration.

Many alternatives suggested themselves. One was a communist takeover (by means of a military coup—a progressive one, of course!—or by a popular uprising, or through guerrilla warfare as in Cuba). Such tendencies could be detected in the Iraqi Communist Party in the 1960s (and also in Indonesia under Sukarno in 1963; the Sudanese communists' attempted military coup in the early 1970s; and the Afghan communists who, heavily influenced by the Iraqi radical argument, staged a coup in the mid-1970s). Another option was to develop the 'national bourgeoisie' stage to maturity before a communist takeover was possible. The idea was that the tasks of the national-democratic movement should be carried out by the national bourgeoisie. Behind the first approach lay a 'leap-forward', 'burn-stages' conception, whereas the second approach revealed an evolutionary, gradualist view of history. A third strand considered the social transformations carried out by the post-colonial nationalists (Nasser in Egypt, Aref in Iraq, and Ben Bella and Boumedienne in Algeria) as, in themselves, socialist transformations; hence there was no need for a working-class party or leadership.

The ideological battles of the 1960s revolved around the following issues. Was the national bourgeoisie, as a social class, capable of carrying out the required tasks? And if so, to what extent should it be supported? Or, if this class was impotent, should the working class step in as it had done in the October 1917 revolution, to undertake both democratic (i.e. capitalist) and socialist tasks at one and the same time?

Irrespective of whether these arguments were practical or rational, they indicated a restless search for an alternative strategy, either by immediate action or by longer-term efforts. The theory of 'non-capitalist development' put forward by Soviet scholars in the mid- and late 1960s was meant, among other things, to resolve some of these dilemmas. In essence, this theory removed (or modified) the leadership of the working class and its communist party from the set of conditions fixed by the Third International as a criterion for any genuine 'socialist revolution'. (These conditions were meant to draw an ideological, political and organizational line distinguishing the radical communist from the reformist–social democratic parties in Europe in the post- First World War era.) These conditions had become articles of faith, and probably all communist parties in the Middle East excluded new converts to Marxism-Leninism unless they met them. (This applied to Nayef Hawatmeh's Democratic Front for the Liberation of Palestine (DFLP) and to George Habash's Popular Front for the Liberation of Palestine (PFLP) from 1969 onwards, when both declared their conversion from nationalism to Marxism-Leninism.)

With the introduction of the non-capitalist development theory, the leadership of the socialist revolution was shorn from the working class (i.e. the official communist parties) and assigned to a new stratum termed the revolutionary democrats, i.e. the ruling nationalists in Egypt, Syria, Iraq, Algeria, Yemen and Somalia (the latter under General Siad Barre). It extended beyond that to other African countries such as Angola, Mozambique and Zimbabwe, not to mention the many examples in Latin America.

It was in accordance with this theoretical formula that the Yemeni Socialist Party was formed, endorsed and admitted into the college of official communism in the late 1970s and early 1980s. But if the Yemeni radical nationalists (or revolutionary democrats, to use the official Marxist jargon) were converted to Marxism-Leninism (willingly, it should be stressed), the communists in Iraq, Syria, Egypt and elsewhere in the Arab world were under varying degrees of pressure, manipulation and persecution to convert to some eclectic form of national socialism, whether that of Nasser, Saddam Hussein or Hafez al-Asad. They came under heavy pressure to give up all independent activity and act more like an appendage to their respective ruling nationalists. The Egyptian communists did so voluntarily in the mid-1960s, after the nationalization of domestic capital. A faction in the Iraqi Communist Party known as the August Faction (Khat Ab) followed the Egyptian example in 1964 and on the same basis. An identical argument was used by them under Ba'th rule from 1974 onwards. Similar positions surfaced among sections of the Syrian Communist Parties (as they did in Algeria, Tunisia, Iran and elsewhere).

What the ruling radical nationalists in the Arab countries did was simply to build a socio-political model that bore a great resemblance to the Stalinist one, although there were differences of course. In both cases, there was a corporate state: in other words, a state economic sector, or a collective entrepreneur making up for the lack of dynamic private capital. In both models, there was one-party rule, and both claimed to be socialist. But whereas the Soviet model placed its legitimacy in the representation of the working class, the Middle Eastern model pinned it on the nation. The former had its roots in Marxism, the latter in Arab nationalism. The socialism of the first was based on universal postulates; the socialism of the second was based on Arab exclusivism. The ideological gap between the two models was too wide to bridge. Structurally, however, the divergence between the polities of the two models was fairly narrow. There was very little difference between Iraq and Romania, for example.

To some extent, the radical nationalists could truly claim that what they had achieved (a large state sector, agrarian reform, state farms, one-party rule, and so on) differed little from the situation in most socialist countries in Eastern Europe, and that there was no reason why their society could not be claimed as socialist too. The Iraqi and Syrian Ba'th even rejected the Soviet concept of non-capitalist development, seeing it as humiliating for them since it denied the socialist character of the transformations they had carried out. The struggle between the communists and the radical nationalists was not only acute, but in some cases bloody: many examples could be given from Iraq and elsewhere.

It is obvious from the foregoing that the Soviet model of development, the so-called socialist model, or the system of enforced homogeneity, was used against the communists themselves. This was clearly the case in several Arab countries in both the Maghreb and the Mashreq, with the exceptions of Jordan, Lebanon and Palestine. (The traditional Gulf states are always an exception.)

The Palestinians had to make a difficult shift to join the armed resistance against Israel and build their own (national) communist party, which they did belatedly in 1982 after de-linking their cadres from the Jordanian mother party. As the Palestinians were still far from the post-colonial phase, the whole argument about the socialist model and its implications was highly theoretical. The Palestinian communists could even discard the idea of socialism altogether without damaging their political prospects in the least. They could justifiably argue that what they were struggling for was simply to achieve their national independent state.

The Lebanese Communist Party was founded in a society whose polity rested on the pre-modern, communal configuration: the residue of the Ottoman *millet* system (the communal or confessional system). This structure was moving inexorably towards a crisis due to the social changes undermining its stability, coupled with other destabilizing regional and international factors. De-segmentation (or de-communalization of the polity, to put it another way) on the one hand, and the anti-Israel national struggle on the other hand, were at the core of Lebanese communist concerns. The socialist model was thus an academic issue.

It is clear that the national setting played a major role in determining the reaction of each of these Arab communist parties towards the changes in the Soviet Union during the reforms of the 1980s, and during the final collapse of most East European communist regimes, including the Soviet Union itself.

Dilemmas and Euphoria

Perestroika and *glasnost* were generally welcomed by Arab Marxists and, despite some reservations, the general reception was euphoric. The proceedings of the 'Seminar on *Perestroika* and the Arab World', organized in Damascus in 1988 by the Centre for Socialist Studies in the Arab World, show negligible disagreement with *perestroika* and *glasnost*. These two theoretical postulates envisaged a return to market mechanisms (reminding the communists of Lenin's NEP in the early 1920s) and a democratization of the political system as a precondition for reform.

It is clear that when the concept of socialism becomes unthinkable without a democratic, pluralistic setting, the ideological pillars supporting the single-party model are shaken if not uprooted, as had happened in the case of the Ba'th Party in Syria and Iraq (and also their counterparts in Algeria, the Algerian Liberation Front; the Tunisian Socialist Constitutional Party; and the Nasserite National Union, later the Socialist Union, in Egypt). Wherever the communists had suffered from single-party, Arab socialist hegemony, *perestroika* extended help. The collapse of communism would be even more helpful in this ideological respect.

But the same market-socialism concept disrupted the long-held communist view that the state sector should continuously expand. Any laxity in this respect had been termed a 'right-wing tilt', sometimes 'regression' or even a 'débâcle'. Thus the contraction or expansion of the state sector, in itself a giant capitalist employer and producer, had for a long time been seen by communists and leftists in the Middle East as a yardstick of reactionary or revolutionary action. Liberal nationalists could give the Soviet–Gorbachev argument of the market economy in favour of liberalization and privatization processes that had so far been timidly pursued. From that moment on, the battle between public and private ownership reemerged, but this time the odds were not wholly in favour of the state as sole economic agent.

The organizational reforms in the Soviet Communist Party—notably, plurality of opinion and renewal of leaders and cadres—had an impact, and soon the pillars of the old democratic centralism (no factions; no right to self-expression for the minorities; the total submission of the minorities to the majority, and of lower to higher committees) were shaken. Most communist parties started to renew their old, sometimes ossified, leadership bodies by means of these organizational reforms. Needless to say, the ossified structures of the higher leading bodies (whose membership had frequently changed only with the death of cadres, or because of cadres being arrested or schisms within the leadership) led to grave problems.

Any sociological reading of the composition of the leading bodies would certainly have shown an ossified rigidity in, say, the Syrian, Jordanian and to some extent Iraqi communist parties. The Lebanese Communist Party had made two reshuffles earlier on and so managed to avoid the immobility that deprived these movements from the energies of their younger members and created a generation gap within the organizational setting, to mention only two negative side-effects.

The organizational reforms that *perestroika* appeared to encourage, or actually encouraged, were warmly welcomed by the younger generation of party cadres, by party members and even by supporters whose upward organizational mobility had been blocked. If *perestroika* and *glasnost* were widely and generally welcomed, however, the third element of the Soviet reforms, the 'new political thinking', was viewed with great suspicion. The core of the 'new thinking' dealt with international relations, i.e. a new cooperation between the two superpowers instead of rivalry and the dogma of the ultimate triumph of world socialism over world capitalism. Arab sceptics were suspicious of a superpower deal behind their backs. These fears were aggravated by the exodus of Soviet Jews to Israel and the Soviet withdrawal from Afghanistan, both of which were seen as a 'retreat of socialism' in the face of the 'imperialist onslaught'.

The phase of general euphoria was soon overshadowed by a bitter scepticism, which increased with each collapse of a socialist regime, whether with the fall of the Berlin wall or the spontaneous uprising that culminated in the execution of the Romanian dictator, Ceauşescu. The final blow came with the abortive coup attempt in 1991 and the humiliating dismissal of the initiator of the reforms, Gorbachev himself, who had lost faith in the socialist model and the philosophy it represented.

If that period had any paramount feature in the life of the communist parties in the Mashreq, then it was surely the incessant debate, or rather, the growth of a home-grown intellectual debate and research to cope with changes and find a way out of what looked like the apocalypse. It also paved the way for certain organizational, ideological and even political changes that made these parties more acceptable in some cases—for example, the Jordanian, Tunisian and Algerian communist parties gained legal recognition for the first time. (It should be remembered, however, that other factors were also in operation at that time: there was a move towards political, pluralist reforms in these countries both before and after the new developments in the communist bloc.)

As most communist parties in the Arab world were deeply rooted in the academic and intellectual traditions of Soviet thought, the intellectual debate was conducted in a vicious circle of theory versus practice. One tendency maintained: theory was right, it was only Soviet practice that had deviated from the 'true path'. Or, if this dualistic approach was not adopted, then a new dichotomy was created: theory *was* right, but it needed renovation. This had not been done, and so Soviet and socialist praxis had gone wrong. The whole debate was locked within the Soviet, Stalinist reading of Marx. At this point the Western-educated intellectuals put forward a way out: a non-Leninist reading of Marx on the one hand, and a post-Marxian reading in economy, sociology, philosophy and politics on the other.

In Search of an Identity

If the changes in form and content of the communist parties in the Mashreq are analysed, two extremes emerge, with a third type in between. The *first* may be characterized as a *full break* with past theoretical doctrines, structural set-ups, and political programmes and alliances; the party was even renamed. This was the case of the Palestinian, Algerian and Tunisian communist parties. Interestingly, a split occurred in the Saudi Communist Party: the organizational wing abroad made no changes, whereas the wing inside the country changed direction, split from the overseas factions and changed its name. The *second* type maintained a *stubborn adherence* to the old pillars of the classical, Soviet-style doctrine in its totality. This was the case of the Jordanian Communist Party and of the Khaled Bekdash wing of the Syrian Communist Party. (In Bekdash's memoirs, he still stresses: nothing has changed; Marxism will win and capitalism will collapse in the end; victory belongs to the working class.)[1] *Third*, there were parties that made *partial changes* and reforms in doctrine, organization or practice. These partial reforms, of course, vary in their depth and extent, but a typical example would be the Lebanese Communist Party, and to a lesser extent the Iraqi Communist Party.

It should be pointed out that the process of change is far from complete. In general, the Arab communist parties have lapsed back into nationalism, liberalism and social democratic pragmatism. This is not to say that each change or fixity, in any party, is devoid of an anti-thesis: an oppositional group that either challenges stagnation or objects to changes that it sees as too radical.

Issues under Debate

Most of the Arab communist parties had hardly ever convened a general congress more than once every five or even ten years (the Jordanian Communist Party had only convened one congress in half a century). During 1991–95, however, in the wake of the collapse of the Soviet Union, they all rushed to organize such congresses: the Lebanese Communist Party held two conferences (one labelled 'urgent') in June 1993, and the Jordanian Communist Party held one in April of the same year. The Syrian, Palestinian, Yemeni, Bahraini and other communist parties in the Mashreq had held their congresses or conferences earlier. The Iraqi Communist Party was the last to hold a congress on 12 October 1993, the outcome of which was in line with the above categorization.

Apart from internal political questions, the range and nature of issues discussed and debated were almost identical among the various parties, but the responses were different due to differences in the national situation and the actual problems at hand. We shall outline a number of these issues and trace the changes in the various communist parties towards them.

A Change of Name?

Almost all the Arab communist parties discussed (publicly in most cases) whether or not to keep the 'old' title of 'communist'. There was a strong reaction against deleting the word 'communist' in the Mashreq, with the sole exception of the Palestinian Communist Party. The implications of the change of name were discussed by Bashir Barghouthi, the party's general secretary:

> At the beginning, when our party was re-established in 1982, we had to adhere to the same name—the Communist Party—as a way of preserving continuity with the Palestinian Communist Party, established in 1920, and its successor, the League of Liberation Movement, founded in 1943. But this was unrealistic. All communist parties focus on social problems; we, on the other hand, have to focus on the struggle for land and a homeland. We need a country before we can wage a social struggle. That is why we have renamed our party the Sha'b [People's] Party . . .[2]

The Tunisian and Algerian parties also changed their names, although the shift there was not to nationalism but to a form of liberalism. The other Arab communist parties stopped short of renaming in spite of considerable pressure to do so.

Theoretical Sources and Authority

Here, as elsewhere, the Palestinian Communist Party was the most extreme example of change in the Mashreq. According to Barghouthi:

> So-called Marxism-Leninism was in fact no more than the conclusions and views of the Soviet state . . . We do not accept Marx's work as a theory . . . We have removed the sacred mantle from Marxism, and Marxism is no longer our intellectual source. We seek our resourcefulness in the Arab revolutionary heritage, the human heritage and that part of Marxism we see fit for our purposes . . .[3]

By contrast, the Syrian and Jordanian communist parties adhered to the theory–practice dichotomy: in other words, theory is right but Soviet practice was wrong.

The partial change in position was typified by the Lebanese and Iraqi parties. Karim Muruwa, a veteran member of the Lebanese Communist Party's Political Bureau, commented in September 1993:

> Our theoretical resources are not confined to Marxism-Leninism, but have been expanded to encompass the whole range of Marxist thought—Kautsky, Rosa Luxemburg, Gramsci, Mao, etc. We need, of course, to develop the theory in order to cope with the changing world.[4]

Almost the same position was expressed by the Iraqi Communist Party in its draft programme published for discussion in 1991.

In the Maghreb, the Tunisian and Algerian communist parties distanced themselves radically from Marxism-Leninism. The Mashreq seems conservative when compared to the Maghreb. It should be remembered, however, that intellectual trends in the Maghreb are in closer contact with, and under the greater influence of, West European forms of Marxist and anti-Marxist debate. Nowhere is the influence of French structuralism, post-structuralism and deconstructionism more deeply felt than in the Maghreb, where most party cadres speak French and have studied in France. In the Mashreq, on the other hand, cadres have tended to receive their academic training in the socialist bloc.

The Concept of Socialism

Whether or not a particular Arab communist party rejects traditional Marxism-Leninism, the concept of socialism itself has not been totally or directly omitted from the programmes of these parties. However, it is frequently mentioned as some vague, remote objective which, in fact, amounts to an omission of the idea of socialism itself. This is the position of the Palestinian, Tunisian and Algerian parties. Other parties have clung to the orthodox concept of socialism, and the predicted triumph of the working class the world over. This the case of Khaled Bekdash and his rival Yousef Faisal, the leader of the splinter group of the Syrian Communist Party.

The positions of the Iraqi and Lebanese communist parties seem more hard-line than the Palestinians but less so than the Syrians. Socialism is still professed as an important and ultimate target, objective or stage, yet it is not urgent. This remoteness of socialism is either attributed to economic backwardness or to the lack of the necessary global conditions. In both cases socialism is prudently dropped, but certain social demands from old programmes are kept.

The Correct Response to Capitalism

Whereas most communist parties in the Mashreq have been critical of their own modern nation-states, particularly their economic policies, and have derived much of their criticism from the anti-capitalist arsenal, the very logic of distancing themselves from the socialist project and the ongoing globalization of the market economy has left an imprint on their thinking. In the past, these parties called for the expansion of the state sector and cooperative farms, criticizing any growth in the private sector as the evil of all evils. Now, by contrast, the terms 'productive capitalism' and 'the productive sections of capitalism' are in wide circulation in communist milieux. The necessity of the market is also defended from a Marxist perspective: it is seen as a step towards a maturity of capitalism that will lead, in some distant future, to a vague sort of better social organization of society. Not only is the private sector endorsed and legitimized, but a strong criticism of the public sector has also emerged. This, in fact, is a general position. Such shades of opinion as do exist concern the desirable size of both the public and the state sector and other related issues. It is now the radical nationalists and, interestingly, some fundamentalists who are coming out in favour of the public sector (perhaps in defence of their former leading roles in it).

Parliamentary Democracy

The Arab communist parties tended to repeat the classical Marxist criticism of the shortcomings or limited nature of 'bourgeois democracy', whether or not they had parliaments in their respective countries. Even when such representative institutions were abolished by radical nationalists (on the pretext of building a unified nation or people, or introducting social transformations such as nationalization, agrarian reforms and the construction of a state sector), the communists hailed these changes as being more important than political plurality. This problem was particularly acute in Iraq, Syria, Egypt, Sudan, Algeria and Tunisia; it was non-existent in Lebanon and had a quite different character in the Gulf states.

Both the reform and the collapse of the Soviet Union shook the 'seven pillars' of single-party wisdom. Today it is no longer the Arab communists but most of the radical nationalists who are in favour of the single-party model; they point to China's 'success' in reforming the economy and holding political monism intact. (This argument is also put forward by some hard-line, orthodox communists.) The general trend, however, is a strong shift towards democratic, even liberal, norms.

A reluctance to espouse greater political liberalism can be detected not in the Mashreq but in the Maghreb, namely in Algeria and Tunisia. The communist parties in both these countries are greatly concerned by the threat, whether potential or real, of a fundamentalist takeover. Hence their reluctance to adopt a fully liberal stand during the military takeover in Algeria. The resumption of the experiment in controlled democracy may lead to a radical change.

Organizational Norms and Structures

There is a general move towards reshaping the concepts and structure of the Arab communist parties (in fact, steps have been taken to do so). First, there is a rejection of some of the major norms of the Leninist concept of democratic centralism, namely: (i) the subsumption of the minorities to the majority; (ii) the subsumption of lower to higher bodies; (iii) the prohibition on the formation of factions; (iv) the prohibition on public debate; (v) the idea that only one party represents the working class; and (vi) the purity of theory (Marxism-Leninism). These are the pillars of the so-called unity of the party, supported by a unity of theory (or 'purity of doctrine', to use the current jargon).

The organizational structures borrowed from the pre-revolutionary Bolshevik experience were, in some cases, even more complicated than those in the Soviet Union. The Iraqi Communist Party structure, for example, had a more complex hierarchy than that of the Iraqi military or civil service: from top to bottom, there were sixteen grades in the party, compared to ten in the military and eight in the civil service.[5] Movement up the hierarchical ladder was not only fatally slow but a source of schisms and splits. The party has now reduced its hierarchy to five or six levels instead of the previous sixteen. The Palestinian and Lebanese communists have also introduced radical changes within the party: free elections (no appointments), free debates, Central Committee membership for two terms; and the same as far as the post of general secretary is concerned.

These changes are ongoing and derive their theoretical legitimacy, where needed, from Rosa Luxemburg's criticism of Lenin's Central Committee, her attacks on the proposed Leninist central norms of organization and her fears that they would lead to some sort of dictatorship.

According to Barghouthi:

> The organizational form we had was Soviet. It is true that not all Marxists accepted the Bolshevik form of organization. Suffice it to mention Rosa Luxemburg, who insisted on the necessity of democracy within the party and society, otherwise a handful of leaders with a group of active executives would prevail over the vast, passive masses of the proletariat, and this would not build socialism. We omitted the Leninist concept of democratic centralism, which is centralism proper, and built district assemblies instead of committees to form some sort of a parliament.[6]

Internationalism and Imperialism

Even before the fall of the Soviet Union, many communist leaders in the Middle East had felt embarrassed by the existence of various old, perhaps archaic, Marxist concepts in their programmes. 'Proletarian internationalism' stands out in particular among other irrelevant concepts such as 'Marxism-Leninism', 'the socialist camp', 'the international working-class movement' and 'the age of transformation from capitalism to socialism'. Part of the communist movement in the Arab world has nevertheless continued the anti-imperialist rhetoric in one way or another. They see the old bipolar system as being displaced by the American 'mono-system' and feel that they have been exposed, left 'naked among the wolves'.

The innovators within the Arab communist movement hold a different view, or rather, views. The 'new world' is either conceived of as a multi-polar rather than bipolar or mono-polar system. Or it is conceived of as a world that is of a different nature from that of the pre-1917 imperialist globe—not only has the nature of capitalism changed, but the system of international relations is no longer based solely on economic and political factors. To quote Barghouthi again:

> . . . cultural factors [also] have their say, such as the human and civilized norms of respect shown for the sovereignty of small and large nations, a minimum respect for international law, tolerance, plurality, and so on

> . . . [Hence] the old image of the world as being commanded by imperialism is no longer valid. It is very difficult nowadays to pursue an imperial policy. Of course, the new world order is in the process of crystallization and it will not be founded on imperial bases in the old sense of the term. I am confident the world is progressing for the better.[7]

Conclusion

The communist movement in the Arab world (for whom the demise of the Soviet Union was an almost apocalyptic event) seems to be involved in a life-and-death struggle to define, construct and defend a particular identity. Some parties have relapsed into nationalism, others into liberalism. These are only the first, hasty reactions, however: the old dogmas still retain a life of their own, creating a fault line that is too great to neglect. A possible reconciliation may well lead to a conscious shift towards some sort of social democracy on the West European model; otherwise further schisms lie ahead.

Throughout the Arab world, only the communist parties in Iraq and Sudan have managed to gain widespread popularity. Both, however, have been subject to continued assaults from 1960 onwards, with the bloody Ba‘thist coup in Iraq in 1963 and the Numeiri counter-coup in Sudan in 1971. The two parties have now gone underground, the first operating clandestinely under the single-party Ba‘th tyranny, and the second under the fundamentalist one-party regime in Khartoum. The Iraqi Communist Party, however, enjoys freedom of action in Kurdistan. It has a seat in the local Cabinet, and its own television and radio stations, and enjoys considerable influence among the urban intelligentsia and lower middle classes. The party bosses estimate the number of votes won by the party in the first free elections in Kurdistan in May 1992 at around 45,000, or 4.5% of the electorate.

Almost all the Arab communist parties now take an active part in the controlled democratic process that has been initiated in several Arab countries, even holding a handful of parliamentary seats. This applies to Morocco, Algeria, Tunisia, Egypt, Jordan, Syria, Lebanon, and of course Yemen, where the Socialist Party was the second most important parliamentary grouping. The Yemeni Socialist Party was the strongest in the Arab world, but was destroyed after the North-South civil war in 1994. The influence of the communist parties in the Arab world is relatively weak, however. A more thorough study may provide information on their sources of support, a support which relies only marginally on the working class. In certain cases, the local communist movement can hardly speak of any solid relations with the working class.

It should be noted that the admission of some Arab communist parties to the parliamentary process had started, in certain cases, long before *perestroika*. This was the case in Morocco, Tunisia, Lebanon and Syria, whereas the Jordanian and Algerian parties have only been admitted very recently. One of the factors that has permitted this new-found 'acceptability' is that there is no longer any fear of the communist parties orchestrating a 'red conspiracy' now that the Cold War is over.

Underground activity is still the order of the day in some other Arab countries: Saudi Arabia, Bahrain, Oman, Iraq, Sudan and (in the case of the Palestinian Communist Party) the West Bank and Gaza Strip. With the possible exception of the Palestinians, clandestinity may well mean that even the existence of loose, disconnected cells scattered here and there is a great achievement. In other cases, a wider range of activities is possible: in addition to the main body of the party, this may mean networks of student, youth, women's, writers' and workers' organizations or clubs.

Before 1991 socialism and socialist perspectives, with their concomitant ideological implications, were the main focus of attention for the Arab communist parties. The focus has now shifted towards democracy and (particularly in Algeria, Tunisia and Sudan) the dangers posed to democracy by Islamic fundamentalism. Democracy, the Arab communists now contend, is the central slogan, the struggle for which covers a historical epoch. Most, if not all, see themselves as the true guardians of authentic democracy and true patriotism and, in certain instances, as a counterbalance to the obscurantist threat posed by the fundamentalists. (Some communist parties have forged alliances with the fundamentalists, however: in Palestine on the basis of anti-Israel nationalism, and in Iraq on the basis of the anti-fascist struggle.)

As mentioned above, the two main tendencies that have recently crystallized within the Arab communist movement are nationalism and liberalism with social-democratic leanings: it is within these frameworks that the communists see themselves, their role and their future. Almost all Arab communist parties have their own daily, weekly or monthly papers, and most of them also produce literary and intellectual journals either as part of their social activities and/or as a source of funds. All are very active in non-government associations such as professional bodies and trade unions, fighting the Islamists or the ruling party for influence in these fields. They are also active among students and in the students' union movement, among the youth, at sports clubs and in writers' clubs, and so on. Wherever possible, they try to act as a pressure and interest group, using their own media in addition to the traditional means of exerting influence such as letters, appeals, meetings and demonstrations. With the two major exceptions of Iraq and Sudan, there has been no attempt by the Arab communist parties to penetrate the army and build networks inside its ranks. The Iraqi Communist Party has its own armed, partisan units which until recently were stationed in the mountains of Kurdistan, but are now located in urban centres.

Most Arab communist parties are now very flexible in terms of social and political alliances, tactics and actions. Some form of European-style social democracy is gradually emerging. It might, in the end, prove not only necessary but also feasible.

Part Two

Globalization, Development and Planning Dilemmas

8. Globalization in Question*

Paul Hirst

Introduction

'Globalization' has become an increasingly fashionable concept in the social sciences. It is widely supposed that the process of economic 'globalization' has taken place or is taking place, leading to a situation where most economic activities have been internationalized and the nation state has lost its capacity as a locus of economic governance. A truly 'global' economy would thus be a new stage in economic relations, qualitatively different from previous structures of the international economy. This chapter asks whether there is such a thing as a globalized economy. It further asks: if not, then how are we to characterize the present state of the world economy?

In the first place, we examine whether such a process of globalization can be specified with some degree of rigour and assessed against the available evidence of international economic trends, thus enabling us to determine whether this phenomenon is taking place or not. To do this we have constructed two contrasting economic types: a fully globalized economy, and an open international economy that is still fundamentally determined by processes occurring at the level of national economies. These types enable us to clarify the issues, and conceptually to specify the difference between a potentially new global economy and what are merely

* This chapter is based on collaborative research with Dr Grahame Thompson of The Open University, UK.

extensive and intensive international economic relations. Evidence of the latter is too often used to substantiate the former.

Second, having specified the ideal types, we consider the main trends in the international economy and how they fit with the ideal type of globalization. Third, we examine both the constraints on and the remaining forms of effectiveness of national economic management, given the current conjuncture in the international economy. In assessing the possibilities of governance at the international level, we then examine supranational trading blocs and the possibilities of coordination through cooperation on the part of the major players.

A Globalized Economy: What Would it Look Like?

An 'Inter-national' Economy

An 'inter-national' economy is one in which the principal entities are nation states, and involves the process of the growing interconnection between national economies. It involves the increasing integration of ever more nations and economic actors into market relations. Trade relations, as a result, take on the form of national specialization and the division of labour. The importance of trade is, however, progressively replaced by the centrality of investment relations between nations, which increasingly act as the organizing principle of the system. The form of interdependence between nations remains, however, of the 'strategic' kind. That is, it implies the continued relative separation of the domestic and the international frameworks for policy-making and the management of economic affairs, and also a relative separation in terms of economic effects. Interactions are conceived of as the 'billiard ball' type; international events do not directly penetrate or permeate the domestic economy but are refracted through national policies and processes. The international and the domestic policy fields either remain separated as distinct levels of governance or they work 'automatically'. In the latter case, adjustments are not thought to be the subject of policy by public bodies or authorities, but are a consequence of 'unorganized' or 'spontaneous' market forces.

Perhaps the classic case of such an 'automatic' adjustment mechanism remains the Gold Standard (GS), which operated at the height of the *Pax Britannica* system from the mid-nineteenth century to 1914. Automatic is expressed in inverted commas here to signal the fact that this is a popular caricature. The actual system of adjustment took place very much in terms of overt domestic policy interventions. The flexibility in wages and prices that the GS system demanded (the international value of currencies could not be adjusted since these were fixed in terms of gold) had to be engineered by governments through domestic expenditure reducing policies to influence the current account and interest-rate policy to influence the capital account.

It is important to recognize that the GS and the *Pax Britannica* system formed merely one of the structures of the international economy. The First World War destroyed British hegemony, accelerating a process that would have occurred far more slowly merely as a consequence of British industrial decline. It resulted in a period of protectionism and national autarkic competition in the 1930s, followed by the establishment of American hegemony after the Second World War and the reopened international economy of the Bretton Woods system. This indicates the danger of assuming that current major changes in the international economy are unprecedented and that they are inevitable or irreversible. The lifetime of a prevailing system of international economic relations in the twentieth century has been no more than thirty to forty years. Such systems have been transformed by major changes in the politico-economic balance of power and the conjunctures that have effected these shifts have been large-scale conflicts between the major powers. In that sense, the 'inter-national' economy has been determined both in its structure and in the distribution of power within it by the major nation states.

The period of this worldwide international economic system is also typified by the rise and maturity of the Multinational Corporation (MNC). The important aspect of these MNCs is that they retain a clear national home base; they are subject to the national regulations of the mother country, and by and large they are effectively policed by that home country.

A Globalized International Economy

A globalized international economy is a distinct ideal type from that of the worldwide economy and can be developed by contrast with it. In such a global system, distinct national economies are subsumed and rearticulated into the system by international processes and transactions. The 'inter-national' economy, on the contrary, is one in which processes that are determined at the level of national economies still dominate, and international phenomena are outcomes that emerge from the distinct and differential performance of the national economies. The 'inter-national' economy is an aggregate of nationally located functions. Thus while there are in such an economy a wide and increasing range of international economic interactions (financial markets and trade in manufactured goods, for example), these tend to function as opportunities or constraints for nationally located economic actors and their public regulators.

The global economy raises these nationally based interactions to a new power. The international system becomes autonomized, as markets and production become truly global. Domestic policy-makers, whether private corporations or public regulators, now have routinely to take account of the predominately international determinants of their activities. As systemic interdependence grows, the national level is permeated by and transformed by the international. In such a globalized economy, the problem this poses for the public authorities is how to construct policies that coordinate and integrate their regulatory efforts in order to cope with the systematic interdependence between their economic actors.

The first major consequence of a globalized economy would thus be the fundamentally problematic nature of its governance. Global markets are difficult to regulate, even supposing effective cooperation by the regulators and a coincidence of their interests. The difficulty is how to construct both effective and integrated patterns of public policy to cope with global market forces, since in order to function, such policies would need to be coordinated from the level of international regulatory agencies down to key regional governments. The interdependence of states and markets would by no means necessarily result in a harmonious world integration in which world consumers benefit from truly independent allocative mechanisms. On the contrary, it is more than plausible that the populations of even successful and advanced states and regions would be at the mercy of autonomized and uncontrollable (because global) market forces. Interdependence would then readily promote disintegration—i.e. competition and conflict—between regulatory agencies at different levels. Such conflict would further weaken effective public governance at the global level. Enthusiasts for the efficiency of free markets, and the superiority of corporate control over that of public agencies, would see this as a rational world freed from the shackles of obsolete and ineffective national public intervention. Others, less sanguine but convinced that globalization is occurring, may see it as a world system in which there can be no generalized or sustained public reinsurance against the costs imposed by market distributions or market failures on localities.

It is also clear that this ideal type highlights the problem of weak public governance for the major corporations. Even if such companies were truly global, they would not be able to operate equally effectively in all markets and, like governments, would lack the capacity for reinsurance against unexpected shocks from their own resources alone. Governments would no longer be available to assist 'national champions'. Firms would, therefore, seek to share risks and opportunities through inter-corporate investments, partnerships, joint-ventures, and so on. Even in the current internationalized economy, we can recognize such processes emerging.

A second major consequence of the notion of a globalizing nternational economy would be the transformation of MNCs into Transnational Corporations (TNCs) as the major players in the world economy. The TNC would be genuine footloose capital, without specific national identification and with an internationalized management, and at least potentially willing to locate and relocate anywhere in the globe to obtain either the most secure or the highest returns. In the financial sector this could be secured at the touch of a button and in a truly globalized economy would be wholly dictated by market forces, without reference to national monetary policies. In the case of primarily manufacturing companies, they would source, produce and market at the global level as strategy and opportunities dictated. The company would no longer be based on one predominant national location (as with the MNC) but would service global markets through global operations. Thus the TNC, unlike the MNC, could no longer be controlled or even constrained by the policies of particular national states. Rather it could escape all but the commonly agreed and enforced international regulatory standards. National governments could not thus adopt particular regulatory policies that diverged from these standards to the detriment of TNCs operating within their borders. The TNC would be the main manifestation of a truly globalized economy.

Julius and Ohmae both consider this trend towards true TNCs to be well established.[1] Ohmae argues that such 'stateless' corporations are now the prime movers in an Inter-Linked Economy (ILE) centred on North America, Europe and Japan. He contends that macroeconomic and industrial policy intervention by national governments can only distort and impede the rational process of resource allocation by corporate decisions and consumer choices on a global scale. He further argues that such corporations will pursue strategies of 'global localization' in responding on a worldwide scale to specific regionalized markets and locating effectively to meet the varying demands of distinct localized groups of consumers. The assumption here is that TNCs will rely primarily on foreign direct investment and the full domestication of production to meet such specific market demands. This is in contrast to the strategy of flexibly specialized core production in the company's main location and the building of branch assembly plants where needed or dictated by national public policies. The latter strategy is compatible with nationally based companies.

A third consequence of globalization would be the further decline in the political influence and economic bargaining power of labour. Globalized markets and TNCs would not be mirrored by an open world labour market. Thus while advanced companies might well continue to locate in the advanced countries, with all their advantages, rather than merely seek low wages, the trend of the global mobility of capital and the national fixity of labour would favour those advanced countries with the most tractable labour forces and the lowest social overheads relative to the benefits of labour competence and motivation. 'Social democratic' strategies of enhancement of working conditions would thus only be viable if they assured the competitive advantage of the labour force, without constraining management prerogatives, and at no more overall cost in taxation than the average for the advanced world. Such strategies would clearly be difficult to implement and the tendency of globalization would be to favour management at the expense of even moderately organized labour and, therefore, policies sympathetic to the former rather than the latter.

So far we have sought to clarify what would be involved in claiming either that we are firmly within a globalizing economy, or that there are strong globalizing tendencies. To establish this firmly is a difficult task. It is made doubly so (and the outcome is quite uncertain) because of a number of changes in the international economy in the post-First World War period. Chief among these have been the change in hegemonic leadership during the inter-war period and then the decline and possible collapse of the *Pax Americana* in the post-1970s period.

The *Pax Americana* as it established and consolidated itself in the immediate post-1945 period heralded the beginning of the liberal multilateral market system that supported the international economy during the long boom. But the American hegemony displayed a number of dimensions. Militarily it is arguable that the US is still hegemonic: this was clearly the case in the context of the 1990–91Gulf war. In addition, the US still serves as the powerhouse of world demand and acts as the guardian of the world open-trading economy. But it no longer has monetary hegemony. No other power or combination of powers can yet challenge this residual hegemonic power that the US displays. It may not be able to command the tight loyalty of the other Western powers that it did during the period of the Cold War, but it retains considerable genuinely hegemonic strengths.

Both of these developments—the change and then the undermining of the hegemonic order, accompanied by the totally floating rate regime—provided the conditions in which the logic of the 'international economy' might be thought to have been undermined. These developments led to the abandonment of exchange controls, and the liberalization and then deregulation of international financial markets. But the floating exchange-rate regime began to exhibit quite perverse 'overshooting'. It was accompanied by the supply-side shock of the oil price hikes, with consequent massive increases both in the liquidity of members of the Organization of Petroleum Exporting Countries (OPEC) and in the Third World countries' desire to borrow (given negative real interest rates) in order to finance their current account deficits, leading to the so- called 'Third World debt' problem. These features also provoked a serious recession in the international economy more generally, with a concomitant increase in government indebtedness. A chronic structural problem of the balance of payments between the US and Japan in particular also emerged as the US became a massive capital importer to finance its deteriorating trade balance.

The totally floating rate period did not last for long. In 1979, for example, the European Community (EC) set up the European Monetary System (EMS) to provide a zone of stability for the main European currencies (except the UK pound) against the vagaries of the US dollar. In addition, the Louvre and Plaza accords between the Group of Seven (G7) countries in the 1980s set in motion an attempt to monitor and 'manage' fundamental disequilibrium in the exchange rates between its members. Explicit policy coordination at the world level was initiated in this case. This has not reversed the main trend, which has been to further undermine the old post-war multilateral order. These events register the contingent nature of many of the phenomena that have been used to argue for a structural transformation in the international economy. Many of these trends could be reversed or interrupted as the international economy evolves. We should be cautious in ascribing too much significance to what might be temporary changes, dramatic though some of them have been.

The Present International Economy

Here we examine the main trends in the international economy and ask how they fit with the globalization thesis.

1. Within the contemporary international economy, the important relationships remain those between the more developed economies, the members of the Organisation of Economic Cooperation and Development (OECD). Indeed, these economies have increased in relative importance over recent years in terms of their share of world trade and investment. In 1989 over 80% of world trade was conducted between the OECD economies, and this rose to 85% if the ex-East European and Soviet economies were included. The Group of Five (G5) main economies accounted for 75% of foreign direct investment. Thus for all practical purposes, it is the advanced industrial economies that constitute the membership of the 'global' economy, if that entity can be said to exist. The Less Developed Countries (LDCs), and even the Newly

Industrializing Countries (NICs), still constitute a very small part of the international economy. The primary producers are almost totally dependent upon the More Developed Countries (MDCs) for markets and investment, a position that has not changed significantly for many decades. Foreign Direct Investment (FDI) and trade flows thus remain distinctly 'lumpy'. Capital is not fleeing from the advanced countries; thus 14% of the world's population accounted for 75% of FDI in 1980–91 and for 70% of world trade in 1992.[2]

2. There is little doubt that there has been a progressive internationalization of money and capital markets since the 1970s, and this represents a marked change in relation to the post-1945 period. Many people have seized upon this as a sign of the radical change towards a globalizing economy. It has led to the argument that national economies are no longer governable because they have become increasingly penetrated by 'international financial capital'. This inability to control capital flows, it is claimed, undermines any remaining credibility of the policies of national macroeconomic management.

   But the implications of this internationalization of financial markets are not unambiguous. For example, Tomlinson presents data showing that the international financial penetration of the UK and other economies (in terms of openness to capital flows) was greater between 1905 and 1914 than it was between 1982 and 1986[3] (and similar results emerge for foreign trade as a percentage of GDP). Thus it is important to remember that the international economy was hardly less integrated between 1870 and 1914 than it is today.

   The principal reasons for the admittedly phenomenal recent growth of international financial flows and liquidity are as follows: (a) the floating of exchange rates; (b) the oil price hike and consequent Third World debt problem; (c) the unexpected emergence of vast and mobile OPEC funds; (d) the international recession and the growth in government debt throughout the 1970s; (e) the emergent structural imbalances in the balance of payments for a number of large economies; and (f) the liberalization and deregulation of financial markets by national governments. All these features increased the extent of international capital flows. If we were to single out one central feature, it would be the floating of exchange rates. Many of the other features followed as a consequence of this (for example, the integration of trading on world currency and equity markets, which is a new feature of the present period).

   This demonstrates how many of these changes may be far from irreversible. First, volatility on the international currency markets could diminish. Indeed, the volatility of the early 1980s was diminished as the EMS and the G7 monitoring system was installed. All the major international currencies are now more or less 'managed' currencies, which has seriously cut speculative activity (a factor that promoted volatility and exchange-rate uncertainty). The continuing difficulties of the EMS do not necessarily contradict this statement, since the root cause is the divergent performance of economies in the European Union (EU) and a Bundesbank policy that has put price stability in Germany above the maintenance of stability within the EMS. The problem is not speculators, but public policies that prompt speculation, by leading to uncertainty and to anticipated changes in exchange rates. Second, after an initial enthusiastic embrace of market liberalization and deregulation, the authorities are recognizing that there are undesirable consequences and the trend now is for re-regulation. The struggle between public policy and the major foreign exchange markets will continue until and if a new system of fixed exchange rates is created or a speculators' tax[4] is introduced by the major nations. However, the outcome of this struggle is by no means settled in favour of the markets.

3. There has been an increasing volume of trade in semi-manufactured and manufactured goods between the industrialized economies. Most markets for major industrial products are now international, and major economies both import and export significant volumes of such goods, whereas before the 1960s home sourcing was dominant and export markets were more specialized. This has had an inevitable impact on the ability of individual economies to exercise national macro-management strategies. This point is considered below: because domestic demand can be sourced from a wide range of foreign suppliers, then strong national expansionary policies can be choked off as demand is met by rapidly rising imports.
4. One of the main concomitants of the growth in interdependent trade relations is the progressive development of internationalized companies. The role of the TNCs in undermining national governments' conduct of an independent economic policy has already been raised. But again the extent of these developments is questionable.[5] Most international companies still only operate in a small number of countries, or at most regionally. Typically, most major manufacturing multinationals account for two-thirds of their sales within their home region; moreover, there seems to be no tendency for this ratio to diminish.[6] There are few truly TNCs and the MNC form continues to dominate. The few exceptions to this do not yet make the rule. Thus the examples of transnational companies, while of interest, do not alter the aggregate statistical picture constructed from the best available data. In addition, most MNCs adapt

passively to government policy rather than continually trying to undermine it. The real question to ask of MNCs is not why they are always threatening to leave a country if things go badly for them there, but why the vast majority of them fail to leave and continue to stay put in their home base and major centres of investment. MNCs are very reluctant to uproot themselves because they become entrenched in specific national markets, and with local suppliers and dealers. This makes it both difficult and expensive to leave given national markets unless there are fundamental structural disincentives, rather than conjunctural difficulties or specific policy constraints imposed by national governments.

Nor is direct foreign investment as important as is often believed. We might take the case of Japan, for example, which is often thought to be heralding a new global assault on both the industrial and the underdeveloped world with its investment strategies. A recent study[7] tries to examine the character of direct Japanese foreign manufacturing investment: it is fairly small-scale compared to the total volume of Japanese capital abroad, and it is mainly aimed at providing transplants that have a high import content from Japan. The aggregate growth of direct investment is small in relation to Japanese trade growth. Moreover, it is no more efficient or profitable than indigenous manufacturing. In general, the most successful industrial nations (such as Germany and Japan) have shown a great reluctance to develop core manufacturing activity abroad; they keep the bulk of their value-adding capacity at home. This is for a variety of reasons, not all of which can be summed up in market efficiency or balance-sheet terms. German and Japanese financial capital still remains largely 'nationalistic' and is committed to its domestic manufacturing sector in a way that Anglo-American capital is not. German and Japanese firms still have a strong commitment to highly skilled and motivated national labour forces. A 'deal' between labour and capital to sustain prosperity was, in different ways, a core part of both countries' post-1945 national politico-economic settlements. Both countries would have a massive political price to pay were a major part of manufacturing to be shipped abroad and the prosperity of recent decades to falter.[8]

5. Perhaps the most significant post-1970s development, and the most enduring, is the formation of supranational trading and economic blocs. One initial question, however, concerns exactly how to specify these blocs. Clearly the EU and the North American Free Trade Area (NAFTA) can be considered genuine blocs, or proto-blocs, but are there any others? Japan is often seen as the centre of a proto-bloc

encompassing much of the South-East Asian Pacific rim countries. But an examination of trade and investment data shows this to be premature. Initially therefore it may be better to consider Japan as a single-country bloc. Many ad hoc combinations of countries that might form (limited) trading and economic blocs around the Pacific rim and in the rest of Asia have been suggested, but so far these remain largely speculative.

A more regionalized international economy would increase the possibility of protectionist attitudes and policies on the part of at least some of the trading blocs. Such protectionism would weaken and even perhaps reverse some of the other trends towards economic internationalization identified above, such as the growth in interdependence in world trade flows and the continuing integration of financial markets. The general issue to consider here, however, is the likely form of the global economy as the liberal, multilateralist regime of the post-1945 period is replaced by other institutions. Will globalization, in the sense of open and unregulated world markets, replace the old regime of managed liberal multilateralism? The present author suggests that it will not. The outcome is likely to be a messy mixture of liberal regulation (General Agreement on Tariffs and Trade, or GATT) and the growing importance of regional blocs—both being dominated by the triad of NAFTA, the EU and Japan. The 'G3' will continue to dominate general international regimes and continue to bargain bilaterally between themselves and with lesser parties. The world economy will thus be governed, at least partially, and is unlikely to correspond to the ideal-type of an open global system.

Consequences and Implications: Managing the New International Economy?

In this section we consider the prospects for the general management of the 'regionalized' world economy and, on a more limited scale, the future for the EU as an entity capable of regional economic governance. What are the prospects for national state regulation in a rapidly internationalizing economy?

Economic Management, the Nation State and Globalization

The consequence of internationalization and the accompanying volatility of markets has been to limit the effectiveness of the strategies of national economic management developed since the 1930s. Both the traditional Keynesian strategy, and the newer 'national monetarist' strategies which succeeded it in the late 1970s, have become less and less effective. Traditional Keynesian policies of stabilizing economic activity by stimulating domestic demand in periods of downturn by means of fiscal and monetary policy have become severely constrained by the effects of such policies in producing inflation rates that diverge from those of dominant competitors, by the effect of sucking in foreign imports of manufactured goods when domestic demand has been stimulated, and by the consequent balance-of-payments constraint and exchange-rate constraints generated by such boosting of domestic demand. The policies of the French socialist government in the early 1980s and their subsequent abandonment have demonstrated the difficulties of 'national Keynesianism'; so too has the experience of the US during the Reagan administration in following an expansionary policy, producing the current American budget and trade deficits. International Keynesianism—involving coordinated policies on the part of a number of major states—is inherently unlikely, given the divergent interests of the major players in the international economy and the absence of a single hegemonic power able to underwrite the expansion of the international economy as the US did between the end of the Second World War and 1972.

At the same time, 'national monetarist' policies have also failed. The other advanced industrial countries are forced to follow the lead in monetary policy of the two most successful countries, Germany and Japan. Before the crisis of 1992–93, the Exchange Rate Mechanism (ERM) limited the scope for monetary policy for all members of the EC, who were directly tied to the monetary regime of the Bundesbank. Controlling the money supply is inherently difficult, given the internationalization of financial markets, the abolition of exchange controls, and the dominant role of credit money generated by the loans policy of financial institutions. The UK abandoned strict monetarism in the early 1980s; its effects had been severely deflationary. During the 'Lawson boom' of the mid- to late 1980s, rapid expansion of domestic credit led both to high growth and to a substantial rise in imports of both consumer and capital goods, and thus to a worsening trade deficit. By the late 1980s the UK government had returned to a (rather traditional, quasi-Keynesian) tight interest-rate policy in its attempt to control the money supply and inflation; interest rates affect the demand for money in the first instance, not its supply. This too was deflationary. Monetarism was intended as an expansionary policy, allied as it was with positive supply side measures. But these twin policy advances failed as an alternative to Keynesianism, because they have had severe deflationary rather than expansionary effects.

The result of this argument is that there is now no doctrinally grounded and technically effective regime of macroeconomic management that can produce substantial and sustained expansionary effects. It might appear that national macroeconomic management has ceased to provide a viable means of steering national economies in an internationalized system and that the nation state has lost its importance in the face of 'globalization' and supranational economic blocs.

This conclusion would be superficial. The mechanisms of national economic regulation have changed but government policies to sustain national economic performance retain much of their relevance, even if their nature, level and function have changed. In the EU, for example, the (uncertain) prospect of monetary union and a single currency by the end of the twentieth century, with the free movement of capital, labour, goods and services under the Single Market policy that took full effect after 1992, along with a common regulatory framework imposed by Brussels, obviously have restricted or will further restrict some hitherto important areas of national management for most member states. But they make other areas of national policy more important—giving a new significance to non-monetarist fiscal and supply-side policies, for example.[9]

While national governments may no longer be 'sovereign' economic regulators in the traditional sense, they remain political communities with extensive powers to influence and sustain economic actors within their territories. Technical macroeconomic management is less effective, but the role of government as a facilitator and orchestrator of private economic actors remains strong. The political role of government is central in the new forms of economic management. Neither the financial markets nor the Brussels bureaucracy, to take the case of the most coherent trade bloc, can impose or secure the forms of social cohesion and the policies that follow from them that national governments can. National governments can still compensate for the effects of internationalization and for the continued volatility of the financial markets.

There are three key functions which stem from government's role as orchestrator of an economic consensus within a given community. States are not like markets; they are communities of fate, which tie together actors who share certain common interests in the success or failure of their national economies. Markets may be international, but wealth and economic prosperity are national phenomena. They depend upon how well national economic actors can work together to secure key supply-side outcomes. National policy provides certain key inputs that cannot be bought or traded on the market. The market is embedded in society and governments remain a crucial element in the success of their societies—providing cohesion, solidarity and certain crucial services that markets of themselves cannot.

The three key functions are as follows:

1. If the state is to influence the economy, it must construct a distributional coalition; that is, it wins the acceptance of key economic actors (and the organized social interests representing them) for a sustainable distribution of national income and expenditure which promotes competitive manufacturing performance (among other things). The major components of such a coalition are: the balance of national income devoted respectively to consumption and investment; a broad agreement on the level of taxation necessary to sustain state investment in infrastructure, training and collective services for industry; and a framework for controlling wage settlements, the growth of credit and levels of dividends such that inflation is kept within internationally tolerable limits.[10]
2. Such a distributional coalition is only possible if the state performs another function: the orchestration of social consensus. Such coalitions only work when they emerge from a collaborative political culture in which the major organized interests are accustomed to bargain over national economic goals, to make lasting commitments to determine policy by such bargaining and to police their members' compliance with such bargains. Industry, organized labour and the state achieve a successful balance between cooperation and competition; such a system is not devoid of conflict, nor are interests wholly coincident, but there are mechanisms for resolving such differences. Such an overall consensus only works if it is also keyed in with the effective operation of more specific resource allocation mechanisms, such as the system of wage determination and the operation of capital markets. Such a national consensus may now be difficult to achieve through corporatist coordination through peak associations, but this difficulty does not obviate the need for firms, public bodies and labour interests to strike an ongoing and renegotiated balance between cooperating and competing. Consensus may have to be both more local and provisional, but it remains necessary to provide those inputs vital to an effective economy that markets themselves cannot provide.[11]
3. The state achieves an adequate balance in the distribution of its fiscal resources and its regulatory activities between the national, regional and municipal levels of government. The centralization of EU policy is promoting the increasing importance of effective regional government. The regional provision of education and training, industrial finance, collective services for industry and social services is gaining in importance. Regional governments are more able to assess the needs of

industry because they possess more localized, and therefore accurate, information and because they are of a scale where the key actors can interact successfully. Regional government cannot be seen as something inherently opposed to national economic management, but as a crucial component of it. It is the national state which determines the constitutional position, powers and fiscal resources of lower tiers of government. Those national states which allow a considerable measure of autonomy to regional governments tend to have the best and most effective supply-side regulation at the regional level. Germany and Italy offer obvious examples. The most prosperous *Länder* like Baden-Württemberg and Bavaria, or the most successful Italian regions like Emilia-Romagna, have achieved a high level of devolution of the tasks of economic management.[12]

The main problem concerning the nation state's continuing importance as a locus of economic management is that such activities now depend on social attitudes and institutions that are not equally available to all states. The new mechanisms of economic coordination and regulation give primacy to the high level of social cohesion and cooperation that the state can both call upon and develop. The new methods of national economic regulation in a more internationalized economy are not like Keynesianism, that is, a technique of macroeconomic management that was in principle available to every substantial and competently administered modern state if it chose to adopt such a strategy. Rather, the new methods rest on specific ensembles of social institutions and these are more difficult to adopt or transfer by deliberate choice. States are thus largely trapped by the legacies of social cohesion that they inherit. Countries like the US cannot simply decide to adopt the more solidaristic and coordinative relations between industry, labour and the state that have hitherto been characteristic of Germany and Japan. Analysts have sought to impose alternative national models on failing economies into the early 1990s, claiming that if they adopted certain institutions or practices they could meet competitive pressures. Learning from Japan is commonplace, but so too are models like the 'Rhenish capitalism' of Michel Albert.[13] Such models are increasingly seen to be mirages, not least because all advanced economies are facing difficulties and the current tendencies favour more decentralized forms of coordination.[14]

This means that between blocs and within blocs there will be fundamental differences in the ability to respond to competitive pressures and changing international conjunctures. Those societies that emphasize short-term market performance, like the UK and the US, are threatened by the competitive pressures of societies that have concentrated on enhancing long-term manufacturing competitiveness and have had the social cohesion to achieve it, like Germany and Japan. The political process and the interest-group culture in societies like the UK and the US does not favour rapid adaptation in a more cooperative direction; rather, it emphasizes competition and the dumping of social costs on those who are both least organized or influential and least able to bear them. This also pushes such societies away from effective international or bloc cooperation.

The problem, then, is how far the more favourable conditions for effective national economic management are to be found either in the existing national economies of the EU or as component parts of the evolving EU supranational economic management structure itself. (We shall return to this issue below.) First, we deal with the emergent management system, such as it is, at the international level.

A Regulated International Economic Environment?

What are the prospects for a more regulated international economic environment if a more orderly pattern returns to the relationships between markets, countries and blocs? As indicated above, there is still great volatility and increased uncertainty when compared to the very stable position before 1972, but nevertheless the indications are that not all the adverse trends giving rise to these uncertainties are set and robust. The inauguration of the EMS (and particularly its ERM component) in 1979 initially decreased the volatility of the members' exchange rates. In addition, the G5/G7 summit system of policy coordination has seen some successes, particularly in its early days and in 1991.[15]

These instances of policy coordination have been of only limited scope. They have involved monetary issues almost exclusively, though in recent years the monitoring of real variables like growth rates has been added to the agendas of such bodies. But 'monitoring 'is far from an active cooperation to change policy. The G5/G7 countries have largely gone their own way on domestic economic policy issues, and the divergence of basic philosophy and approach has been evident in the late 1980s and in the 1990s. We should not dismiss outright the attempts at limited exchange-rate and monetary coordination, but nor should we exaggerate their importance or success.

The problem lies in the divergent interests that still characterize an international economy where, despite the claims of the 'globalization' enthusiasts, the nation state and (increasingly) trading blocs remain the dominant players. If nothing else, the underlying economic conditions of the Japanese and American economies should testify to a divergence of interests that will limit active and positive cooperation between them. Similar remarks can be made in the context of Germany and the rest of Europe.

This is not to suggest that complete non-cooperation will ensue between the major players in the international economy, only that cooperation will be minimal, or that it will be cooperation by default as policies in the stronger economies dictate those in the weaker ones. Added to this are the very obvious differences in economic policy frameworks and outlooks that typify the main international trading countries and that will inhibit wider agreements on more developed cooperative ventures. In many cases, the domestic frameworks are simply not available to implement policies agreed within an international negotiating structure, even if they were more actively canvassed there. Fiscal policy initiatives are an obvious example. It is unlikely that a properly functioning fiscal federalism could be rapidly constructed within the EU, for example.

But these caveats should not blind us to the extent of integration within the international economy—an outright return to overt protectionism between the blocs, while still a possibility, remains unlikely. The case of the financial balances between the major blocs illustrates this point.[16] These show that the EU has been in rough balance on its savings and investments over the period 1960–90. Such was also the case for the US and Japan up to the early 1980s, but then the US went into a dramatic international 'deficit' as its savings collapsed while investment remained high (to finance its balance of payments/budget deficits). This twin deficit was financed by the Japanese, and to a lesser extent by the EU in the mid-1980s. Thus despite some volatility in the overall trends, which show large swings in overall proportionate totals, the three main bloc powers appear to be locked together in a certain way. In particular, Japan could hardly continue to exist in its present form without the US markets for its manufactured goods (though see below), while the US needs Japan as a source of international finance.

These points are reinforced if we look at the structure of trade within the blocs. Consider the percentage of total trade that each bloc leader conducts with its immediate client countries.[17] The most integrated bloc is the EU, with nearly 74% of its traded activity being conducted with other European countries. But the US and Japan do not trade to such an extent with their immediate 'bloc associates'. Indeed, at 33% and 30% respectively, their intra-bloc trade is small. The US and Japan must still look to the wider international environment for their trading partners. This should reinforce their mutual commitment to a more 'open' trading environment. The US may have much to fear from Japanese import penetration in its manufacturing sector, but it remains a major exporter of both manufactured goods and primary products and it relies upon a liberal regime of world trade to do so. Japan may be a virtual trade policy captive of the US, but the

US is still committed to free trade and will remain so, up to and until the time that Japanese competition threatens a catastrophic collapse of the American domestic manufacturing base.

What is remarkable about the trade to GDP ratios of three main economies/blocs between 1960 and 1994 is the way the proportion of both exports and imports for all three sets of economies moved closer together in the late 1980s. This similarity in levels of trade to GDP ratios for the three main players as a whole indicates a symmetry that could once again lead to a somewhat more accommodating outlook. The most vulnerable economy remains the Japanese. This is signalled by the consistently greater importance of its exports to GDP ratio, and the recent rapid increase in its import penetration ratio. The Japanese economy still relies upon trade for its prosperity to a greater extent than do the other two main players, even though they all share a generally similar combined aggregated total of trade to GDP ratios.[18] Japanese export trade in particular is concentrated in a small number of sectors (motor vehicles and consumer electronics, for example), which makes it very vulnerable to US trade policy.

Finally, the three country groupings also display a growing similarity in the ratio of externally held assets—denominated in their respective 'domestic' currency unit (the US dollar, the Japanese yen and the EU ECU)—to GNP. Between 1981 and 1988 the ratio of the share in currency portfolio of world financial wealth to GNP fell from 1.94 to 1.59 for the US, while it rose from 0.21 to 0.34 and from 0.44 to 0.71 for Japan and the EC respectively.[19]

The point of this analysis is to indicate the emergence of three dominant players in the international economy. They are all roughly of the same economic size and standing. Potentially, this encourages a better prospect for management of the international economy. It is easier to generate agreement between three players than the G5/G7 for example. But that does not mean that new agreements will necessarily be easily forged. There are still significant policy differences on the form and style of economic management between the three main players, for example, which could inhibit a more serious attempt at coordinating or cooperating on international economic management issues. In addition, a more active management style presumes that the blocs will form up into coherent managerial/regulatory entities themselves.

At this stage, the analysis suggests that a modified multilateralism will prevail in the immediate future. It will be modified in the form of a dominant trilateralism between the three main players, but with additionally emergent bilateral negotiations between these three on important issues, and between them and other minor parties as well. Quite what the full consequences of this configuration for the management of international economic affairs might be remains an open question. But it does not seem that overt and widespread inward-looking protectionism is likely in the immediate future. A minimal level of modified multilateral cooperation would seem enough to ensure the continued 'openness' of the international economic system, even as it moves further away from the traditional post-war type of full liberal multilateralism.

Conclusion

We have tried to define the concept of a globalized economy and assess whether current trends in the international economy justify the use of this concept. The answer seems to be that globalization has not taken place and is unlikely to do so. The international economy is imperfectly governed through the limited cooperation of the major trade blocs and nation states, but it is governed nonetheless and in a way that limits the power of the main financial markets. Nation states can secure high levels of international economic activity and satisfactory external balances through appropriate mixtures of policy. Such policies increasingly tend to diverge from the Keynesian macroeconomic instruments of the 1945–73 period and they depend on governments' capacities to coordinate and mobilize social actors. The result is that not all states are effective at meeting and mediating international competitive pressures through national policy resources. National success has depended on specific distributional contexts and on sources of social solidarity that are unevenly distributed between states; the US and the UK lack such capacities to a considerable degree while Japan and Germany continued until recently to benefit from them. However, in both the latter cases, continued success in economic management depends on their developing their present forms of social cohesion into looser and more decentralized institutions. Should that capacity for cooperation established by their post-1945 settlements falter through the defection of firms, labour dissatisfaction or other causes, then Germany and Japan's capacity to manage their relationship to the international economy to their own competitive advantage could decline.

Trade blocs are at an initial stage of formation. Even the most advanced, the EU, is unlikely to become a superstate that is capable of exploiting the potential of a continental scale of economic organization. Whether blocs will come into conflict and radically weaken the current liberal regime of trade between the advanced industrial economies is still an open question, but such an outcome seems unlikely. If the concept of 'globalization' has had any merit, it is as a negative ideal type that enables us to assess the shifting balance between international economic pressures and international government regulation and national and bloc-level economic management. We do not have a fully globalized economy, but we do have an international economy and national and supranational policy responses to it.

9. *Intentional Development and Marx*

M. P. Cowen and R. W. Shenton

> Like earlier generations of Californians who waxed fat from the natural wealth of the land, today's bourgeoisie lives off the fruits of social investment and labour involved in their spectacular success. Little do they realize that California needs an industrial policy, or a set of investment strategies and mechanisms of sectoral governance, geared to long run innovation, improving business organization, upgrading labour skills, providing collective infrastructure, and enlarging markets, for keeping the state on the high road of development.[1]

The above passage, excerpted from an article by Richard Walker in the once avowedly Marxist *New Left Review*, is emblematic of the extent to which the political left now begs for the institution of a project of positive state development as the means to escape the prevalent social and economic malaise. Even more striking is that this plea to redress the destructive legacy of a 'triumphal epoch' of a past that is now seen as bearing heavily 'down on the present' is being made not for Bangladesh or Kenya but for southern California, that erstwhile land of dreams, which since 1990 has witnessed a sudden sharp increase in unemployment and poverty. It is here—rather than some global Third World ghetto of continents of mass poverty with which our common-sense understanding of development has become associated since the end of the Second World War—that has become, for Walker, the setting of the demand to keep the state 'on the high road of development'. It is California, which little more than two decades ago was deemed to be fantastically rich in all senses of the word, for which Walker pleads for action to bring back 'light and hope to this microcosm of the national malaise' that is 'so symptomatic of a misguided economy and disintegrative social order'.[2] The appeal is for a design of development to compensate for the destructive propensities of the development of capitalism.

Embodied in Walker's appeal are two senses of the word development.[3] The first, which is implicit, is perhaps more familiar within the Marxist tradition. Here, development is an immanent process, inherent within the phenomenon in question. To think of the 'development of capitalism in Russia', the very title of Lenin's well-known book of nearly a century ago, is to think about the historical formation of industrial capital, the movement of capital to and from town and countryside, and, among much else, changes in the organization of labour-power including the emergence of a modern wage-labour force. Such historical processes are part of an immanent process of change that lacks any coherent plan or intent.

The immanent sense of development has been treated time and again in post-Second World War texts on economic development in the Third World as if it were a synonym for progress. Yet this is fundamentally mistaken. Unlike progress, the immanent sense of the idea of development involves destruction, decay, decomposition and death as well as creation and growth. It gives the same weight to that which negates life as to that which creates and renews the conditions for improved human existence. Immanent development has a long history in Western thought. In classical Greek thought, to take one example, human development was analogous to the process of natural change. Development was a set of sequences within the life cycle, just as a plant, after a period of growth towards maturity, deposits a seed containing all the necessary information for the course of new life before it dies. The seed germinates and grows but growth is merely one sequence within the cycle. Immanent development then, unlike progress, encompasses decay and destruction as well as expansion and growth.[4]

A key difference between the modern understanding of development and the older classical idea is that while, in the latter, the four phases of genesis, growth, maturity and decay are sequential, in the contemporary world, the two phases of development are simultaneous in that while development may happen within the same period of time, they act in different places. Forces acting for destruction and decay act at the same time as those forces which allow activity to grow and expand, but in different locations. The industrialization of Singapore or South Carolina is simultaneous with the de-industrialization of New York City. The rise of the computer chip industry is simultaneous with the decline of the production of manual typewriters.

It is precisely the phenomenon of decay and destruction which so riles

Walker and many others and leads them to call for a practice of intentional development in which the state—or agencies associated with the state, at all levels of jurisdiction from local to regional and national government—is implored to confront a misguided economy and a disintegrative social order. The plea to keep the state on the high road of 'development' means to act against the destruction of immanent development. Intentional development is the second sense in which Walker uses the word 'development' in his plea for state action to regenerate the Californian economy. It should be emphasized that the plea for intentional development is the direct result of what is perceived to be the destructiveness and decay of immanent development. Moreover, unlike either progress or development in its immanent sense, the intent to develop is inextricably linked to the idea of trusteeship.

The concept of trusteeship is commonly associated with the world of colonialism. Trusteeship was, after all, the doctrine used to explain, account for and justify imperial rule in the former colonial world. British colonial administration, for example, regarded itself as in the position of a 'trustee' for indigenous or 'native' populations. Nowadays, in a post-colonial world, the idea of trusteeship is seen as repugnant. We see through the imperial self-justification and understand that it embodied the supposed right of a self-selected group (in this case, Europeans) to impose themselves upon other peoples who were regarded as insufficiently developed to rule themselves.

However, the idea of trusteeship predates the colonial experiences of the late nineteenth and twentieth centuries. While trusteeship may have later come to be assimilated with colonial trusteeship, especially by the early Fabian socialists in Britain, the social source of trusteeship as a doctrine was independent of colonial experience. Rather, its origins were bound up with the problem of intentional development in Western Europe in the early nineteenth century. It was there and then that social trusteeship came to be inextricably linked to intentional development.

Most significantly, trusteeship formed the basis of the doctrine of intentional development espoused by the Saint-Simonians who, it should be remembered, Marx referred to as 'scientific socialists' in contradistinction to Robert Owen and those others he deemed to be 'utopian'. The Saint-Simonians believed that it was possible to plan for industrial society. And it was August Comte, the last of the Saint-Simonians and coiner of the very science of sociology, who brought intentional development to bear upon the means by which industrial society could be planned upon the basis of trusteeship.

Time and again in his writings, and particularly in his *System of Positive*

Polity, Comte wrote of progress being but 'the development of order'. By 'order', he meant the ideal of social order. Development was the means to re-establish this ideal out of the same kind of malaise of the disintegrative social order that Walker underlines in the present-day case of California. The Saint-Simonian idea of trusteeship was developed by Comte through his positive laws of knowledge. Those who considered that they had both the desire and the capacity for knowledge, and could set out the laws of social phenomena from positivist precepts and procedures, saw themselves as able to predict the future course of events. As such, the positive commitment to knowledge carried a social duty to act on behalf of the population as a whole. Unlike other kinds of socialists, who harked back to a pre-industrial past and sought for the means to organize society as if it belonged to a world without industrial capitalism, the inheritors of the Saint-Simonian tradition accepted industrial life as a given. Indeed, they regarded themselves as the fitting trustees of social capital who would act for the benefit of persons of labour-power, the workers and producers in factories. In England, John Stuart Mill attempted to marry the utilitarianism that he had inherited from his father with the positivist, and especially Comtean, thought that he learnt at first hand from the Saint-Simonians, and especially from Comte himself. It was thus that trusteeship came to lie at the heart of much utilitarian thought of the past and present.[5]

Because economics is itself so suffused by utilitarian ways of thinking, orthodox textbooks on economic or social development, which usually begin by asking the question 'What is development?', claim as a part of their answer that while development as an *end* lies in the process of enlarging people's choices, the *means* of development consists of rational procedures to calculate what kinds of economic activity will so enlarge choice. This answer is plausible but deceptively simple. For since the end of development, namely the process of enlarging choice, becomes the means for making development possible, the end of development has to be at the beginning of the process for development to happen. Moreover, individuals not only have to express the desire to exercise choice, but they are obliged to have the capacity to choose and the knowledge of all possible objects of choice as well. If any one of these conditions is missing, then a gap of development has to be filled. The filling of this gap is the process whereby capacities are developed by trusteeship. The same textbooks insist that until people can exercise choice, they will not be autonomous, and that without the autonomy to make rational decisions, they cannot engage in a process of true development. Development thus become a tautology.

The rhetoric of 'empowerment', no matter how uplifting in tone, merely replicates the conundrum of development. Either people have the desire, capacity and knowledge to exercise choice—in which case there is no need for them to be empowered—or they do not; and the task of empowerment is the same as the logical problem of development. Trustees continue to act, whether in the name of development or empowerment or transformation, on behalf of those without the conditions for development. What applies to the individual is considered to apply to social choice exercised by the state in the name of the 'community'. As long as individuals, whether singularly or collectively in the name of the state, do not have the desire or the capacity to exercise choice rationally, to pursue one policy rather than another, then development, it is argued, cannot truly happen.

Interestingly, in the realm of theology a distinction between a true and a false course of development was made in 1845 by John Henry Newman in his *Essay on the Development of Christian Doctrine*. What Newman called a 'false' or 'corrupt development' is what we now refer to as underdevelopment. Corrupt development was one process of development which was devoid of active belief that a principle, namely Christ's revelation of God's authority, could be developed through the variations of historical experience. Newman understood development to be the bridge between the variations of history and the principle which could be explicated by developing its identity through various historical forms of experience. Although Newman started out with positivist tests of development, to attest cases of true development, he later came to reject the basis of what he called 'liberal religion', including the 'religion' of utilitarianism which substituted knowledge and altruism for belief. Thus, in ending up with an idea of development which stood as a 'hypothesis to account for a difficulty' (the difficulty being that incomplete, and thereby uncertain, sets of empirical 'facts' could not be tested), Newman proposed that development stood as the substitute for incomplete processes of history.[6]

If Newman did much to anticipate twentieth-century critiques of utilitarianism, then his different idea of development, and the critique of utilitarianism that he inspired, may have impinged upon the positivist basis for trusteeship, but the utilitarian solution to the fundamental problem of development has not been fundamentally dislodged. Intentional development continues to be the means to fill the gap between the conditions for what makes a process of development possible and what is actually found in an immanent course of development. In filling this gap, those who consider themselves to be developed, who have the desire, knowledge and capacity for exercising choice, take it upon themselves to act on behalf of the others—those without such desires, knowledge and/or capacities.

Marx, Neo-Marxism and Intentional Development

Marx poured scorn on the various nineteenth-century attempts to resolve the logical problem of development through trusteeship. This was fundamentally because his own idea of free development, which was contained within his vision of communism for a world of possibility rather than necessity, was not simply that one fishes in the morning, reads in the afternoon and makes music in the evening. Rather, it was that if one had the desire to do any of those things, then one's capacities or capabilities would have been realized to make it possible for the desired activities to be pursued. In the historically given world of capitalism, the world from which positivists and utilitarians took their bearings, activity was and is made necessary through the remuneration of income necessary for subsistence. The possibility for choice is thus inherently limited and the conditions for exercising choice are so rigorous that they are unlikely, with few exceptions, to be met in practice. One had, of necessity, to become a fisherman, academic or musician in order to subsist rather than being able freely to carry out any, none or all of these activities.

Early writings of Marx, especially *The Holy Family* and *The German Ideology* of the late 1840s, can be read as a heartfelt attack on the ideas of trusteeship that were associated with intentional development.[7] Marx used Hegel's principle of development against the doctrines of intentional development espoused by left Young Hegelians and True Socialists. Hegel had made an important distinction between what he called 'natural development' and what he referred to as 'the principle of development'. His debt to Kant notwithstanding, Hegel made his own understanding of this distinction perfectly clear. Natural development was development according to the old classical metaphor for change through phenomenal expansion and decay, a process in which events happened, but only in so far as the same phenomena reappeared in the same form, as Hegel put it, through endless repetition and boredom. No new potential was created. All the potential of the plant, to go back to the classical metaphor, is contained within its seed, and as it expands and grows, it does not create new potential in and of itself.

Kant's distinction between what Hegel called 'relative or external, and internal purposiveness' was what became the basis of the principle of development. The principle of development was the potential of the human mind, the Idea or Spirit, to find a purpose in change and create the basis for new potential. The principle of development brought the internal purpose of determination, namely the capacity for acting upon self-knowledge, to bear upon a logic of history. Aware that Kant's internal–external distinction suffered from the problem of re-creating a duality between the internal world of the mind and the external world of the body, Hegel rested his principle upon the logic by which the active capacity for self-knowledge (which is what consciousness is all about) develops by internalizing the external world through concepts of the mind. Hegel's end of history was the state which embodied the absolute Idea in which all had consciousness of knowing the will of all others, and, as such, there was universal freedom for all to pursue their interests in life. Therefore, the end of history dissolved the distinction between external and internal purposiveness.

Whereas the Hegelian inheritance in nineteenth-century social idealism was a one-sided treatment of Hegel's principle of development, his original idea was that development was the unfolding of new potential through what he called the 'doubling' of both external existence and the concepts of self-knowing. History moved through the triad of concepts—from family to civil society, culminating in the state. Yet in rejecting the idea of progress, with its metaphor of a slow, peaceful process of growth towards human improvement, Hegel insisted that development was a struggle between the external and the potential for self-knowing. Alienation was the essence of the struggle whereby the 'old concept', such as that of family, was made abstract when history moved from family to the 'new' concept of civil society. Thus the individual, in coming to be being-in-itself in civil society, posited the concept of family and all that is entailed by trust, custom and belief as the content of external reality. Consciousness is developed as the external limits of the old concept are discovered when the final concept, that of the state, arrives through the struggle of inner determination of self-knowing.[8]

Marx's idea of true development took Hegel back to his original reworking of Kant and placed the social organization of capitalism within the ambit of the relative, or external, of history and the proletariat of labour within the inner determination of development. However, more than a century later, when Marx himself was used as a source of inspiration for underdevelopment and dependency theory, a different gloss was put on the fundamental distinction between the internal and external of development.

It was Gunder Frank, probably the most renowned twentieth-century underdevelopment theorist, who brought the internal–external of development to the idea of the difference between the source of true and false development. In general, underdevelopment theory saw the situation in England, for example, as true capitalist development. Producers were separated from the means of production in land and other assets, and then reabsorbed within a capitalist production process at far higher average levels of labour productivity. False or 'corrupt development', called under-development, happened simultaneously with development in time though in a different place. Producers were separated from their means of production here as well but they were not reintegrated into industrial production other than through the will, or, to use Hegel's inner determination, an already existing capitalism. Places where the old is destroyed but not recreated in the image of the active principle of development, and allusions to the chronic condition (mass poverty and unemployment) of what are disarticulated by the false capitalist development, mirror the images of Newman's corrupt development. They are deemed to be peripheral to the external condition for true development and thus underdevelopment.

The capitalism of the centre, viewed by underdevelopment theorists as external to the internal basis of the potential for development in the periphery, develops through an active belief in capital accumulation. But 'capitalists' who control (or are alleged to control) trade and production within Latin America, for example, are deemed to be devoid of both belief in, and the capacities for, accumulation which has been throttled by the external condition of development. Any attempt at intentional development only reproduces the original condition for the chronic course of capitalist development—the development of underdevelopment. Thus the only basis for true development in Latin America requires a revolutionary break with the chronic course of capitalist development through the social organization of the economy upon the internal basis of the mass will of Latin America itself.

In reply to his early critics, including Giovanni Arrighi and Ernesto Laclau, Frank quoted from, and implied that he adopted the views of, Mao Zedong on the question of the internal and external of development. In doing so, he unwittingly opened an old can of worms. Mao had dealt with the internal–external of development during the course of a 1937 speech, which was published as the essay, 'On Contradiction'. In conjunction with other directives to the Chinese Communist Party (CCP), the argument ran as follows: the external condition of development was the mass of given things, in being relatively scattered through an external world of discrete, real matter. Internal development was the basis of change in so far as the active determination of the mind could create the potential for unifying the scatter of matter into a coherent whole.

Since Mao presupposed that the 'mind' was embodied in the CCP, and that development consisted of a procedure of practical knowledge whereby the external condition of matter was to be apprehended and changed through practice, the result of the procedure was to create the basis of policy. Development was intended to be the bridge between the mass of material body and the 'mind' of the party in order to develop a coherent policy for a programme of action.

It might seem that Mao was correct in claiming that he was faithful to the Hegelian principle of development within a Marxist tradition. However, Mao had moved far from Hegel's principle and into a neo-Kantian tradition of idealism. Mao not only resurrected the dualism between mind and body, inherent within Western philosophy, but he also inverted the relation between mind and body as it had come to be understood by Marx via Hegel. In 1937 the external of development was Japanese imperialism in China, namely that which had no basis for the necessary self-movement of Chinese historical change. Later, things in the external world of matter became ideas of the 'masses' within China. Scattered ideas of the masses, as if of the mass of the body, were to be apprehended by the party, whose mind had the singular capacity for inner determination. Discrete, incoherent ideas of peasants and workers were to be unified within the body of the CCP. As such, the party, in determining a coherent programme for action, would act for the mass. Mao's doctrine of development was built upon a variant of the nineteenth-century idea of social trusteeship.[9]

Marx was particularly scathing about the kind of doctrine that Mao came to represent because of the same way in which the Young Hegelians and True Socialists of the 1840s had used the internal–external of development to resurrect and then invert the dualism between body and mind. In the case of the Young Hegelians, Marx's accusation was that Hegel's principle had been subverted in that the mass was embodied in the mass of manual working people, who literally became 'the mass', while 'mind' was inserted into the person of intellect who was equipped with the capacity of self-knowing to direct the mass. Furthermore, self-knowing was reduced to the mere process of expansion and that which was indicative of natural development, while the mass, the antithesis of Spirit, was deemed to be spiritless, indolent, complacent and devoid of any active reflexive knowledge. Though he did not use the word 'trusteeship', Marx's invective was directed against the handful of intellectuals who took it upon themselves to assume the basis of trusteeship, the mantle of active Spirit which acted in the name of self-determination for the mass.

True Socialists, Marx pointed out, saw the distinction between mind and body as that which corresponded to an inherent difference between the subjectivity of the person and the objective force of society. Society became the external condition of development for the individual person, who was supposed to find inner determination through the duty and obligation which were given him or her by society. Marx had found it logically absurd that True Socialists should assert the development of personal individualities while demanding of 'society' a 'transformation' that was deemed necessary as part of this Saint-Simonian-inspired and constructive critique of the 'free competition' which inhered in the capitalist development of society.

While Marx was engaged in his critique of socialist trusteeship, he tore apart another version of trusteeship, also of Saint-Simonian inspiration, but moving along a different trajectory. Friedrich List's doctrine of the national economy was damned by Marx precisely because it was a version of bourgeois trusteeship. List, as much as Newman, anticipated twentieth-century underdevelopment theory—albeit in a different manner. Ostensibly List had offered a programme of late-industrialization for countries threatened by the earlier industrial development in Britain. The nation, for List, was both the categorical entity which stood between the individual and the universal world, and the site in which the productive force of individuals was associated. In contradistinction to Smith (whom List held responsible for the cosmopolitical 'science' of economics which justified British industrial supremacy), List maintained that it was within the nation that the social division of labour made manufacturing industry the basis for the development of productive force. Loss of productive force, through the threat of emigration due to industrial competition from capital in Britain, was what List feared for Germany and what gave the impetus to his programme of state-protected industrialization.

Given that an agrarian site of production had no potential for associated productive force other than in association with manufacturing industry, List referred to a nation that exchanged agricultural exports for manufactured imports as akin to a one-armed individual who was subject to the caprice of a 'foreign head'. Only in Britain were the arms of the existing productive force reconciled with its head. With the significant exception of the 'torrid zone' of tropical countries which perforce had to remain raw-material producers, all other nations, List argued, had to reconcile head and hand by means of an industrial policy.[10]

List's doctrine of intentional development was, for Marx, nothing other than a case of special pleading by a bourgeoisie which sought state protection against competition. It was no intellectual accident, Marx commented, that List had attempted to validate Smith's concept of value for exchange within the nation but had jettisoned labour value for exchange between nations. True socialism was to socialist trusteeship what List's system of national economy was to bourgeois trusteeship. List hoped for a German bourgeoisie which would act as trustees for the people of a nation while directing the labour of productive force within its enterprises in the nation. Since List had shifted the image of the mind–body metaphor to national terrain, it was not surprising that Marx should have objected so strongly to the same philosophical idiom that he had found in the theoretical underpinnings of socialist trusteeship. If Marx used Hegel's principle against the Hegelian proponents of social idealism, he also used it against Hegel himself. Marx had earlier noticed the fundamental contradiction between Hegel's triadic order of concepts of logic and in history. The state, as the concept of logic, developed after civil society but it was clear from a reading of Hegel that the state had to be a historical condition for the existence of civil society and had, thereby, to precede it in the order of history. What Hegel had done, therefore, was to imbue the state with such objective power that, instead of serving as the concrete source of universal freedom for all, he had posited it as the source of negation of the reason for true individual subjectivity. The alienated concept of family had come to serve as the reason why there should be an active source of positive obligation, of positive service, towards the state. As such, Hegel's system had culminated in the very alienation that the process of development was meant to end in history, and the very idea of progress was impeded or arrested by the logic of development.

By the time he arrived at *Capital*, Marx had realized where the source of Hegel's alienation was to be found. Having earlier imbued the Young Hegelian and True Socialist 'mass' with the life and restless struggle of active work and made it the internal of development, Marx later made inner determination reside in the body of labour-power. However, Marx was no crude materialist and it was not simply that the products of active work were alienated to the body of money-capital which assumed command of the production process. Marx made his famous Hegelian inversion by depositing the 'Spirit' in the abstract commodity of money but denuding it of the principle of development. In so far as mind dominated matter, it was the transformation of money into capital which established the capitalist production process, but in commanding the 'mind' of labour-power, Hegel's principle of development had been inverted.

Capital was of natural development, developing according to the metaphor of repetitive change but devoid of intent. Capitalist development, claimed Marx, developed naturally since its only purpose was the expansion of value through profit; and any intent of development, to change the purpose of work according to the principle of development, was negated by the production process of capitalism. As if of nature, capital determines the work of the body of labour-power where inner determination to develop resides. Productive force developed through capitalism, but the potential of productive force to allow the free play of physical and mental powers in work was subsumed by what had alienated the internal of development to the abstract mind of exchange-value.

G. A. Cohen, who has done much to unpack Marx's principle of development through his analysis of productive force, has also criticized

Marx for not making an adequate distinction between free and full development.[11] Cohen suggests that Marx's vision of free development (which for Cohen implies that everyone is free to develop activity in any direction) is both tantamount to licence and a human impossibility. Full development, on the contrary, is consistent with human possibility in that the fullness of development envisages that anyone is able to develop in any direction but according to the capacity of that person. Development, therefore, must be contained by external form, the boundary of matter which establishes the limits of human capacity and individual capacities.

By postulating an overriding external of development which subsumes the social existence of matter, in social or economic form, Cohen, and the school of analytical Marxism with which he has been associated, appears as the twentieth-century version of true socialism. After all, it is social or economic form which makes capacities scarce in relation to the development of productive force which is achieved through the development of capitalism. However much scarcity may be absolutely diminished in general, scarcity of human capacity is relatively increased by what makes the development of productive force possible under capitalism. Thus, in his critique of Cohen, Shamsavari is able to show that in abstaining from Hegel's procedure of doubling in favour of the analytic method, Cohen loses the realization that the external and internal of development become part of each other. In early capitalism, Shamsavari suggests, productive force appears as the external condition of development; in later capitalism, productive force becomes interior to development. Underdevelopment, by this reasoning, is the condition under which the external existence of productive force has not been socially assimilated into the interior basis of development.[12]

Marx had brought Hegel's 'doubling' to bear upon the genesis of capitalist development, and it is the doubling of the concept which enables us to see the significance of the official schemes of state development practice. As Marx put it, the negation of landed property, in the early course of capitalist development, was both the positive condition for wage labour (by separating labour-power from its own means of production) and the negative condition for maintaining the relative surplus population, which was surplus to wage labour employed in the capitalist production process. To dissolve private landed property, which was a limitation upon the valorization of production according to the profit-making criterion, and take it under state ownership was entirely consistent with the development of capitalism.[13] Landed property could now be used as a condition to establish peasant and/or artisan-based schemes of production, thereby absorbing the relative surplus population and making 'the unemployed' responsible for reproducing their own means of subsistence.

The rapid industrialization in East Asia, together with de-industrialization resulting in mass unemployment elsewhere over the past two decades or more, may be part of the immanent process of development. However, there has been no social intention to make the expansion in East Asia cohere with destruction in Europe and America. If we go back to the Saint-Simonians, Comte and their successors, we see that the trusteeship of intentional development was founded on the search for just such a means of equilibrating creation and destruction within a single supervised process of development.

In this regard, Joseph Schumpeter's idea of creative destruction is important. This idea, which he owed to Marx and which was embodied in arguably the first self-conscious text on economic development written by Schumpeter in 1912, attempted to explain the process of capitalist development in which older industries died at the same time as new industries emerged. Usually, when Schumpeter is summoned up, his name is immediately associated with that of the entrepreneur. The entrepreneur, we are told, is the hero of development who makes things happen. In fact, for Schumpeter, it was the banker, and not the entrepreneur, who was the heroic figure of development. Schumpeter called the banker the ephor or supervisor of development, who supervised the process of development by advancing finance to new enterprises at the same time that credit to old firms was cancelled with the intent to liquidate them. Schumpeter's theory of economic development rested upon the idea of the banker as a trustee who bridged the economic system and social order of capitalism. While he started out to analyse capitalism as an immanent process of development, and continued to refuse any positive means to resolve the social problem of unemployment, Schumpeter ended up by bringing back intentional development through the back door of trusteeship.[14]

Proponents of land reform—in Europe during the nineteenth century and elsewhere, especially Africa, during the twentieth century—have sought to find the means which enables the official problem of poverty to be resolved by the constructive purpose of development through the kind of schemes which Marx had in mind when he referred to what the negation of private property might mean. We can also take 'doubling' further. Small-scale household production is seen as the 'old' labour process, which is historically subsumed through the development of capitalism. When small-scale production, whether as peasant or artisan enterprises, reappears as part of the intent to develop, then it the old concept of production which is being re-created as the palliative for the destructive propensities of the new. The unemployed, of the relative surplus population, are to be absorbed in development schemes when the 'misguided' and 'socially disintegrating' economy cannot find the means of accumulation to engage all who are potentially available for wage work.

To go back to the start, we should be aware of the significance of a political programme that appeals for the state to go back to the high road of development. In contemporary North America, as in Europe, development schemes of relatively large-scale manufacturing industry are proposed as the means by which the problem of mass unemployment and urban poverty might be resolved. The late-twentieth-century programme is no different in essence from what was proposed in Europe for small-scale household production during the nineteenth century. Such development schemes are neither of full nor of free development. They stem from the intent to develop on the basis of social trusteeship. Marx damned social trusteeship in the 1840s; there is no reason to go back to it at the end of the twentieth century, 150 years later.

10. *Planning and Markets*[1]

Sami Daniel

In this chapter I re-examine the view that planning and markets are alternatives, one suited for a socialist society and the other exclusive to capitalism. This view has often been put forward in conjunction with the argument that capitalist firms are not only increasing in size and relying on more centralization and planning at the expense of markets, but that in doing so they also facilitate the transition to a new economy, which can be likened to one big factory.

I start by looking at the relationships between firms, planning and markets. I then revisit an old debate on planning and markets which involved Ludwig von Mises, Oskar Lange and Friedrich Hayek (among others).[2] This is followed by a review of three important developments in the capitalist system: intensifying competition, changing organizational structures, and the use of non-market mechanisms for coordinating inter-firm activities and relations. I conclude by suggesting a framework that gives a less ambitious scope but a more flexible role for planning, one that builds on markets and recognizes their limitations.

The Firm and Planning

Planning is the direction of productive resources and the coordination of economic activity. Because it involves direction and conscious coordination, it is often regarded as an alternative to the impersonal and unconscious coordination of resources and activities provided by markets. Sometimes this coordination is denied in the phrase 'anarchy of markets'. The concept of the firm plays an important role in this debate because firms are institutions that plan and manage, coordinate and direct economic resources, in a production–distribution process,[3] a process aimed ultimately at the consumer.

The conscious coordination which takes place within firms is seen by many Marxists and most economists as an alternative. Indeed, the Nobel Prize laureate Ronald Coase saw the firm as arising because of the cost of conducting transactions in the market: the transactions cost associated with finding relevant input prices, and negotiating and enforcing a large number of separate short-term contracts. In the firm there is an absence of market signals. Instead there is conscious coordination.[4]

While the firm directs, and direction involves planning, we should be careful not to equate the firm with planning. Not only does planning extend beyond firms' boundaries and involve coordination between firms, but planning by an individual firm may include activities which are not directed and controlled within the confines of the organization.

There are different kinds of planning. The type that has been attacked most severely is directive planning, with administrative allocation of inputs, the kind of planning that can be called Soviet-type directive planning when applied to a whole economy. The debate examined here, however, is about another type of planning, that envisaged by Lange and other socialist economists: a market model with prices. Managers of enterprises responded to these prices, but the prices were set by a Central Planning Board. Planning was concerned with major investment decisions of structural importance within an economic system with markets in consumer goods.

I shall consider two aspects of the market–plan debate: informational requirements of planning and the consequences of combining political power and economic management. Can we eliminate market relations without creating in the process an enormous, economically inefficient, powerful and dangerous bureaucratic hierarchy? The apparent theoretical justification of central planning in the market–plan debate largely bypassed the major critique of planning by von Mises and Hayek. But as Hayek pointed out, the issues raised by the information requirements of this type of investment planning are similar to those involved in a command economy: the solutions to the information requirements problem were seen to involve both of them swimming or sinking together.[5]

The Economy as a Firm

Marx had little to say about problems of 'production for need' under socialism, and what he did say was fairly orthodox in its approach:

> After the abolition of capitalism . . . under socially organized production, value determination remains dominant in the sense that the regulation of labour time and the distribution of social labour between different sectors of production, and the accountancy that encompasses all this, become more important than ever.[6]

But this is not to say that Marx and Engels gave no indications of the shape of the future socialist economy. Unfortunately, these indications were misleading because they gave the impression that socialist 'evaluation' could be based on the labour theory of value. Where they were explicit, they were very naive and utopian.[7] Marx distinguished between division of labour in the firm and economy-wide division of labour: commodity exchange was absent in the first and present in the other and mediated the division of labour. Indeed, the division of labour within the workshop is an 'entirely specific creation of the capitalist mode of production'.[8] The analogy between the conscious coordination required in firms and in an economy without prices is correct in one respect: resources need to be managed and directed. But it is wrong to see the whole economy under socialism, as Engels and Lenin did, as 'one big factory' in which planning as it exists in a factory replaces the law of value and market anarchy.

The polarity between the 'anarchy of markets' and organized and planned production was later mistakenly translated into a view that the diminution of the role of markets in a capitalist economy (because of the growth of large firms) is a sign of the growth of socialist tendencies. But even in a regime of 'monopoly capital' no firm can produce everything. A centralized command economy organized like the old Ford company will not work because Ford produced only motor vehicles rather than the immense range of commodities of a modern economy, and it did so by purchasing many of its inputs from the 'sea of markets' in existence.

There are real limits to the central control that can be exercised in the process of expansion of individual firms. Companies that have diversified have found a need to decentralize decisions and adopt some form of divisionalized structure. Solutions to problems of coordination as firms diversify and expand do have relevance to those of a planned economy: they stress the importance of decentralization. But economy-wide coordination raises much broader issues and begs the question of the role of prices and markets in this context.

Firm, Plan and Market

Is planning the same thing as control or coordination within a firm? Marx was reluctant to give details of a socialist society, but nonetheless gave some indications of the kind of economy that might emerge. It is clear that it was not only Lenin but Marx himself who thought that socialism and the market were incompatible.

To claim, as Coase does, that the distinguishing mark of the firm is the suppression of the price mechanism means that firms can take the place of markets. This presupposes that markets can exist in the absence of firms. But:

> this is impossible because the non-existence of firms implies no production, which in turn implies that markets have no function, i.e. they will not exist. In short, Coase's analysis is based on an inconsistency because of the view that firms and markets are alternative methods of coordinating production.[9]

The view that firms and markets are alternatives arises because Coase defines the firm as a multi-person organization, thus ruling out one-person firms.[10] It is interesting to contrast Coase and Marx here. In my view, Marx would probably have said, 'yes, a market can exist without firms': this is the case with pure commodity exchange. We can have pre-capitalist production and markets, with one-person firms. The critical distinction concerns the *type* of production: pre-capitalist or capitalist. This is a discussion about the labour process (what orthodox economists call the employment relation). What distinguishes Coase from Marx is the fact that Coase's firm/market contrast is between the firm as a system of organizing multi-person production, with a market coordinating self-employed producers.[11]

We could also talk about the type of firm: capitalist or non-capitalist; or a firm in a capitalist society and a firm in a socialist society. The relevance of all this to the debate about planning is that production would normally take place in advance of knowledge of consumer needs and wants.

It remains true, however that 'firm' and 'market' cannot meaningfully exist without each other. They are necessary for each other. They exist in a symbiotic relation, heavily dependent on each other.[12] Indeed, as Auerbach, Desai and Shamsavari argue:

> the richness and extension of markets are contingent on the kinds of planning decisions that are made by central administrative agencies and by individual firms. It is also true, however, that successful planning by

> the capitalist firm has taken place in the context of market alternatives, and with an awareness of their existence.[13]

The Planning Debate

Marx's main concern was the analysis of capitalist relations. As Nove puts it, 'he was not concerned with calculation, evaluation, criteria, choice, rational decision-making or its organization, under socialism'.[14] Given that economic calculation, opportunity cost (what we give up in order to have more of a particular good) and choice between alternatives clearly have to exist under socialism, Marxian value theory has little to tell us about them. There was no Marxist political economy of socialism.

Von Mises had issued a challenge to socialist economists. The question he raised in 1920 and that led to the famous planning debate in the 1930s was: how can a society produce the products that people need without prices and markets? Von Mises' challenge was: how can you obtain the information needed to plan without the competition that is provided by markets? And how can you use this information to make rational calculations? This challenge was so powerful and generated so many ideas that it led Lange to propose that a statue be erected in honour of von Mises in the great hall of the Ministry of Socialization or the Central Planning Board of the socialist state. What followed says something very interesting about the development of Marxist and socialist economics in the West.[15]

Lange's response to this particular challenge was couched in a 'neoclassical' general equilibrium setting. This offered an elegant theoretical solution which assumed that all the relevant information was available. It becomes possible to arrive at an equilibrium where all demands by individuals and firms are satisfied and all supplies are purchased. From a resource allocation point of view, it was shown that it is possible to work out 'equilibrium prices'. The response therefore adopted a static equilibrium framework instead of a disequilibrium framework. This may have been the price paid for the rejection of the subjectivism of the Austrian School (which required private ownership) in favour of a less individualistic approach. The debate resulted in some odd alliances: Marxist economists adopted a static neoclassical stance against the non-neoclassical Austrian critics of planning.[16]

Hayek's main criticism was that the board would never be able to give good instructions to managers because it could not possibly know everything that was relevant (it lacked 'particular knowledge of time and place', the detailed information possessed by the 'man on the spot'). Hayek later put the point much more clearly, arguing that the signals are the *changes* in prices.[17] Price changes are signals that something has happened, that things have changed. This function, of processing information and signalling change, is an important function of markets and is a fast, cheap and efficient way of communicating information about changes in the economy. This point about the informational content of price changes was missed in Lange's suggestion that a planner can arrive at prices that reflect consumer evaluation through 'trial and error'. The most interesting feature of the debate was 'where do we get the necessary information from'? The answer, based on a very elegant theory, appeared to be that we assume that information is there in the first place. What has been lost is the disequilibrium approach. But more significantly, the problem of information and coordination is virtually avoided in Lange's 'trial and error prices'.

The odd thing about the socialist response was its un-Marxist, static character. The interesting feature of the Austrian School, characteristically reflected in the challenge, is its concern with a dynamic process, a process of economic change, closely related to the Marxian tradition. It is not concerned with a world of equilibrium, but deals with a world which is constantly changing. The neoclassical nature of the socialist response ensured its acceptability to economic orthodoxy, which conceded that planning was theoretically possible, though very difficult in practice. Most accounts of the debate consider the theoretical battle to have been won by advocates of planning. But the planning model ignored dynamics and avoided the crucial issue of information.[18]

Even though Lange was dealing with a market socialist system with central planning of investment, the impression was given that the theoretical possibility of any kind of central planning had been established. I therefore agree with the late Alec Nove:

> marketless socialism can only mean *centralized* planning, in which large and necessarily hierarchical and bureaucratic organization issues instructions, allocates and coordinates. Such a form of organizing production can only have as its counterpart the hierarchical and bureaucratic organization of politics.[19]

The next step is not to produce what is needed, but what the planner thinks the consumer will or should have.

Markets, Prices and Information

The debate would appear to be at a dead end. There remain nagging worries that too much may be expected of markets in terms of information transmission. The problem with the Lange solution was not only that it did not deal adequately with the problem of information, but that it had too much faith in prices and markets, and particularly in the way that managers of enterprises would respond to the prices set by the Central Board. In a different way, the Austrian treatment also places great faith in price information (though recognizing that there are limits to what prices, as a concentrated form of information, can do). The recently developed perspective of the economics of information suggests, however, that price information is not sufficient to bring about a desirable allocation of resources. Roemer, who is greatly impressed by the relevance of the arguments about imperfect information and incomplete contracts developed by Stiglitz (a key figure in this field) in the debate about socialism, neatly sums up Stiglitz's position thus: 'real market economies are characterized by an incomplete set of markets, asymmetric information, and incomplete contracts, only enforceable at considerable cost'.[20]

While placing great emphasis on competition and decentralization, the economics of information perspective also analyses the methods and institutions used under capitalism to carry out economic activity when prices are not sufficient. The role of institutions is, of course, also a feature of the Austrian School, which has emphasized an evolutionary argument for markets and institutions: evolutionary forces work not only to select firms but also to select institutions. Unlike the Austrians, the perspective of the economics of information does not presume that institutions will emerge (through a process of selective adaptation) that will lead to the desirable allocation. As Stiglitz has suggested, 'there is no reason to believe that evolutionary processes have any optimality properties. Indeed there are strong arguments suggesting that evolutionary processes are far from optimal.'[21] Instead, the analysis suggests that there is still a case for substantial intervention in the economy. 'While government ownership is clearly no panacea, there remains scope for further experimentation.'[22]

Industrial Diversity

What are the new features that characterize capitalist society today? My proposition is that competition continues to provide capitalism with its dynamic force. And there is no sign yet of an impending general crisis.

Capitalist economies are now more competitive than ever, with flexible organizational and production structures, and an array of external architectures (relationships with other firms and customers). Some of these features may well be short-lived. Some of them will develop and continue. Some of them contain tensions.

Some of these features have implications for the types of planning that may be used. Can we talk of a developing new regime? Can it be characterized as post-Fordism, 'Toyotism' or 'Sonyism'? One view, provided by the French Regulation School, sees Fordist regulation as counterproductive, particularly in terms of the disadvantages of rigid hierarchies. Three challenges, recognized by Coriat and Petit,[23] are: the potential of information technologies; the major role of flexible high-volume production;[24] and the internationalization of markets.

Boyer refers to the change from Fordism to 'Sonyism' and suggests a number of features that characterize this change.[25] First, there is permanent product and process innovation. Second, there is now a highly skilled and committed workforce with long-run employment. Third, an implicit compromise exists over the sharing of the surplus. Implicit or informal planning within and outside the firm is a fourth feature. Fifth, there is multiple tier contracting with networking but also with competition between subcontractors. Finally, there are long-term strategies which are shared by manufacturers, bankers and civil servants.

It is likely, however, that there will be industrial diversity based on the coexistence of different forms. Some arrangements can be both transitional (for some types of firms) and more lasting (for others). Similarly, there are varieties of capitalism that are likely to coexist.

Varieties of Organizational Forms

The changes noted above are not confined to production and exchange. The internal organization of firms has also been undergoing dramatic change. One explanation is to argue that firms have been trying to reduce management costs. One way of reducing these costs is through successive attempts at decentralization and delayering, with a reduction in middle management. But firms can also invest in what may be termed organization costs: costs incurred in order to encourage trust and cooperation within the firm (and which reduce production costs). All of these are examples of 'internal architecture'. But there has also been an emphasis on 'external architecture', which includes planning outside the firm and may also involve organization costs of 'networking'. We can then have an array of arrangements involving trust costs within firms, trust costs in networks, and so on.

In the theory of the growth of the firm advanced by Penrose, a firm develops a distinctive capability in one or more activities.[26] Richardson distinguishes between similar activities that utilize the same capability and complementary activities that utilize unrelated capabilities—thus extending Penrose's theory to inter-firm activities as an alternative to market or hierarchical coordination.[27] The firm will internalize similar activities and externalize complementary activities. To benefit from their specialization in complementary activities, firms must develop collaborative relationships with producers of different components. 'The choice for a firm is not simply to make or buy, but whether to make, buy or collaborate.'[28]

There is a range of non-market arrangements which foster cooperation between firms. There is nothing new about inter-firm arrangements: price agreements and output-restricting cartels, though unstable, have a long history. The increasing number and range of these arrangements, however, have been important features of the business scene over the last twenty years. These arrangements take a variety of forms: franchises (which tend to apply to small businesses, particularly services: Body Shop, McDonald's); single sourcing (using one supplier as part of an implicit long-term contract); technology-sharing cartels, networks, and so on. These arrangements have led a number of people to talk about another type on the continuum between market and hierarchy: hybrids (or networks) existing in a market environment but involving non-market relations designed to secure cooperation between firms. Some refer to three ideal types: market, hierarchy and hybrids (or networks). Opinion is divided about the nature of these arrangements. Some see them as an extension of control by large firms: an attempt at domination through dependency. Others regard them as providing a model of dynamic capitalism, which may even have portents for a future socialist form of enterprise relationship and planning along the 'industrial district' model.

A case in point is strategic alliances: companies that wish to expand their geographic, customer or product reach adopt a strategy of forming alliances with other firms. According to Bleeke and Ernst, the number of such alliances (domestic and cross-border) has grown by more than 25% per annum over the last five years.[29] They find the term 'alliance' a misleading description of the arrangements: the median life span is seven years, and most of them end in a sale by one of the partners. Their analysis of the nature of these alliances explains the findings. Some are alliances that involve the core business of two strong companies that are direct competitors (ending in dissolution, acquisition or merger). Others are alliances of the weak (a failure as firms usually grow weaker); disguised sales (weak partner taken over by stronger one); or evolutions to a sale (strong partners who become competitive, with tensions developing). The alliances that tend to last longest are the alliances of complementary equals who remain strong during the course of the alliance.

Varieties of Capitalism

It is now widely recognized that there is more than one form of capitalism. The role, conduct and scope of the private sector are not the same in all capitalist economies. These economies also adopt differing relationships between government and the private sector. Sjostrand considers that it is plausible and fruitful to talk of the 'many faces of capitalism'.[30] Economists have contrasted capitalistic market economies with other kinds of economies but have not laid much emphasis on the internal diversity of these capitalist economies—even though this diversity is dealt with in comparative analyses of economic systems.

Albert compares two models of capitalism: the 'neo-American' and the 'Rhein' models.[31] The latter has a different view of the role of the state and accommodates different roles for the social security system (in Germany and France it is guaranteed by a compulsory assurance system, in Japan it is provided by the large companies, and in the Nordic countries it is provided through the public sector).

Chandler discusses the corporate and institutional differences in three countries (the US, Britain and Germany).[32] He argues that there are many important differences in the organization of markets and of market-based relations among different societies, i.e. there are differences in the institutional structures of these economies. He identifies different capitalist features in each of them: competitive capitalism (US), private capitalism (Britain) and cooperative capitalism (Germany).

For Best, the 'new competition' (based on features of firms in Germany, Sweden, the 'third' Italy, Singapore, South Korea, Taiwan and Hong Kong—as well as Japan) is manifest in a variety of inter-firm complexes which range from groups of small Italian firms, linked by cooperative associations for joint marketing, technological advance and financial underwriting, to giant organizational structures (the Japanese 'Shiatsu' or group) that coordinate trading companies, banks and manufacturing enterprises.[33] Best sees the new competition as based on the 'entrepreneurial firm',[34] the firm as a collective entrepreneur, and builds on the idea of Schumpeterian competition.

Conventional economic theory uses the market–plan dichotomy: consecutive production phases coordinated either through the market or through hierarchy. But we can have consultative supplier relationships. This does not mean the end of price competition: the struggle over prices may take place within a long-term relationship based on established norms of mutual responsibility (i.e. shared network norms). Norms can of course be eroded unless violators can be successfully punished, but a variety of special arrangements are possible.

Sector institutions or 'extra-firm infrastructure' (as Piore and Sabel call them) facilitate inter-firm cooperation. Firms not only compete: they can also cooperate to provide common services such as trade associations, apprenticeship programmes, employee education facilities, joint marketing arrangements and technology cartels. Best argues that a healthy industrial sector depends on combining competition with cooperation. Cooperation ensures that commitments are made to the long-term infrastructural development of a sector, while competition keeps firms innovative and responsive.

Portents for Planning

I have tried to present a view of capitalism which is undergoing a great deal of institutional change. Much of the organizational change can be attributed to 'transaction cost economizing within an evolutionary dynamic'.[35] There are clearly tensions and contradictions: 'ownership' of initiatives for change, employee involvement, empowerment, teamwork and cooperation may all lead to a loss of management control which (top) management may try to reassert. Similarly, inter-firm cooperation may either be a lasting feature of relationships or be short-lived and affected by cyclical fluctuations.

But these non-market arrangements, which involve networking and in many cases cooperation on the industrial district model, increase the range of arrangements that may be used within a planning framework. Rosenberg stresses the strategic role played by the freedom to experiment in the process of economic growth and industrialization.[36] We can see this variety of organizational and institutional arrangements as the result of 'economic experiments'. Rosenberg's focus is upon:

> the freedom to perform economic experiments, understanding the expression in the broadest sense to include experimentation with new forms of economic organization as well as the better-known historical experiments that have been responsible for new products and new manufacturing technologies.[37]

Rosenberg's notion of economic experiments may be extended to the planning debate. Such an extension suggests that a planning framework which builds on the existence of a variety of non-market arrangements must ensure that there is wide scope for the freedom of action available to consumers and individual firms. Such freedom is essential for the operation of markets. It is also required to enable experimentation with, and development of, non-market arrangements to cope with the limitations of markets discussed in this chapter.

Part III

The West Versus the Other

11. Marxism and Deconstruction: The West Versus the Other

Some Thoughts on Jacques Derrida's Specters of Marx

Kate Soper

As my title suggests, the present chapter offers some thoughts on the encounter between Marxism and deconstruction as this is instantiated in Jacques Derrida's book, *Specters of Marx.*[1] By way of providing some contextual background to the discussion, I shall begin with some more general remarks about the situation of Marxism today, and the impact upon this of the theory and politics of what may be broadly termed postmodernism.

Few people would dispute the fact that the combined intellectual and political convulsion of recent years—notably the ascendancy in the West of postmodernist modes of thinking together with the collapse of 'actual existing socialism' in Central and Eastern Europe and the consequent demise of the Cold War power structures—have dramatically altered the context addressed by any form of socialist argument. Indeed, some on the left have even argued that we should no longer attempt to salvage a philosophy that has been doubly discredited. In the light of events in Eastern Europe, such people argue, we should accept the truth of the postmodernist analysis of Marxism as a 'grand narrative' credo which was bound to issue in totalitarian practice, and henceforth forswear such grandiose schemes of social amelioration. Others have adopted an antithetical line of response, arguing that there is nothing about this altered context which should be allowed to disturb the equanimity of Marxist thinking. They have suggested that the essential arguments and agendas of socialism have in no sense been threatened by the collapse of a regime that is so far removed from an 'authentic socialism' or by postmodernist theoretical modes which are simply the reflection of the commodifying logic of capitalism and the most recent form of expression of bourgeois liberalism. There is nothing here, according to this view of recent events, which calls for any kind of reconstruction of socialist or Marxist thinking. On the contrary, the duty is to reaffirm its essential credos all the more loudly as a counterweight to the creeping liberalism of the left.

Both these reactions, I would argue, must be rejected. Both mistake the complexities of the situation in which we now find ourselves, and both—though drawing quite different conclusions from it—rely on too simple an opposition between 'socialist' and 'postmodernist' perspectives. The first type of reaction ignores the directly regressive quality of much that has ensued since the heady days of revolution in 1989. Actual existing socialism may have been seen off, but the space it vacated has scarcely been flooded by that pluralist utopia of proliferating difference to which the postmodernists have beckoned us in their assaults upon Marxism and its 'totalizing' logic. On the contrary, it can be argued that what has been squeezed out and denied any serious political representation in Central and Eastern Europe are all those counter-cultural forms of dissent (feminist, ecological, anti-militarist, democratic-socialist) which aspired to the establishment of some 'third-way' transcendence of the Cold War binary opposition. In this sense, we have been witness not to the inauguration of an alternative logic to the capitalism-versus-communism antithesis, but to a developing economic and political momentum which threatens to absorb all oppositional 'difference' within the 'identity' of the Western-style market society.

But to put the objection to the first response in these terms is to draw attention to what the second, orthodox Marxist, type of response is guilty of overlooking: namely, the importance and constructive character of those forms of 'difference' politics which challenged the way in which Marxist orthodoxy had ignored the issues of peace and ecology, of gender, racial and sexual oppression—or sought to subsume them within the politics of class. Insofar as the new social movements which emerged out of this challenge may be described as 'postmodernist' in their assertion of new 'identities' and political agents, and in their questioning of certain forms of Enlightenment humanism and scientism, I would argue that the impact of postmodernist thinking on orthodox socialism has by no means been wholly negative. It was indeed important to question the Enlightenment rationality, the faith in science and technology and the conceptions of the 'good life' which it has inspired, not least because it has encouraged a paternalist and technical-fix approach to human welfare and stimulated patterns of growth and consumption which are fast becoming ecologically unsustainable and generating ever more explosive global divisions of wealth.

Equally we needed (and still need) to challenge the humanistic idea in the sense that we need to be aware of the groups and communities which are excluded or marginalized by its universalist—and at times decidedly imperialistic—pretensions. The impulse to assert difference over identity, to expose the colonizing tendencies of humanist discourse, and to raise the problem of the 'totalitarianism' inherent in totalizing theory, has, in these respects, been important for the left; and the shifts in the approach to science, power, subjectivity and language which it has influenced can be dismissed as so many forms of 'bourgeois revisionism' only at the cost of closing off Marxist thinking from an engagement with those issues and constituencies from which it may renew its strength.

We must recognize nevertheless that the postmodernist impulse has a dynamic which has propelled it into theoretical positions which now place its argument at loggerheads with many of the cultural developments it first helped to promote. The logic which challenged certain kinds of 'identity thinking' and deconstructed specific notions of truth, progress, humanism, and so on, has pushed on to question the very possibility of objectivity or making reference in language to what is not the effect of discourse. This is a logic which asks us not only to renounce glib assumptions of solidarity and common interests, but to view any ascription of solidarity as suspect. To attempt to offer any general political diagnosis or remedy is supposedly to be caught up in 'totalizing' theory and hence to lend itself to totalitarian practice. In other words, we have a 'theoretical' dynamic which pulls the political rug from under the original insistence embodied in the new social movements that we think in terms of new 'identities'. Pushed to its uttermost, the logic of differences rules out any holistic and objective analysis of a kind which allows us to define them as 'capitalist', 'patriarchal' or indeed 'totalitarian', together with the transformative projects such analyses advocate.

The philosophical correlate of this is a total relativism, which invites us to disown the very aspiration to truth as something unattainable in principle, not even a regulative idea. Theories are, after all, only narratives and between narratives we choose subjectively what seems most useful or gives us most comfort. From this perspective, moral judgements become matters of personal preference, and we are denied any objective grounds for either endorsing or denouncing any particular cultural practice. The result, critics have argued, is that postmodernist theory removes the possibility of remaining in any kind of critical engagement with our times; and that in refusing any grounding for values, it in principle condones the most oppressive traditions and reactionary forms of policy.[2]

Perhaps it would be more accurate and fairer to say (since advocates of postmodernist pluralism have almost always defended this as the basis of a more democratic politics) that what is raised here is a question about the extent to which the political rhetoric of postmodernist argument is consistent with its ontological anti-realism: to what extent can it coherently sustain its professedly democratic and egalitarian commitments while refusing to recognize any extra-discursive, non-normative features of the world and ourselves which might explain and justify the moral option in their favour?

It is impossible to deny the abuses that have been perpetrated under the cover of liberal humanist rhetoric, or the extent to which the interests of specific power elites have been hypocritically protected by a projection of them as universal to human society at large. But we must surely ask what we are doing when we expose the iniquities of Western imperialism, or the forms of cultural dominion on our own doorstep, if we do not deplore the failure of such practices to observe the humanity, dignity and rights of those they tyrannize. In other words, it is difficult to see how we can offer any coherent criticism of oppression without, at least tacitly, acknowledging a communality of human needs. If we bend the stick so far in favour of difference and cultural relativity that we deny any universal moral values or common qualities of being human, then not only do we undermine the very grounds of any empathetic solidarity with the sufferings of others, we are also invited to view any and every distinction of persons as intrinsic to them, as an indissoluble aspect of their individual identity. In short, if we are obedient only to the logic of difference, we surely remove the grounds for any claims that different identities come with equal entitlements to the same forms of recognition: we deconstruct the grounds upon which any democratic politics can conceivably be promoted.

It may be argued that it is precisely Derrida's sensitivity to the self-subverting nature of the 'politics of difference' that has led him to refrain hitherto from any definitive statement on the ethics and politics of deconstruction. But, at the same time, he has shown himself to be sensitive to his critics' accusation that deconstruction has too long pretended to a leftish ethical and political commitment while refusing to acknowledge it explicitly, or grant it philosophical legitimacy. Hence the interest of *Specters of Marx*, since it is here that Derrida finally rises to the challenge of those who have charged him with prevarication on these issues and offers some illumination on them.

I want to begin by noting three of the more relevant aspects of *Specters of Marx* in this respect. In the first place, it offers a definite statement of political affiliation. Derrida makes plain here his distance from the celebrants of the demise of Marxism and from all those who would echo

Fukuyama's triumphalist prophecies about the 'end of history'.[3] He is very ready to acknowledge that if we measure the 'out of jointness' of our times[4] by the degree of human misery already incurred or impending, then our times are indeed askew. In his ten indictments of global capitalism,[5] he also makes it very clear that he subscribes to a broadly Marxist view of the sources of the disorder.

While endlessly pursuing the philosophical issue of what it means for the times to be either 'in' or 'out of joint', and advising us, indeed, that it is a mistake to attempt to define what it would be for them to be 'in joint' (since that would be to ontologize, to impose a body on a spirit or spectral promise which is distorted in the very attempt at incarnation); while endlessly refraining, in other words, from any definitive pronouncement on what it would be like to be 'in joint' together with pronouncements on the more practical means to any such adjustment, Derrida nonetheless, in his more straightforward critical moments, clearly deplores the exploitation and oppression of the contemporary world order, regards the capitalist economy as at the root of the problem and thus far aligns himself with Marx.

Secondly, Derrida here engages for the first time at some length with Marx's writing and offers a number of pertinent readings in the process. Some of these are hardly very original (the deficiencies of Marx's realist account of ideology, for example, in *The German Ideology*, have received extensive attention from earlier commentators). But there are other more uniquely Derridean critiques, notably the extended commentary he offers on the largely ignored section of *The German Ideology* in which Marx engages in his obsessional exorcism of the 'spooks' of Max Stirner's egoism.

Several commentators have pondered why it is that Marx devotes such a profound scrutiny to Stirner's defence of the 'uniqueness' of the individual in his book, *The Ego and His Own*.[6] Derrida goes some way to providing the solution in his suggestion that Marx is here locked in a self-denying struggle with himself—with a doppelgänger, or doubling of his own ideas. What was perhaps fundamentally at stake here, though Derrida does not put it in these terms, was the extent to which Stirner's defence of egoism drew upon the self-same arguments that Marx and Engels had themselves used against Feuerbach's abstract humanism and its communist pieties. (Indeed Engels was so far 'taken in' by the book that he wrote to Marx in 1844 that 'only a few trivialities' needed to be stressed against Stirner, 'but what is true in his principles we have to accept'.) If Stirner's book was troubling to Marx, it was because it required him to demonstrate how one could reject abstract humanism while at the same time defending communism against the charge that it involved a sacrifice of the individual to the abstraction of the community. Stirner's book stung Marx into showing how the communism to which they aspired was not only consistent with the realization of individuality but was the only possible route to individual self-fulfilment.

Derrida might well not agree with this, but it seems to me that part of his interest in the Marx–Stirner contestation, and part of the interest of the engagement with it in *Specters of Marx*, is that it targets the point in Marx's writing where Marx himself is struggling with a sort of proto-deconstructivist assertion of 'individual' difference against the conflations of communist collectivism.

The third noteworthy feature of Derrida's book is that it acknowledges that if deconstruction is to be associated with an ethics and a politics, then it is itself reliant in its argument on an element which is irreducible and resistant to deconstruction; it must in some sense be value-grounded. Or as Derrida himself puts it, a certain 'messianism', a certain idea of justice and democracy, is essential to an emancipatory politics:

> What remains irreducible to any deconstruction, what remains as undeconstructible as the possibility itself of deconstruction is, perhaps, a certain experience of the emancipatory promise; it is perhaps even the formality of a structural messianism, a messianism without religion, even a messianic without messianism, an idea of justice . . .[7]

Admittedly, Derrida is quick to assure us that this is no ordinary idea of justice, but a justice that must be distinguished from any of its current concepts and determined predicates. Nonetheless he here explicitly recognizes the need to adopt a certain prescriptive stance—and this is an important concession to those who have for some time been pointing out that there is an inconsistency between the ethical indecisionism of deconstruction and its deployment in support of an emancipatory political agenda. I am not suggesting that Derrida has not previously gestured to the undeconstructible grounding of deconstructive critique, only that in the engagement with Marx he acknowledges more clearly than before the indispensability of fixing in some sense, however sketchily, the future aims or ends in the light of which one is rejecting the actual, and even perhaps of saying something about the means whereby those might be realized.

Where the argument of *Specters of Marx* remains more predictable is in the still purely formal quality of this recognition. Ready though Derrida may be to accept that a deconstructive critique only makes sense against the background, or within the context, of a certain ethical commitment, he still seems very loath to endow it with any content. In the final analysis, the prevailing message of his book is that we must never ontologize, must remain no more than haunted by the spirit of an emancipary politics, must never seek to incarnate it in any set of goods, institutions or strategies, since to do so—it is implied—is inevitably to betray the spirit itself.

What Marx shared with the opponents of communism, Derrida argues, was a fear of its spectre—an antithetical fear to theirs, since it was not a fear that it might take on flesh and become an embodied presence, but rather that it might *not*; in other words, that it might remain merely spectral—but it was nevertheless a common fear of spectrality itself. According to Derrida, what we should be more afraid of, and more wary of, is the exorcizing impulse itself—the urge to clothe the spirit in flesh, to concretize our messianic yearnings. We should love the ghost, embrace the spectre—which means that we should think and act always within the space between the absolutely formal and contentless regulative idea and its embodiment or representation in any 'full' presence. Spectral logic requires us, as it were, to accept that the only site of political virtue is virtuality itself.

Thus we must conduct an ongoing immanent critique of the failure of existing actuality to live up to its own ideals of justice and democracy; but at the same time we should critique those ideals themselves in the light of a justice which is not that of law and right, a democracy which is not to be confounded with any of its present concepts—a justice and democracy that no alternative reality should be expected to realize or represent as actualizable. Rather, we should proceed within the spirit of an indefinitely deferred justice: what Derrida calls a 'justice of the gift', which neither expects nor requires any return from the 'other'; in the spirit of an indefinitely deferred democracy whose 'yes to the stranger' ethic is that of an absolute hospitality which sets no conditions on welcome; an ethic which refrains from all representations of identity and makes no demands on the 'other' to conform to any existing system of rights or legality, or to any pre-given code of honour or justice.

Several points can be made about this deconstructive reworking of the Marxist emancipatory promise. In the first place, we can surely ask in what sense, if any, it could be said to be Marxist, even in spirit. It is easy to accept Derrida's own point (it is hardly a controversial one for Marxists since it has been made by most of them themselves) that a Marxism adequate to our times is a reformed, even radically revised Marxism. But we may still argue that to think in the spirit of Marx is to do more than condemn the actual in the light of the impossible. Or to come at the point from a slightly different angle, we might ask whether there really is such a thing as the spirit of Marx once all his letters—about economic determination, about base and superstructure, about class antagonism and class struggle, about ideology, about materiality, about the 'real men and their circumstances', about, in short, the ontology of the capitalist mode of production and the means and direction of its transformation—have been obscured or spectralized, either denounced as no longer relevant to our times or denied their literal meaning. Derrida refers (and wants to refer us) to Marx, but given this is a Marx whom he deems presentable (presentable to himself, to us, for our times) only if we suspend our belief in his literal meaning, a Marx who in a sense is not only 'not a Marxist', but not Marx, we might ask why: why Marx? When, in short, does working merely in the spirit of Marx cease to be Marxist—and become, say, left-liberalism, or the 'radical democracy' of Ernesto Laclau and Chantal Mouffe,[8] who make no bones about describing themselves as 'post-Marxist', but with whose argument Derrida's de-ontologized version of Marxism would seem to have more affinity than with the actual works of Marx himself?

Just as I do not view these questions as purely rhetorical, so I am not prejudging the answer to them. But there are a number of implications of Derrida's advice that are relevant and that I do want to dispute. First, why should we abide by a logic all of whose emphasis might seem to fall on the compromised nature of any active, hands-on politics, rather than on the gains it can achieve—which might seem to imply that we can be properly politically sensitive only in thought, in philosophy, and never in our actual practice? In my view, Derrida does not sufficiently acknowledge the 'to be or not to be' quality of much political activity on the left: its active and concrete pursuit of a 'third way' through the ontologies of the Cold War, for example; its insistence on being in favour of justice, equality and democracy, but not the justice, equality and democracy of either Soviet communism or liberal capitalism; its commitment to a variety of betwixt-and-between agendas (between Marxism and existentialism; between Promethean and irrationalist responses to ecological crises; between class politics on the one hand, and an 'anything goes' postmodernism on the other). It is not that the specific representations of these political positions are invulnerable to a deconstructive critique: it is, rather, that this critique is too assimilative. By inviting us to view all praxis as damned aforehand by its failure to instantiate a true or authentic democracy, this critique offers no gage or criterion for adjudicating between the more or less progressive character of different acts, practices and institutional forms. Moreover, Derrida takes too little notice of the ways in which leftwing practice might be said to have actualized 'spectrality', to have proceeded in the spirit of some of its scruples. That Derrida envelops his precautions against 'theological' Marxism in a new rhetoric should not blind us to the fact that the general spirit in which they are moved is one that has frequently been registered within the Marxist and socialist camp, and has at times been instantiated in some relatively clean-handed forms of praxis.

But if the logic of the spectre invites us to collapse distinctions within the actualized politics of the left, it is also, and conversely, mistaken in implying that there could be any such politics that did not involve some choice, some decision about how and when to act, and some representation of the other as the condition of that action. If that is dirtyhandedness, then, yes, there is no politics without it. We cannot change the world, however minimally, if we stay obedient to the injunction not to ontologize. Nor can there be any extension of empathy or solidarity with the victims of oppression that is not 'guilty'—if that is the word—of reading or representing their plight in the light of our own identity; in the light, that is, of a conception of how it would be for us were we to be in their condition, of what we would feel were we to suffer their fate. Messianic opening or hospitality to the other is all very well if it is simply thrown out as a caution against over-hasty political assimilations—or as a challenge, for example, to current government policies on immigration. But if Derrida means that we are culpable of some disrespect for the absolute otherness of others in any and every representation of the other as like the self, then this seems a recommendation not for justice or democracy, but for political quietism: we would, strictly speaking, be doing an injury in the very presumption of the other's agony or humiliation at the hands of the torturer or oppressor, and might therefore do better not to intervene.

It will be argued that Derrida himself recognizes the impossibility of what he is advocating, which in a sense is true. Thus he writes of messianic opening that 'it would be easy, too easy, to show that such a hospitality without reserve, which is nevertheless the condition of the event and thus of history . . . is the impossible itself, and this condition of possibility of the event is also its condition of impossibility'. Yet the acknowledgement is made only in the context of an argument to the effect that without this experience of the impossible, one might as well give up on any justice, and on any pretensions to a politics 'in good conscience'. 'One might as well', so Derrida claims, 'confess the economic calculation and declare all the checkpoints that ethics, hospitality, or the various messianisms would still install at the borders of the event in order to screen the arrivant . . .'[9] On the one hand, a just politics or its experience is impossible; on the other, there is no honest or just politics without it.

But one can also claim that the condition of any politics 'in good conscience' is the refusal of this very dichotomy. For as soon as we ask why this so-called democracy of unlimited hospitality is 'impossible', we confront the fact that the idea of the 'impossible' is here obscuring a failure of politico-ethical engagement. It is impossible because, as suggested above, there can be no saying 'no' to the other's suffering if saying 'yes' to the stranger means refraining from any and every preconception of how they are to live. It is impossible because respecting the absolute difference of the other—imposing no conditions on hospitality—would logically deprive the other of any grounds for contesting even the most inhospitable forms of reception; and would require any and every 'host' to accept all those strangers whose strangeness consisted in their radical incapacity to accept or understand the very principles of hospitality, democracy or justice. It is impossible because justice is not a matter of generosity or charity, but a relationship of reciprocity which, of its nature, can only exist in a context of mutual obligations and responsibilities.

One can understand Derrida's reluctance to recognize these conditions on the possibility of democracy and justice in the light of the inequalities and disparities of distribution perpetrated in the name of their existing concepts and determinate forms; but the very critique of these disparities within the global economy only makes sense if it is rooted in an idea of justice as sharing—as involving a commitment to a fair distribution of goods and resources. I do not see how it would be just to transcend such a conception of justice; and I certainly think the rhetoric of 'justice of the gift' is unfortunate if it were to imply that certain forms of unconditional 'givings' through which such justice might be better realized (such as the cancellation of Third World debt) were 'givings' or 'gifts' rather than restitutions for previous takings, thefts and dispossessions.

Derrida's refusal to ontologize, and his reluctance to speculate on the political forms and institutions which might realize his transcendent concept of democracy and justice, leave him open to the charge that he is not really engaging with the ethics of justice and democracy at all—and even to cynical claims that we have had far too much already of 'justice of the gift', most of it in favour of the more affluent and privileged communities of the globe. There is a limit to our acceptance of the notion that Derrida's recommendations for sustaining a politics 'in good conscience' *are* in good conscience in the absence of any blueprinting of their conditions of possibility, or any engagement with the ethical conflicts to which unreserved hospitality offers indefinite welcome.

But there is a further aspect of Derrida's 'yes to the stranger' ethic of which we should be wary: its invitation to erode or collapse conceptual distinctions between the 'human' and the 'animal'; or, to put it more accurately, Derrida's invitation to us to treat all our intuitive demarcations between human and non-human 'others' as a form of unwarranted conceptual policing. In a recent interview, for example, he recommends that the 'someone' addressed in messianic opening is a someone whom we cannot and must not define in advance—'not as subject, self-consciousness, not even as animal, God, person, man or woman, living or dead'.[10] There are a number of similar claims in *Specters of Marx*. But could we even determine what was or was not a 'someone' if we were obedient to this injunction? What would it mean to be a 'someone' in the absence of any definition or determination? In other words, is this a coherent injunction; and, even if it were, could it be ethical, could such indiscriminacy be the basis of a just polity?

I find it puzzling that Derrida should be advocating an ethical perspective that appears at face value to be so ready to abstract from those differences (of language use, or our insertion within a symbolic order) which distinguish humanity from other creatures, and which have been such a focus of structuralist and post-structuralist attention. Is he not arguing here in ways that might align a deconstructivist ethic with some of the more simplistic and reductivist forms of naturalism: with those, for example, who have argued for the extension of the moral community to include non-human primates, or with the opponents of 'anthropocentricity' who have rejected any privileging of humanity over other life forms? Clearly there is a debate to be had around these issues, and a spectrum of positions that may be adopted in regard to them. My complaint is that Derrida gestures at these conceptual erosions of the human–animal distinction without any consideration of their counter-factual difficulties, and in complete abstraction from the important and intense discussions that have been taking place around these issues in environmental ethics.

A final, and perhaps obvious, point: it is one thing to claim, as Derrida does, that 'there is no future without Marx' and another to suppose that we shall ever see a popular mandate for socialism in the future. It is one thing to advise that the foreign debt must be treated 'in the spirit' of Marxist critique (whatever that means) and another to suppose that it will ever be dealt with through a dismantling of global capitalism. If the question whether Marx will come again is interpreted as a question about the return of any commanding support for a socialist programme, then there may well be a future without Marx, at least for a good while to come. Never, in fact, has the spectre of communism looked less like haunting Europe than at the present time. But if anything remotely resembling this ghost is to be kept in the offing as a potential vote-winner in the future, then it will require all those who are committed to its spirit to rebel against the Derridean veto: to put some flesh on this alternative to the actual, to think through the institutional forms that might realize that will-o'-the-wisp called democratic or authentic socialism.

It seems to me that the capitalist order is sustained less by any widespread faith in its capacity to secure the good life, or to ward off the major crises of our times, than by a deep, and in many ways justifiable, scepticism about the practical viability of any alternative. In this sense, one may argue that the problem for the left has not been too much blueprinting, but too little: too much readiness to invoke the idea of an 'authentic socialism' as a way of dissociating oneself from what has been done in the name of Marxism, and too little attention paid to the concrete forms in which such an idea might be implemented. If we do indeed wish to preempt ever more terrible forms of misery, genocide, ecological barbarism and terminal warfare (as Derrida implies that we do), then all the more practical engagements of left theory—the work on market socialism and alternative economic policies, on new concepts of citizenship and forms of democratic empowerment, on the liberation from work and on the institutions of a new cosmopolitanism—seem more helpful than continuous Derridean warnings against preempting the forms in which the future will eventuate.

It is paradoxical that Derrida should be recommending a spectral Marx, given how loath Marx himself was to do more than conjure the spirit of communism, and given his resistance to specifying the political institutions which might realize those famous abstract desiderata: a society of abundance; a future unmeasured by any existing moral yardstick; distribution according to needs; and a rich and all-round development of the individual. Where Marx is closest to the spirit of deconstruction is, arguably, in these formulaic gestures towards a society that had so far transcended existing actuality that its conditions of realization could no longer be conceptualized. Marx *is* spectral Marx in his refusal to envision communism in his envisaging of it, in his anti-utopian utopianism.[11] I am not deploring the vision in itself—a world that no longer aspires to any such political sublimity is an impoverished world. What I am saying, however, is that ontological voids can offer themselves as hostages to fortune, that Marx's refusal to think through the politics of communism created a number of such voids, and that insofar as these came to be filled by 'actual existing socialism' they have played a role in the demise of Marxism itself. Or, to put it in other words, one does not necessarily avoid the horrors of a messianic totalitarianism by refusing to ontologize; one might even be leaving more space for them. Certainly, we should be very wary of all those who know how to change the world, and what it must look like when they have. But since the world will change anyway, there are also dangers in confining oneself too narrowly to the task of 'critical criticism': to a permanent critique of the out of jointness of all times, of the eternal failure of the actual to measure up a rationality that will never arrive.[12] Derrida abhors the politics of the 'full presence', whether it takes the form of a celebration of the end of history or an absolute knowledge of how it should end; and I agree. But it is not, I think, by leaving total ontological vacuums that we best guard against these types of plenitude.

12. Simplicity and Complexity: On the Foundations of Marx's Methodology

Ali Shamsavari

In this chapter I shall attempt to show that the concepts of 'simple' and 'complex' form the cornerstones of Marx's methodology in *Capital*. What makes this topic relevant today is the fact that these two concepts have come to occupy a prominent place on the frontiers of a number of physical and life sciences to the extent that important new theories are cast with the notions of simplicity and complexity as major points of reference. I shall first briefly discuss why these notions have acquired such significance in modern science and then explore in more detail the role of simplicity and complexity in Marx's theory of capitalism.

Introduction

The modern scientific explorations known as the science of complexity, or complexity theory,[1] have emerged partly from chaos theory and in a way complement the latter. What chaos theory shows is that 'simple laws can have very complicated . . . consequences'. On the other hand, complexity theory is about how 'complex causes can produce simple effects'.[2] Cohen and Stewart thus claim that, 'The relation between simplicity and complexity in nature is one of the deepest and broadest questions that face modern science'.[3]

Until the nineteenth century, the physical sciences were dominated by the Newtonian revolution in science. The latter represented a mechanistic-analytical paradigm the main elements of which were determinism, linearity, equilibrium and reversibility (one need only recall the pendulum). In the nineteenth century, when Newtonian science seemed triumphant, the birth of thermodynamics—with its celebrated second law—introduced irreversibility into the physical sciences, thus undermining one of the pillars of this science. In the early twentieth century the development of quantum physics and Einstein's theory of relativity began slowly to erode other pillars of Newtonian science by introducing instability, indeterminacy and complexity (e.g. the behaviour of nucleic phenomena) into the physical sciences.

Outside the realm of the physical sciences, there were also important developments in philosophy and the social sciences. While British empiricist philosophy was constructing a philosophical basis for the Newtonian triumph, German critical philosophy was undermining some of the basic assumptions of Newtonian science. For example, the latter is based on a fixed opposition between the observer, experimenter and 'knower' on the one hand, and nature on the other. It also involves the reduction of complex reality into its simple elements and laws.[4] While Hume's theory of knowledge basically conforms to these assumptions (e.g. his view of causality), Kant problematized the relation between the knowing subject and the known object by posing the question of the nature of experience and knowledge.[5] By introducing the elements of the innate properties of the mind that make experience possible and the active role of the knowing subject, Kant went some way towards resolving the dualism of thought and nature. However, he fell into the trap of Newtonian and Cartesian dualism by postulating the existence of 'things-in-themselves' which are unknowable. Hegel criticized this position and thus transcended Newtonian science and empiricist philosophy.

Hegel's concentration on the study of the human mind, organic nature and historical development led him to question the universality of the empiricist problematic. For example, the organic model shows that there is an intrinsic and internal relation between cause and effect, the internal and the external, form and content, the whole and the part, the implicit and the explicit, the beginning and the end. Today, advances in biology, microbiology and genetics clearly conform to Hegelian perspectives.

In the social sciences, the most important breakthrough was the development of classical political economy. From Adam Smith through Ricardo to the last great classical economist, John Stuart Mill, a systematic approach to economics developed that emphasized larger issues of economic growth and development through historical time. In spite of the Newtonian influences, particularly in Ricardo, classical theory has a significant historical dimension, contrary to Marx's criticisms. This is why Hegel took

Smith very seriously and Marx built his entire analysis of capitalism on the achievements of the classical economists. Let us not forget that both Smith and Mill were philosophers before they came to political economy. Marx is the ultimate case of a theoretician who was almost entirely influenced by theoretical developments that were at variance with Newtonian science (the exception being the Ricardian influence). German critical philosophy, the French historians' view of the French revolution, British classical political economy, and British and continental utopian socialism were among the many influences on Marx. I shall show below how Marx's method involved elements that have become so important today in complexity theory.

Another nineteenth-century blow to reversibility was the Darwinian theory of evolution. Marx even compared his own analysis of historical development to the theory of evolution and admired Darwin so greatly that he wanted to dedicate *Capital II* to him, an offer that Darwin politely refused.[6]

For most of the nineteenth century, philosophy and social science had been ahead of the physical sciences in their explicit or implicit rejection of the appropriateness of the Newtonian paradigm (Hegel, Marx), but by the late nineteenth century the intellectual climate in the social and philosophical sciences had begun to change. While the physical sciences were turning away from the basic tenets of Newtonian science, the social sciences were increasingly converging to the Newtonian paradigm (especially in economics). One reason for this was that the mechanistic paradigm in science (although eroded by the development of thermodynamics and quantum mechanics) still ruled supreme, as many scientific and technological breakthroughs tended to be based on the main elements of this paradigm. It is not surprising that a number of the social sciences (particularly economics in the late nineteenth and twentieth centuries) increasingly turned to this paradigm and made it their own (important exceptions being the work of some of the founding fathers of modern sociology such as Weber and Durkheim).

As opposed to this mechanistic-analytical paradigm, complexity theory is based on opposite elements: indeterminacy, disequilibrium, non-linearity and irreversibility. It also involves the significance of initial conditions, the emergence of complex behaviour from simple initial conditions (chaos theory), emergence, non-reducibility of wholes to component parts, co-evolution and complexity.

Apart from chaos theory, the development of complexity theory can be traced to the pioneering work of Ilya Prigogine in the area of non-equilibrium thermodynamics, in particular the theory of dissipative structures, for which he received the Nobel Prize in Chemistry in 1977.[7]

During the 1980s complexity theory became increasingly associated with the work of scholars attached to the Santa Fe Institute in the United States.[8] The disciplines in which complexity research has made significant inroads are numerous and diverse. Apart from chaos research, prominent examples include molecular biology, genetics, evolution (both natural and social), environmental science (e.g. Lovelock's Gaia hypothesis), artificial life and non-linear dynamics in the physical sciences. A small number of economists have also been involved.[9]

As mentioned above, the notions of simplicity and complexity have acquired a significant place in the new complexity-based interpretations of nature, science and society. Indeed, these notions have become so important that Cohen and Stewart have developed two new concepts to cope with the relation of simplicity/complexity to new developments in complexity research, i.e. 'simplexity' and 'complicity'.[10] Complexity theory has advanced to a point at which it rejects reductionism and the analytical approach; it has also overcome the fixed opposition between the notions of simplicity and complexity. The following quotations should suffice to demonstrate this point:

> An examination of experimental data will lead us to the conclusion that the distinction between physico-chemical and biological phenomena, between 'simple' and 'complex' behaviour, is not as sharp as we might intuitively think.[11]

> Far from opposing 'chance' and 'necessity', we now see both aspects as essential in the description of non-linear systems far from equilibrium.[12]

Thus complexity theory has arrived at a truly Hegelian/dialectical standpoint, as will be demonstrated in what follows. I shall, first, attempt to show the significance of the concepts of simplicity and complexity in Marx's method and, second, examine the precise meaning and functions of these concepts in Marx's analysis of capitalist development as a contribution, from the point of view of social science, to complexity theory.[13]

Marx's Simplicity Model

Marx uses the term 'simple' to characterize a number of concepts in *Capital*: 'simple commodity production', 'simple circulation of commodities', 'simple reproduction' and 'simple cooperation'. Marx also intimates that science begins with simple concepts. The theoretical status of these concepts (hereafter S-concepts) as well as the 'question of the beginning' has found a number of diverse interpretations. I shall try to demonstrate that most of these interpretations have viewed S-concepts in a one-sided way and that, in spite of their differences, these views are based on a fixed opposition between the concepts 'simple' and 'complex'. I shall argue that Marx's concepts are multidimensional and have a complexity of their own.

There are three main approaches to S-concepts, which may be termed historicist, structuralist and rationalist. The historicist approach conceives of 'simple' as a historically 'first' relation; in other words, S-concepts refer to historically prior relationships. The major presumption here is that history develops from simple to complex forms. The structuralist approach views 'simple' as a simple relation, not necessarily historically first but structurally subordinate to a 'complex' whole. The rationalist argument does not interpret S-concepts as representing a reality, i.e. a simple relation that is historically prior or subordinate to a real complex whole. In this approach, 'simple' refers to an abstract idea, or an abstract model representing a mental abstraction from a complex reality, which is then used to explain the latter.[14]

All three approaches capture one particular aspect of Marx's concepts but not the complete notion, thus remaining abstract and one-sided. They all end up by postulating a simple structure which, having been discovered, should serve as a stepping-stone, a departure point or a beginning for scientific inquiry. In the first case, this simple structure is a historically first condition; in the second, it is a simple contemporaneous relation subsumed under a more complex whole; and in the third, it is a simple concept, a logical construct or simple model. After identifying this simple beginning, the journey of inquiry traverses the path from this simple beginning to the concrete or complex end result. In the first case, this journey is a movement in time; in the second, it is an ascent from the bottom to the top of an existing structure; and in the third, it is a progression in thought from a simple to a more complex (and therefore more realistic) model. In all three cases, the end result is a concrete-in-thought which is supposed to correspond to reality. In all three schools, the process of knowing reality—knowing it in as complete a manner as possible—invariably involves a passage from 'simple' to 'complex'.

If we now raise the question as to the criterion that distinguishes simple from complex, it will become clear that no such criterion is provided by any of the schools. We end up identifying complexity with reality (which intuitively makes sense: reality is complex because it represents a multiplicity of events, factors, dimensions, etc) and simplicity with thought.

Ultimately, thinking has to submit to the complexity of reality and somehow 'reproduce' it in thought. Thus thinking as a complex process merely reflects the complexity of reality; it has no autonomy, i.e. it cannot be complex in its own right. Thought is complex only when it reflects a complex reality.

Thinking is denied an autonomous complexity. In these approaches only a reproduction of complex reality can qualify as a complex thought. The upshot is that complexity cannot characterize thinking as opposed to being, and therefore thinking must be 'simple'. The simplicity of thought rises to complexity only when it strives to contemplate 'complex reality'. The reality of simple relations may seem to negate this polarization of simple and complex as reflections of thought and reality. This contradiction, however, is only apparent: in both the historicist and the structuralist conceptions, simple relations are not the 'real' thing—in one case, the simple relation fades away with the coming of the complex whole, and in the other, it subsists as a subordinate relation.

When we turn to Marx, we find that in his discussions of the method of political economy in the *1857 Introduction*,[15] while justifying the latter's manner of beginning with S-concepts, he criticizes the nature of this 'simple' beginning:

> Hegel, for example, correctly begins the *Philosophy of Right* with possession, this being the subject's simplest juridical relation. But there is no possession preceding the family or master–servant relations, which are far more concrete relations. However, it would be correct to say that there are families or clan groups which still merely possess, but have no property. The simple category, therefore, appears in relation to property as a relation of simple families or clan groups. In the higher society it appears as the simpler relation of a developed organization. But the concrete substratum of which possession is a relation is always presupposed. One can imagine an individual savage as possessing something. But in that case possession is not a juridical relation. It is incorrect that possession develops historically into family. Possession, rather, always presupposes this more concrete juridical category.[16]

In this intricate passage Marx develops the concept of the simple category in various directions and presents different shades of meaning with which the concept 'simple' is impregnated. We can distinguish three aspects, sides or meanings of the concept of simple:

S.1 simple as an elementary, historically prior or primal relation ('a relation of simple families');

S.2 simple as an elementary relation coexisting but subsumed under a complex and developed whole ('the simpler relation of a developed organization'); and

S.3 simple as a relation that presupposes a more concrete (complex, many-sided) development, e.g. a juridical relation ('But the concrete substratum of which possession is a relation is always presupposed'; 'Possession . . . always presupposes this "more concrete juridical category"').

The bracketing or subsumption of these three different concepts (S.l, S.2 and S.3) under a single category ('simple'), as attempted by Marx in the passage quoted above, is truly remarkable and defies our conventional, ordinary way of understanding. Obviously, there are semantic and conceptual difficulties in making, for example, a proper distinction between something which is 'simple' because of its elemental nature and something which is 'simple' by virtue of its purity and universality. In the ordinary way of thinking, it is easy to conceive of S.l or S.2 as simple, since these concepts designate a single relation. But when we consider S.3, a category based on the highest development and presupposing the richest possible determinations, it is difficult to justify its characterization as 'simple'.

The question of the common bonds and links between these three determinations of 'simple', i.e. their unity, is addressed below. At this stage I will demonstrate how S-concepts function in Marx's discourse by using two examples.

The Question of the Beginning

Marx begins *Capital* by discussing the concept of commodity and analysing the forms of commodity, such as the commodity form, the money form, etc. The question as to why Marx begins with commodity (which is presumably the common denominator of all commodity-producing economies) and not with capital (which is the feature of capitalism that distinguishes it from other modes of production) has been debated extensively in the literature.[17] According to the historicist approach, Marx begins with commodity because it is historically the first form of human product produced for exchange, and thus a historical foundation of capitalism. If we follow the structuralist approach, Marx begins with commodity because it is the basic elementary structure of capitalism. The rationalist response would be that by beginning with commodity, which is a form common to all commodity-producing economies, Marx intends to abstract from complicating features (such as ownership of the means of production) in order to simplify the analysis of capitalism. Against all these approaches, I have argued elsewhere[18] that

Marx's beginning in *Capital* is neither the commodity as it appears at the dawn of history, nor the one which forms the elementary structure of capitalism, nor is it the simple model that, through a process of 'finite and external' addition (as Hegel would put it)[19] of complicating factors, leads to a developed model of capitalism. On the contrary, the commodity that forms the beginning of *Capital* is the commodity as it emerges not under pre-capitalist conditions, or as a simple substructure or thought construct, model etc, but as it appears as a result (at the end rather than the beginning) of capitalist production. Thus Marx's discussion of the value form in the first chapter of *Capital* presupposes all the advanced features of capitalism. This is confirmed by Marx when he states:

> The commodity as it emerges in capitalist production is different from the commodity taken as the element, the starting-point of capitalist production. We are no longer faced with the individual commodity, the individual product. The individual product manifests itself not only as a real product but also as a commodity, as a part both really and conceptually of production as a whole. Each individual commodity represents a definite portion of capital and the surplus value created by it.[20]

Thus Marx begins with an S.3 concept, i.e. one that presupposes the richest development. One may ask how this differs from the rationalist response as it also begins with developed capitalism. In my view, although the rationalist approach—especially in the version present in the work of Sombart, Schmidt and Rubin[21]—comes very close to S.3, it is different from my interpretation for the following reason. The 'simple' of the rationalist school is, in the last analysis, only a 'generic' concept, i.e. simple commodity production or the law of value as a simplification, a first approximation or model of capitalist relations. But this simple idea or model has been stripped of any inherent or necessary connection with developed capitalism and thus forms the common denominator between all commodity-producing societies. The problem, however, is that Marx never identifies any single mode of production, apart from capitalism, that involves commodity production on any significant scale. Therefore commodity as the dominant form of production belongs only to capitalism. Marx's commodity, like the 'doctrine of being' in Hegel's logic, does not simply presuppose more advanced development, but essentially contains the latter, although implicitly.[22] This brings us to the second example, i.e. the intricacies of Marx's concept of 'simple circulation'.

The Simplicity of Circulation

> Capital can be formed in the circulation process, and must be formed there, before it learns to master its extremes, the various spheres of production between which circulation mediates. The circulation of money and commodities can mediate spheres of production with the most diverse organization, in which their internal structures are still oriented principally to the production of use-values. When circulation process becomes independent in this way, as a process in which spheres of production are linked together by a third party, this expresses a double situation. On the one hand, that circulation has still not mastered production, but is related to it simply as its given precondition. On the other hand, that the production process has not yet absorbed circulation into it as a mere moment. In capitalist production, on the contrary, both these things are the case. The production process is completely based on circulation, and circulation is a mere moment and a transition phase of production, simply the realization of a product produced as a commodity and the replacement of its elements of production produced as commodities. The form of capital that stems directly from circulation —commercial capital—now appears simply as one of the forms of capital in its movement of reproduction.[23]

In this passage, circulation finds a threefold determination that I shall call C.1, C.2 and C.3. C.1 circulation as a historically prior form is a process that occurs between differently organized spheres of production (different modes of production) which are principally oriented to the production of 'use-values' (i.e. products destined for internal consumption, whether personal or productive). This does not mean that no products find their way outside the limited circle of internal use (otherwise no circulation could take place), but it means that exchange does not absorb the entire product of these modes of production: only 'surplus' products are exchanged. Thus, under these conditions, circulation has a merely external relation to production. Since products are not produced primarily for exchange but for internal use, circulation does not reach anywhere near the 'interior' of production—it is not 'internalized'; it only scratches the 'surface' of the production process. In these conditions, in contrast to capitalist production, the role of circulation is a limited one since, on the one hand, it 'has still not mastered production' and, on the other, 'the production process has not yet absorbed circulation into it as a mere moment'. This 'negative' characterization of the function of circulation in pre-capitalist conditions points directly to the characteristics of circulation under capitalism.

We have a double movement between pre-capitalist modes and the capitalist mode of production: the 'simultaneous' movement of the absorption of the production process by circulation and the reduction of circulation to a mere phase of production.

C.2 circulation, as a mere phase of the capitalist mode of production, is wholly absorbed by production. In this form its function is similar to C.1: it basically mediates between different units of production and to this extent remains external to production. However, it is quite unlike C.1 in that its mediation is not between different spheres of production which are not already absorbed by capital. The units between which it mediates, whatever their internal principle of organization, capitalist or not, function in relation to capital. The same observation applies to merchant capital: this form which historically develops 'directly out of circulation [C.1] appears here [under capitalism] merely as one form of capital'.

Under the capitalist mode of production, C.3 circulation relates to production in two different ways: (i) the production process is completely based on circulation; and (ii) circulation is a mere moment and a transition phase of production. Circulation, as the foundation of the capitalist mode of production, explains the internal principles of organization under capitalism. Capitalist units of production produce primarily for the market, for circulation. Circulation thus has taken over all the production processes and reorganized them in its own image.

I shall now attempt to throw some light on the question of why Marx applies the term 'simple' to so many diverse concepts. At this juncture, two interrelated questions arise. First, what are the grounds for identifying such divergent concepts with each other by using the word 'simple'? In other words, what is the basis, if any, for the unity of the three concepts of 'simple'? And second, what is the precise mechanism by which the transition is made from S.1 to S.3?

> Being is simple as immediate being; for that reason it is only something meant or intended and we cannot say of it what it is; therefore, it is one with its other, with non-being. Its notion is just this, to be simplicity that immediately vanishes in its opposite; it is becoming. The universal, on the contrary, is that simplicity which, because it is the notion, no less possesses within itself the richest content.
>
> First, therefore, it is the simple relation to itself; it is only within itself. Secondly, however, this identity is within itself, absolute mediation, but it is not something mediated.[24]

Thus, in Hegel, simplicity has a twofold determination. On the one hand, 'simple' is an isolated and one-sided moment; it is also abstract and unmediated. On the other hand, 'simple' is a characteristic of the universal, or of notion. As such, it has 'the richest content'. In this meaning, simple is pure self-relation, immediacy, which at the same time contains 'absolute mediation'. The following discussion attempts to incorporate Hegel's view of simplicity into the analysis of Marx's concepts.

The unity of the three concepts of simple has two aspects, one formal and the other substantial (essential):

1. *The formal unity* (why all these three distinct concepts are called 'simple'). The 'simplicities' of the three concepts have more or less distinct and different origins. At least two definitions of simple can be invoked here: simple as a self-related, self-contained whole; and simple as an abstract, isolated relation.

S.2 is obviously an abstract relation subsumed under a more complex whole. Thus it would satisfy definition 2 above. S.3 is a self-contained relation because it embraces a complex whole. It is an abstract (thought), ideal representation of the whole. Thus it falls under definition 1 above.

S.1 is a self-related whole but it does not contain a complex whole. It is thus isolated and abstract but not like S.2: i.e. it is not a necessary moment of a larger whole like S.2 but lives on the fringes of larger wholes without a necessary relation to them. It is subordinate (like S.2) but not subsumed (unlike S.2).

Thus S.1 is simple under definition 2 in one sense (isolated) and under definition 1 in another sense (self-contained by default, like the empty set in set theory, because there is no whole to contain it, not because it contains a whole). Thus S.1 is simple in the first sense only to the extent that it is not contained by something else; and it is simple in the second sense only to the extent that it is isolated. But unlike S.3 it does not contain any moments, it is elemental; and unlike S.2 it is not a necessary moment of a larger whole (an 'abstract, one-sided relation').

Since S.1 is neither a necessary moment of a larger whole nor an independent whole containing differentiated necessary moments, it cannot be self-sustaining (like S.3) nor can it sustain itself (like S.2). Thus S.1, by its nature, refers to something other than itself; it has to be mediated. But in being mediated, i.e. related to something else, it loses its identity as a self-contained entity. It is transformed into its opposite or else it becomes a subordinate moment subsumed under a larger whole.

2. *The substantial unity*. The discussion of the formal unity above shows that, even in a formal way, it is impossible to find a common ground for all

the three concepts. This becomes even more true when we consider their essential unity.

The question is whether the three concepts of 'simple' have a common essence; and whether there is a unitary, single system uniting all three in a coherent way such that each functions as a moment of that system. If we consider the three concepts in isolation from each other, there can be no question of the identity of essence. We cannot assume a simple essence of which the three 'simples' are so many forms.

However, when considered in conjunction with each other they become united on the basis of the developed, complex whole. S.3, being based on this whole, has the unifying function since it does not stand apart from steps leading to it; it does not maintain an external existence apart from the 'lower' forms. These forms are absorbed as moments rather than being discarded.

More specifically, first, S.2 is a transformation of S.1, i.e. an accidental, isolated relation is turned into a necessary moment of a complex whole; thus S.2 is the conservation–transformation of S.1 under the complex whole. Second, S.3 is also a transformation of S.1, i.e. an accidental, abstract relationship is transformed into a necessary system of relations. Thus the crucial difference between S.1 and S.3 is the difference between contingency and necessity.

Let us now reflect on the three meanings of the 'simple circulation' analysed earlier in the light of the above discussion. Simple circulation, C–M–C, as C.1 is an isolated phenomenon under pre-capitalist conditions; it appears on the fringes of different forms of production; it mediates between different spheres of production governed by entirely different principles of internal organization. Under these conditions, individual spheres of production can always recede back into their shells, i.e. break with the 'market'. This is because only surpluses of means of consumption are exchanged and not products necessary for their production process (factors of production). Thus C–M–C can easily turn into its opposite, the cessation of exchange, without becoming absorbed into any productive system. Even when trade takes place on a regular basis, because of the existence of the subsistence economy, traders can always fall back on their traditional self-sufficiency if the terms of trade change to their disadvantage. This is also true when the members of the self-sufficient sector have some involvement with an external wage-system: as long as the subsistence sector is not broken up internally or by external compulsion, the exchange of labour cannot become regular. Finally, even when labour-power is exchanged, it is usually in the form of exchange of slaves; after the labour-power has been bought, the exchange ceases.

The same is true of the merchant capital as the historically first form of capital. It is a subordinate form under pre-capitalist conditions but is never absorbed as a necessary moment into a mode of production since, as Marx points out, this form of capital, like interest-bearing capital, is hostile to pre-capitalist forms of production. Thus, as such a fleeting moment, it has either to stand in 'external' mediation with other modes of production or cease altogether. We have thus shown that in the form C.1, C–M–C cannot become the form of the general circulation of commodities, nor can it be absorbed as a necessary moment into any mode of production. The same is true of capital in the form of merchant capital.

It is only with the capitalist mode of production, with its fundamental premise of the separation of the labourer from the means of production, that the general production and circulation of commodities become possible and necessary.

Under capitalism, C.1 goes through a double transformation. On the one hand, it is transformed into C.2 as a necessary moment, as a phase, of the total economic process; as such, it performs a similar function to C.1 under pre-capitalist formations in that it mediates between different units of production (and consumption) but with the difference that the mediation is no longer external, but internal: the units connected by separate acts of exchange are by and large governed by capitalist principles of organization. On the other hand, C.1 is transformed into C.3 but not as a moment, not as a phase in the total production and reproduction process, but as the very social form and foundation of that process, and thus as necessity.

Marx's Complexity Model

In this section I shall first show that Marx conceives of production as a complex totality, rather than an empty generality, embracing its moments, i.e. production in the narrow sense, distribution, exchange and consumption: this stands in sharp contrast to the traditional classical and neo-classical view that conceptualizes the economy as a linear chain leading from production to consumption or vice versa. Secondly, I will argue that Marx's actual historical account of capitalist development involves the notion of co-evolution (a modern concept associated with complexity theory) rather than the traditional mechanistic interpretation of Marx's theory of history, according to which the development of production forces leads to a contradiction between the old relations of production—this contradiction is resolved when the class struggle leading to social revolution introduces new social relations of production as well as a new superstructure in harmony with the new level of the development of productive forces.

Production as Totality

In the *1857 Introduction*, Marx problematizes the notion of production 'in general' and shows how this is an empty generality or, at best, a 'particular' moment of totality:

> Production in general is an abstraction, but a rational abstraction in so far as it really brings out and fixes the common element and thus saves us repetition. Still, this general category, this common element sifted out by comparison, is itself segmented many times over and splits into many determinations. Some determinations belong to all epochs, others only to a few. Some determinations will be shared by the most modern epoch and the most ancient. No production will be thinkable without them; however, even though the most developed languages have laws and characteristics in common with the least developed, nevertheless, just those things which determine their development, i.e. the elements which are not general and common, must be separated out from the determinations valid for production as such, so that in their unity . . . their essential difference is not forgotten. The whole profundity of those economists who demonstrate the eternity and harmoniousness of the existing social relations lies in this forgetting.[25]

As an example of this 'empty' generalization (generic concept), Marx refers to the manner in which economists identify capital, a social relation of production, with the instruments of production:

> No production is possible without an instrument of production, even if this instrument is only the hand . . . Capital is, among other things, also an instrument of production . . . Therefore capital is a general, eternal relation of labour; that is, if I leave out just the specific quality which alone makes 'instrument of production' . . . into capital.[26]

Marx continues by denying the existence of general production: 'If there is no production in general, then there is also no general production. Production is always a particular branch of production—e.g. agriculture, cattle-raising, manufactures etc—or it is a totality.'[27] Thus production is either a particularity (a particular branch of production) or a totality. This is the first time that 'totality' is mentioned in Marx's text. It is clear that Marx is introducing this concept as a category that unites generality and particularity. Thus an economic system is a totality and not a generality. The generality itself is negated and reduced to a particularity and, at the same time, the concept of totality replaces that of generality as a 'true' and no longer empty generality. A totality, unlike the empty generality, cannot be reduced to a particular; rather, particular moments are subsumed under the totality. Marx ends the paragraph under discussion with these words: 'Production in general. Particular branches of production. Totality of production.'

Marx then goes on to elaborate this theme further:

> It is the fashion to preface a work of economics with a general part—and precisely this part figures under the title production [see, for example, John Stuart Mill] treating of the general preconditions of all production.[28]

> But none of all this is the economists' real concern in this general part. The aim is, rather, to present production [see e.g. Mill] as distinct from distribution etc. as encased in eternal natural laws independent of history, at which opportunity bourgeois relations are then quietly smuggled in as inviolable natural laws on which society in abstract is based.[29]

Marx continues the discussion by pointing out that 'quite apart from this crude tearing apart of production and distribution and of their real relationship' one can also generalize about distribution. 'For example, the slave, the serf and wage labourer all receive a quantity of food which makes it possible for them to exist as slaves, as serfs, as wage labourers.'[30] Marx is thus criticizing a conception of the economy in which production always obeys general laws common to all forms of production but where distribution is specific ('production in general plus a specific distribution of income'). His point is that one cannot separate production from distribution and, furthermore, if the laws of production form a generality, so can the laws of distribution.

Next Marx takes up the question of the moments or elements of production:

> The obvious, trite notion: in production the members of society appropriate (create, shape) the products of nature in accord with human needs; distribution determines the proportion in which the individual shares in the product; exchange delivers the particular product into which the individual desires to convert the portion which distribution has assigned to him; and finally, in consumption the products become objects of gratification, of individual appropriation.[31]

He continues by stating that these segments of the economy form a 'regular syllogism': production is the generality, distribution and exchange the particularity, and consumption the singularity in which the whole is combined. Marx grants that this scheme is indeed coherent but states that it is shallow.[32]

Marx is judging the above conception of the economy (as consisting of three or four interlocking segments) in the same way as he treats the idea of 'production in general' discussed above. In other words, this conception of the economy is at worst a tautology and at best a particularity.

In this conception, the economic 'whole' is split up into distinct phases; furthermore, these distinct stages form a linear chain leading from production to consumption, each phase naturally leading to the next one. It turns out that this conception is only applicable to certain particular forms of economy, e.g. 'Robinson Crusoe' types of self-sufficient communities, or what Marx identifies as a 'single subject'. Marx demonstrates the error of generalizing this conception to all economies by referring to Say,[33] for example, for whom 'when one looks at an entire people, its production is its consumption'.[34]

The problem with this conception is that while it attempts to produce a coherent picture of the economy consisting of phases and moments, this coherence suffers from two closely related shortcomings. First, the division between moments does not follow any logic, i.e. it is arbitrary. In reality it is a unitary process divided up into phases in the same way as one may divide an assembly line into arbitrary stages. The distinction between phases merely 'exists' but is not essential. An essential division would involve autonomy and independent activity for each moment. Second, the coherence presumes a strict one-way causation running from production to consumption (or vice versa).

I shall now examine whether Marx is able to offer an alternative view that avoids these pitfalls. Closely following the above discussion on the relationship between production and consumption, Marx states:

> With a single subject, production and consumption appear as moments of a single act . . . In society, however, the producer's relation to the product, once the latter is finished, is an external one, and its return to the subject depends on his relations to other individuals. He does not come into possession of it directly. Nor is its immediate appropriation his purpose when he produces in society. Distribution steps between the producers and the products . . .[35]

Marx now turns to distribution:

> In the shallowest conception, distribution appears as the distribution of products, and hence as further removed from and quasi-independent of production. But before distribution can be the distribution of products, it is: (1) the distribution of instruments of production, and (2), which is a further specification of the same relation, the distribution of the members of society among different kinds of production.[36]

Marx is attempting to overcome the separation between production and distribution by grounding distribution firmly in the conditions of production. But, more significantly, distribution is placed at the very root of production itself. For example, Marx mentions Ricardo, 'whose concern was to grasp the specific social structure of modern production, and who is the economist of production *par excellence*'. Yet Ricardo believed that 'not production but distribution is the proper study of modern economics'.[37]

Thus distribution is not only not separate from production but is a determinant factor of the nature of production itself. Based on Marx's earlier discussion of production, it is obvious that distribution, like production, is either a totality or a part of a totality. John Stuart Mill considers distribution to be specific to each particular society while conceiving production as having laws that are common to all societies. Marx's criticism is that Mill's specific distribution is based on a more fundamental distribution that goes to the heart of production. It is obvious that Marx is 'enlarging' and deepening the concept of production to include distribution: 'The question of the relationship between this production-determining distribution, and production, belongs evidently within production itself.'[38] This clearly confirms that the second concept of distribution is subsumed under production itself; as a result, the concept of production itself has been widened and deepened to include distribution. Marx explains the nature of the relationship between production and distribution in the following way. He says that if it is claimed that 'since production must begin with a certain distribution of the instruments of production', this means that distribution has precedence over production. Marx opposes this argument by declaring that 'production does indeed have its determinants and preconditions, which form its moments'. Thus production, considered not as an empty generality or a particular but as a totality, has its moments, e.g. distribution. But how does distribution (or any 'determinants' and 'pre-conditions') that may historically precede a given system of production become a moment of it?

> At the very beginning these may appear as spontaneous, natural. But by

> the process of production itself they are transformed from natural into historic determinants, and if they appear to one epoch as natural presuppositions of production, they were their historic product for another. Within production itself they are constantly being changed. The application of machinery, for example, changed the distribution of instruments of production as well as of products. Modern large-scale landed property is itself a product of modern commerce and of modern industry, as well as the application of the latter to agriculture.[39]

Thus the process of the production itself determines whether or not a 'natural' pre-condition of production becomes a 'historic', specific moment of the totality. Marx conceives the relationship between production as a totality and its moments in the following way. He says that distribution, exchange, consumption, and so on, 'all form the members of a totality, distinctions within a unity':

> Production predominates not only over itself, in the antithetical definition of production, but over the other moments as well. The process always returns to production to begin anew. That exchange and consumption cannot be predominant is self-evident. Likewise, distribution as distribution of products; while as distribution of the agents of production it is itself a moment of production. A definite production thus determines a definite consumption, distribution and exchange as well as definite relations between these different moments. Admittedly, however, in its one-sided form, production itself is determined by the other moments.[40]

In this remarkable passage, every concept finds a double determination. Distribution is explicitly defined in two ways, i.e. as distribution of products and of means of production among agents: it is in the latter sense that distribution is a 'moment' of production. Clearly this is a distinction between production-determined and production-determining distribution. Furthermore, production itself leads a double existence, i.e. production in its 'antithetical definition' or its 'one-sided form', i.e. material production (the labour process), and as the totality, which is the predominant factor. So far it is clear that production in the latter sense is defined as the totality which determines its own constituent parts as well as the relations among them. What about exchange and consumption? Marx admits that these in fact determine production in its one-sided form. But can we find a determining role for these moments, similar to distribution—an autonomy in relation to the totality? Marx is silent on this question. These asymmetries in Marx's treatment can be represented as in Diagram 1. If these asymmetries are removed, however, then we have a more consistent, coherent and symmetric system as shown in Diagram 2.

The system presented in Diagram 2 shows what I call Marx's complexity model (or C-model for short). In this model, all the elements of the economy appear at two different levels. At level i, these elements are active and determine the totality. At level ii, they are passive and are determined by the totality.

My interpretation can be justified on the following grounds. If production is defined as a system that includes production in the narrow sense, with the distribution, exchange and consumption of products as passive elements, then the totality is abstract (empty) or it is a particular. On the other hand, if every element is allowed the possibility of some degree of autonomy or independent activity, then the totality is no longer abstract but concrete. For example, based on Marx's earlier reference to how changes in the application of machinery changed the distribution both of instruments and of the products, one can say that production in the narrow sense (as in this example), and exchange and consumption as well, are each capable of changing the distribution of the instruments of production and thereby influencing production as a totality. This is the only way to escape a one-sided interpretation based on a fixed opposition between 'parts' and the 'whole' which leads to the determination by wholes on the one hand and determination by parts on the other.

These conclusions raise an important methodological question concerning the relationship between the general and the particular. In the analytical (as opposed to the dialectical) conception, there is a fixed opposition between particularity and generality. This opposition takes many forms. For example, science may be characterized as dealing with general as opposed to particular concepts; or the beginning of a science may be characterized as a concrete as opposed to an abstract object.

The discussion so far has demonstrated that Marx's text precisely problematizes this fixed opposition. Thus one form of generality is turned into its opposite and is characterized as a particular, while particular moments of the social whole are elevated to the position of universality. From this it is clear that Marx is trying to overcome this abstract opposition by positing a higher degree of generality that not only does not stand in opposition to particularities but can only exist in active relation with them.

It will be recalled that in the C-model the elements of the totality appear in two opposing functions, i.e. as active elements (subjects) and as passive elements (objects). The latter were identified with the 'common element' represented by a one-sided abstraction, i.e. the historical 'constant' which

Diagram 1

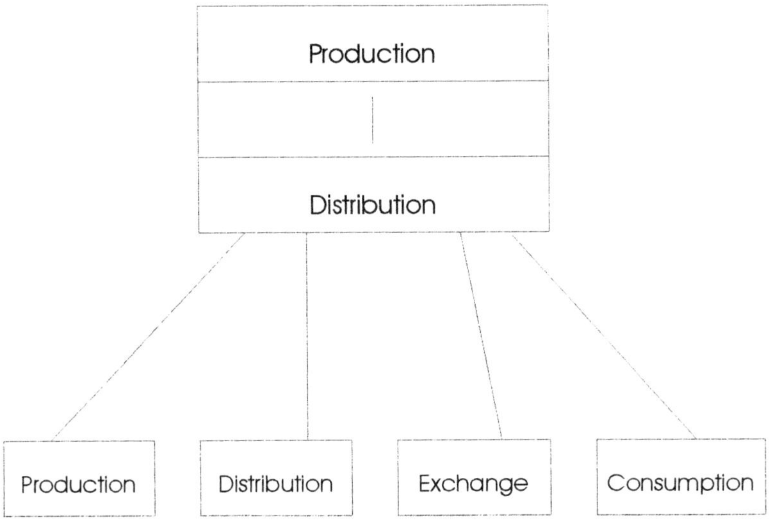

Diagram 2

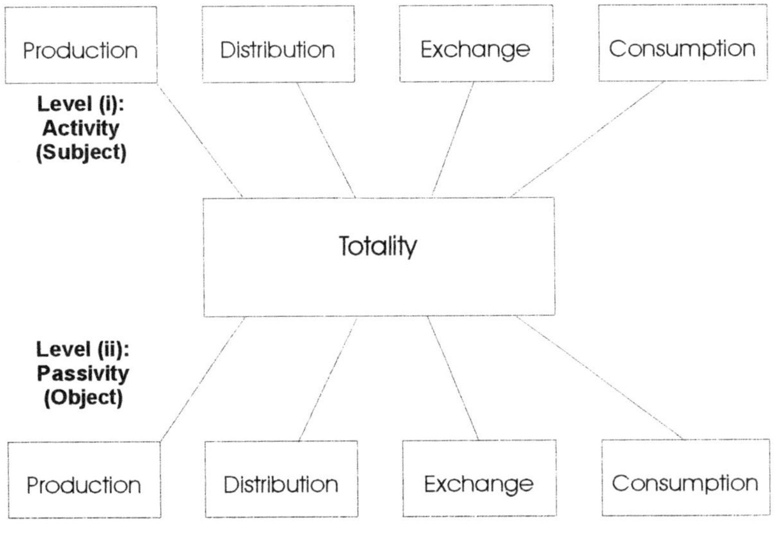

Diagram 3

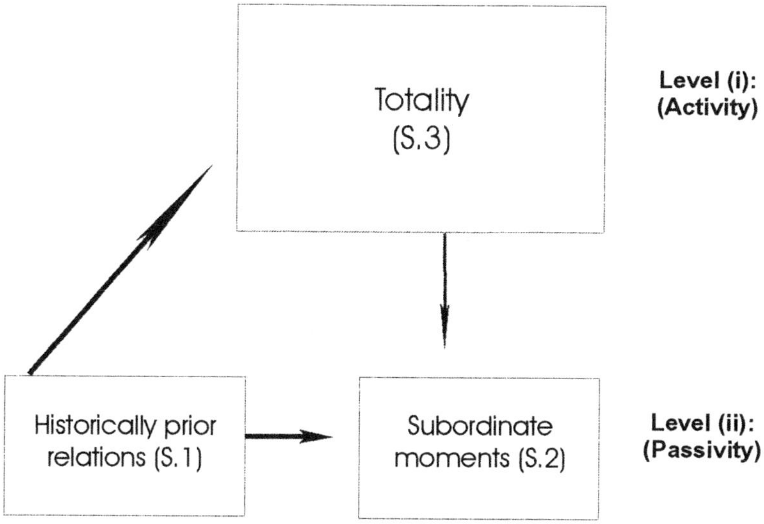

is a particular (if not empty) and not a true universal. The former were identified with activity, subjectivity and autonomy, approaching an identity with the totality itself. Turning to the S-model, we can see that S.3 represents the concrete totality and thus LEVEL 1 of the C-model. It is also clear that from relations represented by S.1 there is a double transformation. On the one hand, the historically prior relationship is elevated to the status of a determining moment of the whole (S.3) and, on the other, it is reproduced as a subordinate and passive element (S.2).

We have seen how Marx's analysis in effect problematizes the fixed opposition between generality and particularity; and then how the rigid opposition between simplicity and complexity, the abstract and the concrete, and the beginning and the end product of scientific activity, are similarly problematized. Here I wish to compare the duality model presented above with the threefold determination of simple concepts in the S-model. Diagram 3 is a representation of this relationship.

Thus the S-model and the C-model represent the same theoretical framework at the heart of Marx's analysis of capital and capitalist development. I shall now try to demonstrate this point by some examples from *Capital I*.

According to the mechanistic conception of historical materialism,[41] it is the growth of productive forces that prompts the development of new social relations of production, which conform to the new level of productive forces, via a revolutionary process that dismantles the old economic structure and social superstructure. This conception has all the hallmarks of the mechanistic-analytical approach that ruled some of the physical sciences wholly or partly until the last three decades or so (i.e. until the rise of the chaos and complexity theories) and has also come to dominate most of the social sciences, particularly in the twentieth century. Thus it involves a mechanistic division of the social whole into fixed and rigid parts and components; a linear, one-way relation of causality from forces to relations of production; and the complete analytical separation of historical modes of production from each another. For example, it denies that new relations of production in a new mode of production or elements of the superstructure can be traced to older modes of production. Yet according to Marx, commodity production and capital relation, as well as wage labour (at least as S.1 concepts) predate capitalism. The same can be said about laws, democracy, ideology, and so on.

Marx's analysis of capitalist development in *Capital I* is anything but mechanistic. Thus it is clear that the whole period of mercantile capital and the corresponding mercantilist policies during the period from the sixteenth to the eighteenth century involved rapid capitalist development and the accumulation of capital without any major technological breakthroughs. It is true that productive forces were improving, for example in agriculture, navigation and shipping. However, some of these improvements had started centuries earlier in China and the Middle East as well as in Europe. This period can be identified as a period of co-evolution of the forces and relations of production, a period in which, by and large, capitalist relations of production were adapting and shaping old forces of production (i.e. the introduction of the putting-out system, its replacement later by large manufactures, and eventually the introduction of the division of labour within workshops) rather than revolutionizing them. Thus the relation between forces and relations of production was much more complicated than a one-way process of causation.

Cultural, social and political revolutions (the Renaissance, the Reformation and the English, American and French revolutions) all occurred before the industrial revolution. Thus both capitalist relations of production and superstructure were more or less in place before the massive growth in productive forces brought about by the industrial revolution. Although the introduction of large-scale, machine-based production, according to Marx, gave capitalism its own independent technical foundation, the further development of capitalism also involved a process of mutual adaptation and co-evolution. All that can be said here is that after the industrial revolution this co-evolution became more internal, necessary and secure (as opposed to the external, almost contingent co-evolution before the industrial revolution). The following two examples from *Capital I* should help to clarify these points.

1. *The technical and social division of labour.* While Adam Smith had a single concept of the division of labour based on the technical division of labour, which he identified with the social division of labour, Marx clearly distinguishes between the two concepts. While the social division of labour involves the production and exchange of commodities (the market), no commodities are exchanged within the sphere of the technical division of labour. In spite of his sharp distinction between the two systems, Marx analyses capitalist development in terms of the co-evolution and mutual symbiosis of the two. Even Smith was aware of the relation between the two: he declared that the extent of (technical) division of labour was limited by the extent of the market (social division). We may add that the expansion of the market is itself limited by the extent of the technical division of labour. Marx shows, for example, how the more detailed division of labour in the factory leads to the creation of entirely new branches of production, i.e. a technical division creating ever new possibilities for greater social division. On the other hand, greater social division and market expansion make further technical division possible. Thus, far from a one-way relation of causation from productive forces (technical division) to relations of production (social division), we have a non-linear (almost circular) relationship between the two. I say 'almost circular' because the interrelations of the two levels fit the C-model above in the sense that technical and social divisions assume an active role one at a time, while the other is passively responding.[42]

2. *The formal and real subsumption of labour under capital.* These two concepts play an important part in Marx's analysis of capitalist development. While formal subsumption is associated with the absolute form of surplus value, real subsumption obtains when the relative form of surplus value is extracted. Marx calls real subsumption the specifically capitalist mode of production, and the associated form of relative surplus value the specific and characteristic form of capitalist exploitation. The apparently curious thing is that while Marx credits Ricardo with having discovered the latter form of surplus value, he accuses him of not understanding it.[43] This apparently contradictory view is only so from the standpoint of analytical thinking, however. Based on either the S-model or the C-model, Marx's critique of Ricardo makes perfect sense. Marx often describes absolute form as the 'foundation' or the 'starting-point' of

capitalist development. At the same time, he states that absolute form is sometimes found alongside relative form. Furthermore, he intimates that absolute form functions as a vehicle of transition from non-capitalist to capitalist forms of production.

Absolute surplus value as S.1 refers to early forms, the starting-point of capitalist production, when, for example, 'handicraftsmen who previously worked on their own account, or as apprentices of master, should become wage-labourers under the direct control of a capitalist'. Here 'a merely formal subsumption of labour under capital suffices for the production of absolute surplus value'.[44] The subsumption is formal because it is contingent, i.e. workers can easily disengage from capitalist production as they still possess their skills or perhaps even their instruments.

Absolute surplus value as S.2 refers to a form that continues to exist after capitalism has become the dominant social form of production. If the capitalist mode of production is the dominant (but not exclusive) form of production, the extension of the capitalist mode to non-capitalist branches of production normally begins with the extraction of absolute surplus value. Certain enterprises, or even sectors, may continue this method for a long time. During the industrial revolution large-scale industry depended heavily on this method. The production of absolute surplus value may thus be viewed as a transitional form under capitalism.

Absolute surplus value as S.3 refers to a form that is the very foundation of the capitalist system, which explains why the relative form becomes dominant at a certain stage of capitalist development. Thus without a theory of absolute form, the relative form does not make any sense:

> The prolongation of the working day . . . is the process which constitutes the production of absolute surplus value. It forms the general foundation of the capitalist system, and the starting-point for the production of relative surplus value. The latter presupposes that the working day is already divided into two parts, necessary labour and surplus labour. In order to prolong the surplus labour, the necessary labour is shortened by methods of producing the equivalent of the wage of labour in shorter time.[45]

Thus the same dialectic that we observed earlier in the case of simple circulation applies here as well. The forms of surplus value cannot be artificially separated from each other. We see a double transformation of absolute form as the 'starting-point', or even pre-capitalist form of exploitation (S.1) to absolute surplus value as a transitional or subordinate form under capitalism on the one hand, and its progression via the relative form to the very essence and foundation of the capitalist exploitation of labour on the other.

Conclusion

I have attempted to demonstrate that the concepts of simplicity and complexity and their relation are fundamental ingredients in Marx's method. Now that these same concepts have become fundamental to the physical sciences, it is high time that the social sciences took dialectics more seriously. As stated in the Introduction, towards the end of the nineteenth century, the social sciences (especially economics) turned to a mechanical paradigm that was slowly being abandoned by the physical sciences. After the Second World War, the 'mathematization' not only of economics but also of sociology, psychology and even economic history further deepened the mechanistic paradigm in social science. Even in the traditionally non-analytical areas of research by Marxist scholars such as value theory, the increasing use of analytical methodology became pronounced (the rise of Ricardian and analytical Marxism).[46] The distancing of economics and the other social sciences from Hegel, Marx and even the classical tradition has complex historical, social and ideological roots. Whatever the reasons, it has cost the social sciences dearly in that a whole century was wasted in the process of a regression to analytical methodology. Perhaps now with the end of the Cold War, the increasing concern over environmental degradation (mainly caused by what I call 'analytical practice', i.e. the modern development of industrial capitalism) and the triumph of dialectics in complexity research, some of the historical, social and ideological reasons behind the banishment of dialectics from the social sciences will begin to wither away.

13. Hegemony and Politics

Ernesto Laclau

The present chapter contains a series of reflections on the category of hegemony which, in my view, is the central category in the understanding of politics. I shall first offer some theoretical observations about what is distinctive in relationships of hegemony. Then in the second part of the chapter, I shall comment on the history of hegemony within the Marxist tradition.

Let us begin with one approach in which all the elements are given for a hegemonic conception of politics to arise, but in which the very bases of this possibility are systematically undermined. I am referring to Hobbes.

The structure of Hobbes' argument consists in showing how, if we start from the true anarchy of the state of nature, there is only one possible form of stable order for the community. Hobbes asserts, first, that in the state of nature there is a war of all against all. And second, that in that condition, the only possibility of permanent order is the concentration of power in the hands of Leviathan. The important point in this approach is that power appears divided from the very beginning because while, on the one hand, Leviathan imposes a certain order, on the other, he represents the *only* possibility of order as such. That is to say that as far as he imposes order, it does not matter what the content of that order is. Hobbes is not concerned with ethical good order for the community. He is only concerned with the possibility of order as such, because what underlies his whole argument is the realization that when people are confronted with a situation of radical disorder, any order will do. The need for order is far more important than the content of that order. So we have two elements: the concrete order imposed by Leviathan, and the fact that what is being imposed is order as such, order in general. Thus there is a basic ontological/differential split in the constitution of any political content. We can say (I return to this below) that for Hobbes all political relations, as a result of that split, consist in giving material content to what we can call an 'empty signifier'.

For example, if we compare Hobbes' conception with that of Plato, we apparently have the opposite view. For Plato there is nothing like an order in general that differs from a concrete content. On the contrary, the very possibility of order is linked to an absolutely determined content, to the point that even the number of inhabitants of the city has to be determined from the start. So in Plato we have an absolutely full content determining the possibility of the community as such; whereas in Hobbes we have an absolute emptiness of the notion of order separated from any particular content. But if we examine the matter more closely, we will see that what Plato and Hobbes share is more important than what separates them. What they share is the fact that politics is impossible as the basis of a communitarian order. For Plato, politics is a matter of knowledge. The philosopher-king is he who knows what is good order. For Hobbes, it is the emptiness of the content of power and its concentration in the hands of the ruler that removes the possibility of politics. So how do we move from this emptying-out of politics to a social arrangement in which politics becomes possible? It is this road which will lead us to the notion of hegemony.

The Hobbesian construction is based on a premise which is the cornerstone of his logical argument, namely that in the state of nature all men have to be equal. There is no difference in power between men in the state of nature, because even if some are physically stronger than others, the others can make an alliance and defeat them. Thus in the final analysis, differences in power are irrelevant and can be discounted. This assumption is central to Hobbes' argument: if this assumption were not there as part of the definition of the state of nature, then differences in power between individuals would create the possibility of a social order based on a societal differentiation of power previous to the establishment of the commonwealth. In such a case, political order could not be concentrated exclusively in the hands of Leviathan. If we modify this Hobbesian assumption, we reach a completely different conclusion without renouncing anything of the Hobbesian analysis.

Let us suppose that there is a differentiation of power in the state of nature. In that case, society will be able to regulate itself, to a certain extent, independently of the constitution of an entirely separate sphere of politics. In other words, the political sphere would still be necessary, because civil society is incapable of ultimate self-regulation, but it is capable of *some* regulation, to give itself *some* order; and in that sense, the demands that civil society will present to its ruler will be much more determined. It is no longer true that because we start from a situation of total disorder, any order will do. Because we are now able to give ourselves a certain order, our demands to the ruler will not only be demands for order as such, but will also impose on that ruler a certain content. If we conceive of society as having achieved a certain relative social order in which the two hypotheses of total organization and total anarchy never obtain, we will have signifiers of power, signifiers of communal order, which at any moment in time will be given a certain content. This process by which a certain particular content within the community, at some point, assumes a function of representation of the communal order in general is exactly what I call hegemonic relations.

Here I should like to give an example that I have often used in my work. In Italy in the early 1920s, at the moment of fascism's accession to power, it was common for people to say that the fascists had succeeded in carrying out the revolution in which the communists had failed. What is the justification for this assertion? There is apparently none, because the two revolutions—the fascist and the communist—would have had completely different contents. So what made such an expression acceptable? It was simply that since the end of the war, all Italians saw that the state that had emerged from the *Risorgimento* (the unification of Italy) was disintegrating and that some kind of radical re-foundation or reconstruction of the political order was needed. In such conditions, revolution meant this radical re-foundation, and whether it was carried out by fascists or communists was, to some extent, a secondary question. This can be seen, among other things, in the fact that during this period there was a far from negligible exchange of personnel between the fascist and communist camps. The idea of a radical, clean cut with the past was part of the collective imaginary. As in the case of Hobbes, we have an empty signifier, with the fullness of the community as that which is lacking. However, the process of linking this need for a certain fullness, for a certain order, to the programme of a concrete social force is the result of a contingent history, of a contingent struggle, which is precisely what I call a hegemonic struggle.

To summarize, the possibility of a politics of hegemony depends on the presence of empty signifiers which political forces then try to fix in one way or the other.

There are several aspects of the hegemonic relation that I consider to be central. When we try to think in hegemonic terms, all the classic categories of political theory will be deconstructed in one way or the other. I shall give two examples. The first is the notion of representation. Traditionally, representation has been conceived as a one-way relationship: we have a 'good' representation when the represented transmit their will to the representative and the representative does not change it. If we consider the matter more carefully, however, we will see that the relation of representation is always a two-way process. This is because the role of the representative, if representation is to be achieved, is not simply to transmit a will, but to express that will in a different medium from the one in which the will had been originally formulated. So what a representative should always do is to create a political language which eventually determines, in some part, the identity of the represented. This double movement (implicit in the relation of representation) is obviously a hegemonic movement, inasmuch as the new language tries to transform itself into an inscriptive surface in which very different demands will be discursively constructed. If we think, for example, of the situation in many Third World countries where civil society has been shattered, and where identities are being reconstructed at the political level, the role of the political leader is precisely to create these languages and to give the people some kind of identity, some possibility of calculating around interests which must be constructed in the first place. Thus the relation of representation presupposes this kind of hegemony displacement.

The second point arises in the relationship between power and emancipation. Whereas we see politics as a practice which cannot be superseded, the relationship between emancipation and power in classical 'liberationist' discourses was obviously a relation of mutual opposition. Emancipation was defined as the elimination of power. Is this a logical possibility, leaving aside the empirical possibility of actually realizing this liberation in the historical arena? I contend that it is not. What does it mean to be free? To be free is to be able to 'self-determine' oneself. For example, I am confronted with the need to take a decision, and if the decision is to be an entirely rational one, it is not me who takes the decision but a structure of rationality that precedes me. If there is an algorithmic answer, the same answer will be repeated by all men, and the very notion of decision loses its meaning. But if the solution to the problem is not an algorithmic one, I will have to decide without any ultimate foundation, and the other possible decisions are simply cancelled out of existence. If you want, I repress the latter. And if one passes from individual decisions to collective ones, and these collective decisions are not the result of algorithmic choices either, in that case this repression of alternative decisions becomes a relation of power. So the condition of being free is that power exists. We act to displace some relations of power, we act to overcome them, but this is always part of a process of creating power. This means, again, that the game of hegemony is inherent in any system of social relations. And it is good that this should be the case, because otherwise we would have reached an entirely reconciled society in which all decisions would be algorithmic. In that case, we would not have any kind of freedom except the obnoxious freedom of being conscious of necessity. Thus a free society and power require each other.

In conclusion, I shall now say something about the way in which the problem of hegemony has emerged in the Marxist tradition. Let us start with the genesis of this image of the community as a totality, which is at the root of the whole debate.

In Hegel's *Philosophy of Right*, civil society is the only realm of particularity. The possibility of universalizing the community as a totality depends on a separate field which is the political sphere. For Hegel, the universal class is the bureaucracy. Marx's critique of Hegel's philosophy of right consists in saying that this is not true: the state is not a separate sphere in which the universality of the community is realized; rather, it is an instrument of the dominant class and, as a result, is one more particular sphere. How can one arrive at a universality of the community, if this is the case? Only if at the very level of civil society there is a process by which universality emerges. The universal class for Marx is the proletariat. The point of view of universality emerges out of the endogenous movement of civil society, and this involves a separation of spheres between state and civil society. This means that society has to be more and more homogenous and the moment of emancipation has to coincide with the moment of the death of politics. It is the moment in which, to use the language of the Saint-Simonians, we will replace the government of men by the administration of things. The history of Marxism has largely been a continuous retreat from this original assumption and the progressive acceptance that class struggle, and in fact any historical struggle, takes place in a terrain which, far from becoming homogeneous, is increasingly complex and fragmented. Paul Hirst said once that the crisis of Marxism started in 1848, a view that I largely support.

I shall give two examples of the progressive emergence of the primacy of politics, which is the same thing, in my view, as the primacy of the logic of hegemony.

The first relates to the theory of combined uneven development. As is well known, the analysis made by Russian social democracy of the stages of development in that country asserted that Russia was advancing towards a bourgeois democratic revolution, but with the historical particularity that the bourgeoisie was incapable of carrying out its own tasks. In those conditions, it was argued, the tasks of democracy passed, to a large extent, from the bourgeoisie to the proletariat. This taking up of tasks from one class by another is what Axelrode[1] and Plekhanov[2] called hegemony.

The logic of the empty signifiers is already operative here, because the less that a democratic revolution is linked to a particular class, the less it has a particular content; it then becomes an empty requirement able to be hegemonized by different historical forces. During the period of the Third International, the analysis of what was called 'combined and uneven development'—that is, the dislocation of stages—was generalized to the entire Third World. The argument was that because of the universalization of conditions introduced by imperialism, countries had the possibility of jumping over stages and articulating social forces and social processes in a way that escaped the sequence of stages through which the Second International had conceived historical development. Trotsky was later to generalize this view by asserting that combined and uneven development —an abnormal combination of stages—is the very historical terrain in which contemporary social struggles take place.

At this point, one might reasonably ask the following question: if all historical development is abnormal development, what then is normal development? Clearly, we are moving here from a logic of the development of productive forces to a logic of the articulation between contingent political forces and contingent political processes. So we find again the logic of hegemony.

My second example relates to Gramsci. Gramcsi's starting-point was the realization that it was no longer possible to carry out revolution in the West following on the pattern of the Bolshevik revolution. Consequently the forces of socialism, in his view, were confronted by a far more complex process, for these societies were increasingly differentiated and a political revolutionary process could not be effected in a single act. This required the logic of articulation, which Gramsci called hegemony. For him, the historical subjects are not social classes but what he called 'collective wills', and these collective wills involve a microphysics of power: that is, a complex aggregation of forces by which elements which do not tend naturally to coalesce in a certain way, could be put together as a result of political initiatives. The vocabulary used by Gramsci at the time—hegemony, war of position, collective will, intellectual and moral reform, and so on—pointed to a logic of history which was profoundly different from that of classical Marxism.

From today's perspective, it is clear that there are limitations to Gramsci's historical vision: he was still assuming that the articulating force would always be a fundamental class in society, whereas the world as we know it today suggests that the very notion of class is a result of complex hegemony construction. Furthermore, Gramsci's vision was also limited in the sense that he thought that the arena of political struggle was limited to the classical terrain of class antagonisms. Today, we can generalize the area of operation of the logic of hegemony to many social fields, and this takes us onto the terrain of what has been called the microphysics of power. That is to say, we have a plurality of smaller aggregating centres producing partial effects and reaching, at the level of the collective imaginary, some higher form of re-aggregation. These forms of aggregation cannot, however, be related to any ultimate content because that content is continuously changing.

14. Marxism and Hope

Jonathan Rée

I have been in the habit of calling myself a Marxist for twenty years or more—ever since reading *Capital* and the *Grundrisse* as part of a serious and convivial 'Marx reading group' of the kind that flourished in Britain in the 1970s. However, I have recently had to face up to the question: what can I possibly mean by continuing to say that I am a Marxist? I was always, I suppose, a 'Western Marxist,' so I did not pin my socialist hopes on the future of Soviet communism, and the events of 1989 and afterwards were not a shattering disappointment to me. On the other hand, my admiration for Marx's way of analysing the capitalist mode of production was conceived in the context of a strong, if vague, conviction that Western capitalism could not survive for many years—and this has certainly turned out to be mistaken. Socialism, if it is defined as the attempt to eradicate the frustration and unhappiness, the poverty and inequality produced by capitalism, may still make sense as a utopian ideal, and also as a general policy orientation; but perhaps we ought to recognize that as far as Marxism is concerned, the game is up. We self-styled Marxists may not be able to change the habit of a lifetime, but when we are all dead, we may have no successors, and historians may look back on us as latter-day mesmerists or phrenologists: convinced devotees of doctrines which, in retrospect, seem so deluded that it is hard to see how anyone was ever seduced by them in the first place.

In fact, it may be even worse than that: it may turn out that Marxism as a political movement, whatever the intentions of its supporters, has in practice been overwhelmingly a force for evil. As far as the Arab world is concerned, it can be argued (as it has been by Fred Halliday) that the main legacy of Marxism is Islamism, with its calls for 'revolution' against the encroaching forces of 'liberalism', 'consumerism' and 'the West'. The populations of the former Soviet Union, of Eastern Europe and of China have little reason to be grateful to Marxism either. And as for Marxism in Western Europe: it may be that if it had not existed, then fascists and nazis would never have come to power, and the holocaust and the Second World War would not have occurred. Marxism, it seems, may have a lot of blood on its hands.

Nor do recent attempts to 'reconstruct' Marxism help. The ideals of 'radical democracy' (of the kind discussed by John Mepham) may be admirable, but it is hard to see how they differ from those of the radical liberals who always regarded Marxism as an aberration. There is little point in calling them 'post-Marxist', unless post-Marxism simply means a doctrine that people happen to have adopted after ceasing to be Marxists. The same applies to the argument (made, for example, by Ernesto Laclau) that classes and other historical agents should be analysed in terms of the 'articulation of contingent forces' rather than by reference to their real relation to the means of production: if this is true, then Marxist analysis was always completely mistaken and needs to be ended, not transformed.

Marxism, then, is undoubtedly caught up in a crisis. But I want to suggest that it is a crisis not specifically of Marxism, but of politics in general, or rather of a certain conception of politics—what might be called the *modernist* conception of politics. Alternatively, one might call it a crisis of *politicism*, that is to say, the habit of seeing politics as the essential hidden truth behind everything, rather as old-fashioned psychoanalysts see sexual secrets everywhere. Under the influence of this idea that 'everything is political', the meaning of the word 'politics' has expanded during the twentieth century, so that instead of referring specifically to affairs of state and party, it now covers all aspects of personal life and social organization, especially those having to do with 'power'. (The fact that 'power' and 'politics' both begin with the same two letters of the alphabet seems to have encouraged a superstitious association between the two.) And this shift in meaning is not a neutral linguistic development; it also entails a confusing conceptual elision between specifically political processes on the one hand, and social issues on the other. The effect is similar to that of using 'academic' as a synonym for 'intellectual', rather than for referring specifically to the procedures of schools and universities—a habit which tends to obscure the fact that intellectual forces may well be in contradiction with the special discursive forms of the academy. The danger of what I would call 'the fetishism of politics' is that it may, analogously, make us forget the possibility that social forces can contradict the forms of politics, or be hidden and distorted by them.

Base and Superstructure

It may seem strange to suggest that Marxism is caught up in a fetishistic overestimate of the scope and importance of politics. After all, the distinction between the 'economic base' and the 'ideological forms' which constitute the 'legal and political superstructure' has been expounded with tedious insistence in elementary courses on Marxism ever since it first became a political movement. The texts in which it is formulated—the *Communist Manifesto* in 1848 and the 1859 *Preface* to the *Contribution to the Critique of Political Economy*—must be the best known of all Marx's writings, and their meaning is perfectly clear: that 'legal relations' and 'political forms', far from being autonomous agents of historical change, are dependent upon 'material conditions of life' over whose development they have practically no influence.

Nevertheless, all the way from Engels to Godelier, Marxists have kept coming back to the doctrine of base and superstructure as if it were the greatest of enigmas. Despite its familiarity and clarity, the 1859 *Preface* has proved to be a profoundly unstable text. Part of the reason is that the programme it suggests is not one that Marx himself adhered to in his own theoretical practice. *Capital* is devoted to political economy, but instead of treating it as an 'ideological form', Marx sought to establish directly the extent to which it provided an adequate 'anatomy', as he puts it in the *Preface*, of the 'economic structure of society'. (The first systematic Marxist attempt at a base–superstructure explanation of legal and political forms, apart from the sketch in the *Communist Manifesto*, is probably Engels' *Origin of the Family, Private Property and the State*, which was published in 1884, a year after Marx's death.)

Given this destabilizing context, the base–superstructure theory has always been open to a kind of double interpretation, and it is precisely this doubleness which explains its canonical status in the history of Marxism. Like religious scriptures, it offers both a public exoteric meaning and a secret esoteric one. In particular, it divides would-be Marxist believers into two groups: a laity of Vulgar Marxists, who are said to impose a 'mechanistic' or 'mechanical' distortion on the Marxist approach to history, and a priesthood of True Marxists, who are able to discern an esoteric 'dialectical' meaning wrapped up inside the exoteric one. Vulgarly, the *Preface* is taken as saying that the superstructure is entirely dependent on the base; but Truly, it is interpreted as meaning that, under the right circumstances, the superstructure—especially political activity—may take command.

The distinction between 'mechanistic' and 'dialectical' interpretations of the base–superstructure distinction has a remarkable history. It was used, for example, by the Third International in order to denounce the Second: the distinctive principle of Leninism, Stalinism or Maoism, or indeed of Gramscism, was always said to lie in their claim that authentic Marxism is really about the primacy of 'practice'—usually identified unquestioningly with politics—rather than about the 'economic base'. But Trotskyists accused the Third International of precisely the same 'mechanistic' and 'economistic' deviation; and 'humanist' Western Marxists laid exactly the same charge against communist theory as a whole: that unlike authentic Marxism, it obliterated the role of politics (or more generally, ideology and consciousness) in the historical process.

Anxiety, Certainty and Political Activism

The ambiguities that have been read into the 1859 *Preface*, apart from serving to fix a certain distance between the politically uninitiated and the party elite, have had the further and more positive function of making room for a graduated presentation of the problem of historical action. The 'mechanistic' interpretation of the base–superstructure model fitted in with a deterministic, even fatalistic, view of historical change. The first principle of this interpretation is that history is essentially the history of modes of production, and of the class divisions to which they give rise. Next it is asserted that every pre-capitalist and capitalist mode of production has only a limited lifespan, because it allows productive forces to expand to the point where they can no longer be contained within existing relations of production. Finally, it is inferred that socialism is bound eventually to come to pass, if only because all other historical options will have been exhausted, and socialism, as the only fully stable mode of production, must eventually triumph and then endure to the end of historical time. It follows from all this that, in the words of the *Communist Manifesto*, 'the fall [of the bourgeoisie] and the victory of the proletariat are equally inevitable'.[1] And since socialism was bound to come about, there was no point in resisting it; all you could do was jump onto the socialist bandwagon and look forward to the certainty of ending up on history's winning side.

Once you began to be initiated into a Marxist political movement, however, the esoteric dialectical meaning of the doctrine of base and superstructure would be revealed and you would learn that, despite all you had heard before about how large-scale historical forces were making the transition to socialism inevitable, political action, or rather activism, was urgently required of you in order to bring socialism about.

In this way, the issue of base and superstructure has sustained a dilemma between 'senile' economistic fatalism on the one hand and 'infantile' politicist voluntarism on the other. This tension between ultimate assurance of victory and immediate anxiety about failure, though perhaps a weakness from a purely theoretical point of view, is clearly a strength from the point of view of political organization: it provides a potentially compelling spur to committed activism, of a kind which is a necessity for any mass movement, whether Marxist or not. After all, no one would make the sacrifices involved in being a political activist without some reasonably solid confidence that political action would eventually alter the course of history, even if it might not bear fruit for several generations.

Marxism and Historicism

As a mass political movement, Marxism has always needed to be able to set its activities within a wide-angled theory of historical change. It has also required an assurance that such change is, by and large, and taking a broad perspective, change for the better; and that the succession of epochs, and especially the imagined transition from capitalism to socialism, is in some way progressive. It is by postulating that the forces of history are on the same side as the ideals of socialism (or communism: I am not making any distinction between them here) that Marxism has mobilized mass militant activism for the socialist cause. Behind their debates over base and superstructure, therefore, Marxist movements have always agonized over another issue: that of meaning and purpose in history—in short, the question of historicism, or rather (since the term may be ambiguous) *teleological historicism*. Historicism in this sense is the idea that history has a definite shape, that it is a journey leading to a clear *telos* or destination, and that this destination will eventually justify or redeem the sacrifices made by progressive movements along the way. This is the sense in which Marxist movements have always postulated socialism as the end towards which human history is moving—an end which, as Marx put it, 'is the solution to the riddle of history and knows itself to be the solution'.[2]

But how is such historicism to be justified? Why should anyone suppose that the fulfilment of socialist hopes is the ultimate end of history? It will be remembered that in the 1859 *Preface* Marx describes political economy as providing the 'anatomy' of modes of production. He also claims (in the *Grundrisse*) that 'human anatomy contains a key to the anatomy of the ape'.[3] These references suggest that applications of evolutionary biological theory to economic development may provide Marxism with the desired assurance that historical processes are leading inexorably to socialism. (And it seems very probable that some such theory can be applied to certain historical transitions, especially in the context of Darwinism and neo-Darwinism.)[4] Such a theory, however, does not show that more evolved kinds of social arrangement are necessarily preferable (in terms of justice and morality or even prosperity) to less evolved ones; and it is very unlikely to point to socialism as the terminus of historical progress. It therefore lacks the capacity to motivate political activity that Marxist movements require from a theory of history.

The only kind of historicism that could answer the needs of a Marxist movement is one that tries to show that human action always essentially, if unconsciously, strives towards the realization of socialist ideals, so that a socialist movement can be conceived as simply helping and guiding human history in the journey it is embarked on in any case. Such a theory was evolved by Sartre in the *Critique of Dialectical Reason*,[5] which distinguishes between two interpretations of Marx's theory of historical progress: that of the external and the internal dialectic. The external version—which would include any attempt to compare social history with biological evolution—sees historical processes as governed by laws of history, just as particles are governed by laws of nature. Sartre regarded this as an Engelsian distortion, and politically stultifying. On the internal interpretation, the Marxist dialectic holds that the whole of human history is to be understood as an outcome of human actions, that is to say, processes in which people seek to bring the world into conformity with the future as they imagine and desire it to be. In practice, of course, human actions are 'mediated' by each other, by institutions and by nature so that they often do not achieve the goals to which they are directed; but the idea is that, other things being equal, the eventual outcome of all these projects will be a society that corresponds more closely to the abstract human desire for freedom—in which case socialism appears, just as Marxist movements need it to, as internally connected with the very nature of history.

Politics and Hope

The point of Sartre's interpretation of history was to rescue the idea that human activity is collectively progressing in the direction of socialism from the metaphysical and quasi-theological notion that human history is bound to conform to an externally specified programme. Sartre's idea that history develops according to a dialectic which is internal to human action is meant to show how there can be an overall process of 'totalization' in history, without presupposing any transcendent power pulling history towards a predestined goal. One might also describe it as offering the prospect of a teleology with no undischarged debts to theology. It is meant to provide, as Sartre puts it, a conception of 'totalization without a totalizer'.

Sartre realized, however, that the 'internal dialectic' as he conceived it came nowhere near to proving that socialist struggles are bound to be crowned with success; and many critics have argued that even Sartre's attenuated kind of historicism is compromised by its reliance on concepts of humanity, history and historical action which are really just old theological themes in disguise.

The general implausibility of socialist historicism, together with the decreasing popularity of socialism in the second half of the twentieth century, are the core of the 'postmodernist' (or 'postsocialist') challenge to Marxism. In the form in which it is usually expressed, however, the challenge is one that Marxists have not been obliged to take seriously: indeed, they can take it as supporting the distinctively Marxist strand of the socialist tradition. The indisputable fact that most of the great socialist experiments of the last 100 years have been disappointments, if not disasters, conforms well enough with the Marxist idea that socialism cannot be achieved until the right conditions have been established. And the fact that ever fewer people are inclined to celebrate socialism even as an ideal does not mean that socialist values will not eventually triumph: after all, Marxists have never thought that values themselves could dictate large-scale historical change. Indeed, one could go further and argue, as Althusser would have done, that Marxist theory never required anything like a teleological theory of historical progress, or a general concept of human action, and that it will be healthier without them.

For these reasons among others, I never used to pay much attention to postmodernism and postsocialism. But I now think that was a mistake. The trouble is that, even if Marxist theory is unscathed by these challenges, the idea of a political movement animated by Marxism is extremely vulnerable to them. The problem is not a loss of theoretical credibility, but a loss of activist hope.

This crisis of hope affects political movements in general, and not just Marxist ones. Political movements are a phenomenon of modernity, and they presuppose a specific conception of politics—the 'modernist interpretation of politics', as I would call it. This was first worked out by Kant at the end of the eighteenth century. For Kant, politics was essentially a struggle for justice and enlightenment. This view of politics could also, of course, be found in Plato and Aristotle; but what made Kant's conception different was his argument that politics is essentially an expression of an inherent 'tendency and faculty in human nature for improvement'.[6] In other words, Kant was able to present politics as corresponding to an aspiration to justice, freedom and autonomy which was built into the structure of human existence as such, and which was progressively making itself manifest in the historical process itself.

The modernist interpretation of politics depends, then, upon a teleological and historicist fusion between political activity and historical hope: it is based on the idea that progressive political action is underwritten, in the long run, by the inherent progressiveness of human history as a whole. (One symptom of its pervasive influence is the obsessive concern with dates in politics. Whatever else it may be, a political movement must present itself to its supporters as up-to-date, or preferably a little ahead of its time: its rhetoric will be filled with heated but empty references to looking forward to the next century, not backwards to the last: that sense of time, one might say, is an intrinsic part of a politicist view of the world.)

Mourning and Tragedy

One of the most eye-catching phenomena of twentieth-century history has been the operation of mass political movements—some of them socialist, most of them nationalist, and many of them a mixture of the two—all of which have been based on the modernist interpretation of politics, with its fusion between political activity and historical hope. But on the other hand, there have also been far-reaching transformations (in particular, new organizations of the family, child care and sexuality, connected in complex ways with the transformation of techniques of production, communication, and information-processing, all set in the context of the intensification, extension and internationalization of markets) which have occurred without being led, inspired or informed by political movements of any kind. The manifest damage being suffered by the natural environment has also drawn attention to the fact that there are unalterable limits to social progress, which no amount of political organization can overcome.

Thus twentieth-century history, one might say, has issued repeated demonstrations of the hubristic vanity of politicism. In the light of these, much Marxist political activity turns out to have been (if not cynical and corrupt) essentially tragic, in the fullest sense of the concept of tragedy: noble, conscientious and intelligent actions, brought to terrible and self-destructive conclusions.

But this conclusion, paradoxically enough, conforms exactly with the plain meaning of what Vulgar Marxists have always taken to be the cornerstone of Marxism: the old doctrine of base and superstructure, according to which social transformations control politics, and not the other way round. If we take this statement at its face value, and not as a coded and paradoxical call to political activism, then it fits in with what I increasingly think of as the dominant theme of Marx's work as a whole—namely, its mood of sombre but wry stoicism, in the context of incomparably sharp-eyed analyses of the opacity and intractability of social processes. A large portion of Marx's polemical energy, after all, was devoted to ridiculing those of his fellow socialists (all of them, it sometimes seems) who imagined that a transition to socialism would be quick and easy; the whole of his social analysis, in fact, tends to show that nothing could be more foolish than the attempt to create a socialist society by an act of political will. There is a need, I think, for a book in praise of Marxism with the title, *Karl Marx: Pessimist*.

Marxist political movements, however (unlike Marx's purely theoretical legacy), have always presupposed epistemological and historical optimism. They have assumed that, with the help of intelligent and theoretically informed political activism, things are bound to get better for everyone, in due course. The reality has been, however, that even to the extent that human life is improving, politics has not usually had much to do with it. Political movements, both Marxist and non-Marxist, which have imagined themselves to be in control of history, or at least to have an indispensable role in guiding it in what they take to be its natural direction, have turned out to be systematically deluded if not fraudulent. As a result, politics is reverting by default to a pre-modern form (even if it is called postmodern), where its function is not so much to help existing social forces continue with their constructive and progressive work, as to prevent them from doing the most terrible damage. The whole structure of modern political hope is fractured, and one of the tasks for a pessimistic Marxist now is to work out how to mourn the end of a deluded hope; but also, of course, how to celebrate it.

15. Fewer Illusions, More Humility: Marxism, Culture and Politics

John Mepham

Marxism and Culture

For many people the main appeal of Marxism was that it expressed a system of values. It answered the question, 'What is it that makes life worth living?' and other questions such as, 'What should I do with my life? Who should I be? How am I to think about the urgent political and cultural questions of the day?' Marxism reminded people that there could be more to life than the tawdry, commodified pleasures offered by capitalist cultural production. It enabled one to resist the definition of human needs suggested implicitly by capital. Among the most sickening of the consequences of capitalism is that, over and above the material impoverishment it causes, it creates in its agents a tendency to lose sight of whatever it is that makes life worth living. Marxism acted as a constant reminder that things do not have to be like this and that one could feel proud of insisting on alternative forms of social life.

Obviously there were many different versions of these values and this sense of alternatives. We each have our own memories. If I think of Marxism as a culture, I think of the Fêtes de l'Humanité organized by the French Communist Party on the outskirts of Paris in the early 1970s. This was Marxism at its best (as long as you ignored, as the vast majority of people did, the men in suits in the Central Committee tent, who staged 'debates' on current political issues). The festivals were huge, bigger than Woodstock, but just as much a celebration of alternative cultures. Angela Davies would sweep by to the applause of the crowd. In one of the book tents Louis Althusser sat at a wooden table signing copies of his latest volume. Groups from Chile played Latin American folk music or Spanish political songs and Algerians sat around chatting about their literacy programmes or the time they went on a delegation to Beijing and shook hands with Chou Enlai. A long queue formed outside the huge marquee that housed the Picasso exhibition—at last, and after many absurd struggles with the *apparatchiks*, modernism had become a permitted form of art. Another long queue of patient, laughing people formed outside the lavatory tents where a sign invited you to 'Piss for the revolution, 10 cents.'

Marxism was never *only* a culture of alternatives and values, of course. There were two other central components, each with many variations, and each of which is now without credibility. Marxism was a *political project*, defined in terms of class, state and revolution ('the proletarian revolution'). It was also a *socio-economic project*—the aim was to socialize the economic activity of society. This meant replacing the anarchy of the market, of encounters on the market between individual producers of exchange value, as the method of regulation of the economic activity of society, by some method or methods of collective control and regulation. This would allow economic activity to be determined by the objective of the satisfaction of needs rather than the production of exchange values.

This second project also existed in conjunction with non-revolutionary models of politics, but it now seems that even these versions of socialism have (perhaps temporarily) lost credibility or viability. For example, in Sweden in the 1970s and early 1980s the project took the form of an intended incremental move towards the socialization of economic activity via 'workers' funds', created by taxes on profits, administered by trades unions and regulated by a social-democratic state. Why is it that even this version of socialism no longer seems to be on the agenda?

A Marxist would have to see this in terms of the development of capitalism itself. The conditions in which viable capitals now form and accumulate do not permit this sort of national system of constraints and regulations. Each national state has to create the conditions to attract international capital, and it has been beyond the resources of socialism in any of its forms to hold out against this and other aspects of globalization for any length of time without the massive loss of value of national currencies.

It is quite possible, if paradoxical, that the best broad analytical framework for examining the long-term shapes of capitalism's development may well be Marxism itself. The crucial aspects of this development are *globalization* and the *unmaking of the working class.* One of the strengths of Marxism was its insistence on seeing political possibility as rooted in the development of forces and relations of production. What we are now witnessing are developments in the forces of production (technical equipment, buildings, skills and knowledge, urban concentrations of population, communications systems, and so on) and in the relations of production (including all those ways in which capital organizes itself on a global scale through money markets, communications systems, the global spread of banking and of contract law, global labour markets, and so on) which undermine the conditions that gave Marx's political and socio-economic projects credibility at earlier stages in the history of capitalism. This credibility rested on two ideas: the control of the economy through some version of state planning; and the formation of a unified working class together with its culture and political instruments. The ways in which these ideas have been undermined are summed up in shorthand in the ideas of globalization and the unmaking of the working class. The political history of the Soviet Union and its satellites has also undermined the credibility of Marxist politics. These developments—over which, as Marx would have predicted, nobody has any control or even understanding—all combine to remove the material, historical basis of Marxist politics, or so it seems. It is as if Marxism itself could draw the outlines of a historical map and chart its own journey towards the point at which it ceases to have the capacity to identify politically possible alternative futures.

So what, if anything, survives of Marxism, or even more broadly of socialism? I shall quote two writers who have answered this question very concisely. The first quote comes from a discussion between the German philosopher Jürgen Habermas and two Polish thinkers, a discussion usefully entitled 'More Humility, Fewer Illusions'. Adam Krzeminski asks, 'You continue to stand up for progress and behave like a "believing optimist" . . . What remains of socialism?' Habermas replies:

> *Radical democracy* . . . I would add the rider that one thing we can still learn from the Marxist tradition today is the *critique of capitalism.* Indeed, this may be even more important today since capitalism has experienced a huge increase in self-confidence, thanks to the collapse of state socialism. Hardly anyone nowadays would venture to criticize capitalism. At the same time, we have 17 million unemployed in the European Union alone, and no one—and that includes me—has any idea how we are going to break out of the cycles of jobless growth. In other words, we need new ideas with which to criticize this system. But *the ultimate criterion must be the creation of a radical democracy* . . .

To which Adam Michnik, a leading Polish dissident under the old communist regime, answers, 'The way I would put it is that we are what we were thirty years ago, except that *we have lost our illusions and gained in humility.*'[1]

The second quote comes from a newspaper interview with John Berger in 1995. Berger has been an important cultural figure for many intellectuals in Britain, not only for his writings but also for the way that he has lived his life as a model of socialist values. He has always been an anti-Stalinist, and his work has displayed and continues to display what he calls his visceral solidarity with the less privileged. When reminded that he once defined his aim as to help, in however small a way, to destroy bourgeois society, he laughs and says:

> And look where that got us! But I stick with the principle although one has to change the term 'bourgeois'. Because what we live in now is no longer bourgeois. It's a kind of multinational network of free market and of profit. I think if one looks at this system, it is clearly not doomed by a proletarian revolution. I think it is probably doomed by its own internal contradictions. It is too narrow, too extremist. It denies too much and it creates such tensions on a world scale that something is going to crack. There are now, for example, 18 million unemployed in Europe and, even when the recession stops, there will still be 18 million unemployed.
>
> The system, as it is, has no solution. Every left-wing and right-wing politician in Europe would love to be able to deal with this. It is not out of heartlessness that they don't, but out of powerlessness. How long can such a situation go on? I don't like to speak like a prophet or a Cassandra. If I say this, it's out of a kind of *faith that so much of the human spirit and human potential is denied by the present system that I can't believe it can survive.*[2]

Although these writers are offering a European perspective on the problems of capitalism, these problems must seem just as destructive if seen from the point of view of the Arab world (though they may be expressed in significantly different forms).

What I take from these two discussions is the following: there is still an urgent need for a framework for the critique of capitalism, particularly a critique of its inability to satisfy even the most basic needs of millions of people, but also a critique of its cultural narrowness and impoverishment. In addition, there is now a vital need for a vocabulary in which to explore the possibility of alternatives, a vocabulary centred on the idea of the radicalization of democracy. What matters is to keep alive the possibility of the critique of capitalism and the exploration of the radicalization of democracy; what does not matter is whether the means for achieving these things are to be found within Marxism or anywhere else, just so long as they are found and kept alive.

What I find helpful in Marxism—perhaps because of my intellectual background and not because it is a unique source for these ideas—is twofold. First, it inculcates certain materialist habits of mind and, second, it offers a cluster of concepts with which one can start (but no more than start) to think about culture, politics and value.

Expanding Democracy

Marx's critique of capitalism circled around the ideas of *knowledge, control* and *needs*. The point of democracy is that people should be able to take control of the conditions of their own lives. This presupposes certain kinds of knowledge, and a certain distribution of knowledge in the population. Capitalism distorts both the development of knowledge and its distribution. A democractic socialist society would have quite different cultural objectives and a differently cultured population from a capitalist society—people would have different, richer and more reliable means of identifying needs as well as the means for bringing this knowledge to bear upon the social organization of economic activity. These three ideas, then—knowledge, control and needs—which underlie the idea of democracy, circle around and mutually clarify each other.

In practice, within Marxist traditions, both academic and political, there was a constant will to tie these ideas down, to forge clear and distinct versions of them, to theorize them. I now think that what is needed is quite the opposite: an effort to keep them open and flexible, to enable them to develop in piecemeal and chaotic, perhaps even contradictory, ways rather than in a coherent way. This is why Marxism can do no more here than get one started, and then the ideas have to be allowed to open up and go all over the place. The crucial point is to see that each of these terms is *open*; there is no single interpretation of them which is to be preferred in all contexts and they are constantly in need of re-invention. Within Marxism in practice they became fixed and frozen, by their association with a monolithically conceived political project or by their association with the institutions and methods of socio-economic planning.

Let us take the notion of 'control', for example. There is no one model of democratic control, no one form of democratic organization and participation which will be appropriate to all activities of collective control within a radically democratic society. So the idea of 'control' is more like an open agenda than a concept.

As for 'knowledge', there was within Marxism, with its Enlightenment heritage, a tendency to close down the idea of knowledge, to define what people would need by way of intellectual resources in terms of the models of science, technique and rational management or administration. Now it seems much better to open up the concept completely, in fact to replace it with the idea of 'culture'. By 'culture' I mean some indefinitely expanding list of things: all those forms of knowledge, meanings, representations, information, values, by means of which people conduct their lives. The question, 'What cultural forms and contents are needed in order to expand democracy?' will always be context-dependent, and the answers might well be not just different but contradictory.

'Needs' has always been a tricky, shifting set of ideas, but it is now clear that it is even more radically difficult than we had supposed.

There is no single model of democracy, there is no unified political project and there is no prospect of a politically unified class to act as the agent of history. So we have to operate with, to think with, *plurality* (nowadays a familiar but not an easy notion). The future is an open field, or rather futures are open fields, of invention and experiment. In terms of expanded or radicalized democracy, some words from Ernesto Laclau sum up some of the foregoing:

> 'Radical democracy', as the extension of the principle of equality to wider social spheres, attempts to be a social imaginary [i.e. not 'a political programme, which is a set of concrete but changing proposals' but 'an imaginary horizon which is made up of visions and values that mould the whole approach of a varied group of social forces'.] I firmly believe that the present crisis of the left is not so much linked to the failure of concrete policies, but rather to the fact that both communism and social democracy, the two classical imaginary horizons of the left, have ceased to galvanize the imagination of the masses and are no longer viable languages for the expression of radical social demands.[3]

Culture, Politics and Technology

I shall now turn to the concept of cultural democracy, in other words, the expansion and radicalization of democracy within the cultural sphere. It is impossible to talk about this in the abstract, in isolation from other spheres of social life, because everything in life is implicated. Thomas Mann wrote between the world wars, 'In our time the destiny of man presents its meaning in political terms.' This implies that the great, decisive question of the day at that time was which of the competing political projects for the future of mankind would be victorious: liberal democracy, communism or fascism. The destiny of mankind seemed to be at stake in the battle between these forms of political organization, and the outcome was not yet determined, whereas now the destiny of mankind seems to be presented in terms of competing cultures. Far from the outcome being settled (as the preposterous 'end of history' thesis would have us believe), it seems entirely open.

A recent Algerian film called *Bab el-Oued City,* directed by Merzak Allouache (1994), tells a story centred around a cultural struggle, or rather a struggle to control the means of production and distribution of culture. A young man who works unsocial hours in a bakery is driven to distraction by religious messages from a loudspeaker mounted on top of his apartment building. The loudspeaker is the property of the local mosque and is controlled by a gang of young Islamists who are building up an intimidatory presence in the Bab el-Oued quarter of Algiers. The young baker secretly rips down the loudspeaker and throws it in the sea, thereby putting his life at risk—he is eventually denounced and forced to leave. The imam also leaves because he can no longer tolerate the increasing violence with which the Islamic culture (rules, values, meanings) is being imposed on the local population. The local newspaper is bullied into supporting the fundamentalists. There is a hint that the leader of the fundamentalist group may actually be an agent for some other, more hidden and sinister force, perhaps some agency of the military state machine. All these people are caught up in a violent struggle for political, cultural and economic power; they are caught between a totalitarian tendency within Islam and a corrupt and violent military state, and this struggle is channelled in part through the loudspeaker. It is the material base for a particular convergence of power/meaning or power/knowledge—a technical medium through which meanings (values, a way of interpreting the world, ways of defining aspiration, rules and prohibitions) circulate, through which the life-world of the people is reproduced.

What I mean by a 'materialist habit of mind' (an expression derived from Marx and which survives the rejection of other aspects of his thought) is that culture is always thought of in relation to the material means of its production and dissemination, and the social relations which define power and control over these means, and the cultural spaces within which contending forces struggle to have their own ways of representing the world heard and accepted. No political power can be sustained, and no control of economic activity effected, without this material cultural life. Culture, the material production and circulation of culture, is a fundamental dimension of socio-economic and political life; the ownership and control of cultural production is vital to economic and political power.

Modern or postmodern struggles no longer centre on, or no longer only centre on, loudspeakers and the power to control messages aimed at the population of the local neighbourhood. We now have to learn to think in terms of satellites and information superhighways, of video and multimedia CD–ROMS, and so on.

Marxism conceives the possibility of social production aimed at the satisfaction of needs rather than the production of exchange values for the profit of capital. As the forces of production develop, they are potentially open to many different uses. For example, consider the technical means of production: how these means develop, the forms they take, and the social uses to which they will be put, depend not just on their technical properties but on the system of social relations within which they are developed and controlled. It is always possible to conceive of alternatives—alternative forms of technical development and alternative use-values. Moreover, as the productive apparatus of society develops under the aegis of capital, there are always created spaces, forms, potentials beyond those intended by capital. There are always struggles around different conceptions of how the productive forces of society are to be used and controlled. This is as true of information technology (IT) and communications as it was of print or loudspeakers.

What follows is one example of a Middle East cultural struggle that poses problems in this new technical context:

> The voice of Kurdish nationalism, effectively banned in Turkey, is being beamed into the country through a new satellite television station based in London. MED TV . . . this week began regular broadcasts of cultural, educational and news programmes in the Kurdish language to the community in Europe and the whole of the disputed area of Kurdistan. [MED TV] is not about political propaganda . . . the first week's schedule includes cartoons, folk music, Kurdish history, a film from inside a typical Kurdish home and . . . two 20-minute news slots.[4]

The point is that satellite television cannot be policed at national borders. New technology allows cultural struggles to break out of old forms of constraint and allows those who control it extraordinary kinds of power, power on a global scale. No baker could rip down and throw away the communications satellites, and they are feared by governments and by progressive peoples because they represent unprecedented forms of power and will have incalculable effects.

We are used to the idea that it is capital which owns and runs the global means of cultural production, and this is certainly true. Yet the Kurdish example given above should remind us that all technology has many different potential use-values and contradictory cultural possibilities. The materialist framework for thinking about culture encourages us to raise questions about alternative potential directions of social development. It allows us to raise as a 'thought experiment' the question of whether, in relation to the present state of development of the forces of production, there are alternative possible futures. And it suggests a way of identifying what they might be and also of identifying the forces pushing society in one direction rather than another. These sorts of thought experiments have had considerable political importance at key moments in the development of modern information and communications technology.

Television, for example, is one of the most influential technical developments in modern cultural life. In the early 1980s the Greater London Council published a report on alternative directions in the development of cable and television technology.[5] The report relied extensively on the work of Raymond Williams, the British Marxist thinker who made a major contribution to the understanding of culture, and in particular to the relationship between culture, technology and the socio-economic context within which they develop. For example, in his book *Television: Technology and Cultural Form*[6] Williams offered a subtle analysis of these relationships that remains a model of materialist thinking at its best. *Cabling London* commented:

> Raymond Williams sees the development of television, and the extension of its technical infrastructure today with cable and satellites, as a process in which there was and is a central and direct thrust on that technology from the direction of social agencies asserting their perceived needs, purposes, problems and practices. The communication system is the outcome of a process in which social agencies identified their needs and purposes, problems and obstacles not on the basis of a developed technology but preceding it and acting as a spur to its evolution in particular directions.
>
> We are so used to living with the mature results of this process that we tend to see them as having been inevitable. 'Sound radio and television . . . were developed for transmission to *individual* homes, though there was nothing in the technology to make this inevitable' [wrote Raymond Williams]. Similarly, many popular versions of the communications systems of the future are based on the idea of the wired and computerized home; they focus on the domestic setting for the

> technology and on its uses by isolated individuals or families. Instead of having to leave the home the members of the family will be able to meet many of their needs via a console and a VDU, as if moving our bodies around in space were an inconvenient inefficiency, and modern communications the means of overcoming it. Sitting in their living room, where the energy systems and security systems are all taken care of by a computer, the family can do its banking, its shopping and its betting; they can play video games instead of going out to play football; they can talk to their friends and relations on the video-phone; they work at home and they study at home; they can worship at home and even organize politically via the video-conferencing facility.
>
> But there is nothing whatsoever in the technology that determines this outcome and makes it inevitable. It is technically just as possible to have an advanced telecommunications system which is accessed by members of the public at community information centres (and it may well be that for most people this would make more sense in terms of their most pressing needs). There is nothing *technically* to prevent the enormous growth of adult education at community centres, at which the resources of modern technology could be provided to enrich this communal experience. There is no technological imperative towards the privatization of education: there is every pedagogical imperative to exploit the resources of communications technology within the context of classroom and school. There is no technical reason why people should work at home, though there are very powerful social forces, backed by the technology serving their interests, which may drive people to do this.[7]

In other words, developments in technology open up alternative possible futures—they do not by themselves determine the shape of those futures. That is determined by struggles between capital and other agencies and interests to establish technical and social frameworks that meet their own needs and purposes, just as in the case of the Algerian loudspeaker, but now at an enormously more effective and technically powerful level.

Democracy and Developments in Technology

All cultural workers, whether in education, book publishing, film or television, are aware of some of the dramatic developments in both forces of production and relations of production that have taken place in the last decade or so. These developments include both the technical 'revolutionizing' of cultural work (the production and circulation in society of meanings, images, information and ideas) via satellite, cable, computing, and so on, and also the 'managerializing' of the social relations of cultural work (the introduction into cultural fields of what Marx called the despotism of the factory). But these developments are moving at such speed and have such contradictory potentials that they are very hard to interpret.

The possibilities for access by millions of previously information-poor people to vast banks of data, knowledge, images and texts are increasing in unpredicted ways and with incalculable results. Contending forces (states, religious organizations, private corporations, individuals and collectivities of all kinds) seek advantage or merely fun in this strange, suddenly image-rich and data-rich world. It is hard to see whether these developments are liberating or are preparing future cultural nightmares of alienation, philistinism and cultural shallowness.

Information and its transmission threaten to break out of the bounds of capitalist forms and to evade national regulation and control, and this makes some familiar legal and accounting forms archaic and inoperable. Capital constantly attempts to invent forms of ownership, control and accounting that can contain all these new developments within understandable and profitable capitalist forms—capital chases after the Internet, desperately seeking for forms of copyright and costing that can bring it back within the world of commodities. There is also pressure to rewrite or rethink libel law and obscenity laws so as to bring electronic publications back within the range of familiar methods of cultural policing. Information seems to break out of the corset of the commodity form. The British Film Institute runs a huge database of film and television information—why is it not socialized and made available free of charge to everybody with a use for it over the Internet? Because the BFI, though it is a public body financed partly through taxation, is required by government to invent ways of commodifying its products although the technology makes this very difficult.

It is interesting to try a thought experiment which involves three factors—the most advanced IT, the openness of that technology to different potential uses including culturally progressive ones, and the idea of radicalized democracy. What opportunities and dangers for the ideal of the radicalization of democracy are presented by innovations in information and communications technology?

What could it be, to bring together the aspiration to extended or radicalized democracy, state-of-the-art information and communications technology and a cultural statement or symbolic affirmation of value, the value of informed and participatory citizenship? I have tried to imagine an answer to these questions because this is a way of trying to concretize and bring alive the idea of radicalized democracy, to make it something other than an abstract idea or a vague slogan. I have tried to imagine how progress in these directions might be facilitated by ease of public access to information via state-of-the-art IT, and by the possibilities for networking and communicating within and among participating groups via access to cable and satellite systems. The idea would be to concretize the idea of civil society and citizenship through the imagined organization of democratic activity, facilitated by socialized IT and communications equipment. It would be like opening up a small space for socialist imagination and research as a result of the development of the forces of production.

Democracy always involves and includes not just formal mechanisms (votes) but also substantial conditions. These include: people with particular kinds of skills, capacities and knowledge; and access to these via education, IT equipment and forms of collectivity/ways of interrelating in such a way as to be able collectively to organize, plan, swap views and interpretations, and so on. Democracy depends upon the developed capacities of the population as well as developed access to varieties of information. This is why building democracy in the expanded and radicalized forms that we are speculating about here is likely to be a long-term project which will move forward slowly and unevenly and might well take several generations. So this 'thought experiment' asks how these prerequisites of substantial and effective democracy might be built around a project for public investment in socialized information and communications.

Several possibilities occurred to me as the bases for research and experiment in this area. First, for topical reasons I thought about democracy in the economic sphere, and specifically within companies. What kinds of intra-company information should be accessible to workers' representatives? The participation of workers' representatives requires both structures and information and one could conceive of this ('employees' democratic information systems') as a field of open, ongoing research under the general heading of radicalized democracy facilitated by IT. Trades-union ballots are expensive and not always effective in encouraging active participation —could IT be designed so as to make ballots, and the information-sharing that should be an essential aspect of them, more effective and easier to operate? In addition, there has been much talk in Britain recently about the rights and powers of *shareholders* in company affairs (putting a brake on the greed of higher executives who loot company funds via share-option schemes and gigantic salaries). Of course, individual shareholders have only formal or nominal power to affect these matters, as was soon discovered. What would be necessary to encourage some elements of substantial shareholders' (or more generally, stakeholders') power, and once again, what contribution might be made by public access and socialized cyberfacilities? Although there are substantial obstacles in the form of lack of access to shareholder registers and the cost of communications, the problems could easily be overcome by computer databases, networks and the Internet. Again, it is easy to conceive of ongoing research in this area.

These ideas could easily be generalized to bring in many other forms of the expansion of democracy via a variety of organizations and models. The important point is to think of this as piecemeal experimentation rather than a search for a single unique solution. Among participating user groups could be NGOs such as those involved with Helsinki Watch human rights issues, ecological issues and women's issues. Many of these NGOs work on an international, even global scale, especially in preparation for global conferences. How might public-access equipment and data facilitate their international work?

The point of all this speculation is not to propose any particular solutions to questions about the radicalization of democracy, but to imagine how the idea might be concretized and made to flourish, and how the idea might be dramatized as a value by locating it in a symbolically powerful installation. The general framework of questions which we would then bequeath to successor generations in the new millennium concern the conditions under which democracy could go beyond the restricted model of political democracy as generally understood. In this model, the democratic agent is an isolated, individualized voter working within a manipulative and deceitful political and journalistic culture. The problem that we pass on is the gradual installation of the cultural frameworks and the organizational/structural forms for an expansion of democratic life.

Culture, Politics and Religion

In some areas of the world today, the greatest obstacle to the development of democratic cultures and institutions, let alone the radicalizing of democracy, is not capital but fundamentalist religion. The implications of this require thorough study by champions of democracy in the West, some of whom assume that democracy is a universal value, rather than a Western value which will clash with the values of other cultures, particularly within cultures dominated by religious belief. There are many people in the Middle East and North Africa who would see these values as Western and not universal—how are we to answer such people? It should be stressed that everything that follows here amounts to a series of questions, and that I cannot claim to have any answers.

In the West, speculation about socialist democratic values takes place within a broadly liberal democratic context—the value of democracy is proclaimed and the problem is how to realize and expand that value rather than to defend it. Some form of liberal political democracy is assumed as the basis for the expansion of democracy into other areas of social life. In the Middle East there are highly polarized societies, with large sections of the population suffering extreme deprivation, marginalization and hopelessness while small elites amass vast wealth and power within protected islands of high development. Under such circumstances, it is not surprising that the option of democracy can seem neither urgent nor possible, nor even relevant to the needs of the majority of people. It is precisely the failure of modernizing states in the Middle East to carry through credible projects of social development that has opened the way for a different form of political movement, based on Islam. Those states which opted for secular modernity (for example, Turkey, Algeria and Egypt), but have now produced a situation of extreme social polarization, are threatened by forms of religious/political aspiration which merely become more extreme and popular the more that violent repression of them is attempted.

A choice seems to have arisen between political projects based on incompatible categories of thought: on the one hand, Western ideas and values, including democracy; and on the other, ideas derived from a religious view of value and authority. Abdullahi an-Na'im explains why there seems to be such a stark choice within Muslim cultures between these two incompatible ways of thinking about political authority—*either* divine law *or* secularism.

> Although Muslims have in fact lived under varying degrees of secularism for most of their history, the ideal of an Islamic state in full accordance with the *sharia* (Islamic law) has always been kept, even invoked, by secular rulers to legitimize their power. Nevertheless, if confronted today with a categorical and immediate choice between an Islamic *sharia* state and an openly and unequivocally secular state that relegates *sharia* to the purely personal and private domain, most Muslims would probably opt for the former since most find it extremely difficult openly to oppose the application of *sharia* in public affairs.
>
> Without ruling out the possibility altogether, it seems highly improbable, given the present predilection for majority rule and self-determination, that a strictly secular state could be sustained in the Islamic world today, at least in countries with an overwhelming Muslim majority. Whatever degree of secularism earlier authoritarian rulers like Ataturk of Turkey or Bourguiba of Tunisia were able to construct, the prospects of open secularism appear to be diminishing: the failure of

> post-independence secularism and nationalism gave Islamic fundamentalism its impetus. Using the tools of 'modern' political organization, international finance and the technology of mass communication, Islamic fundamentalism is now confronting an increasing number of Muslims with a stark choice between the 'divine' law of God and the 'anti-religious' law of man.[8]

The author of this quotation argues that this stark choice is in fact an illusion and that these two ways of thinking about the law are not in such absolute opposition as they are made to appear. But is this so? This opposition derives not only from the authoritarian inflexibility of Islamist views but also, of course, from arrogant claims to the universalism of Western definitions of value and political rights. The example of Marxism illustrates this quite clearly.

Marx's thinking about religion was based on an Enlightenment assumption which I have always shared, but which it is no longer so easy to accept. This was the assumption of a basically progressive narrative that saw the development of science- and technology-based secular societies as the inevitable direction of historical development. Religion arose, Marx thought, in contexts of ignorance and superstition and impotence in relation to nature. It became institutionalized as a cultural mechanism contributing to the smooth reproduction of the relations of power and ownership in society by validating and legitimating forms of social dominance and subjection. This Marxist framework contained the assumption that the development, first by 'the great civilizing force of capital', and then by socialism, of scientific knowledge and the technical mastery of nature would engender the possibility of a cultural and political world no longer dominated by enslavement to religious belief and authority.

Secular, modernizing democracy and fundamentalist religion do seem to be utterly incompatible: they represent mutually exclusive political and cultural projects. They are two ways of thinking about the world that have hardened into absolute opposition. Fundamentalist religion is a force of cultural exclusion. It is censorious. It aims to control meanings. It is against plurality, because it believes in the one text and the one authority. It is thus against democracy and it is against the forms of equality that are presupposed by democracy, especially the equality of women.

The Rushdie affair is a perfect example of this. On the one hand, a religious authority takes upon itself the right to pronounce a death sentence in the name of a single truth, a single sacred text, a single way of understanding history, and indeed as a function of 'a revolution against history' as Rushdie himself saw it. On the other hand, there is the novel, that most democratic of cultural forms, 'the privileged arena of conflicting discourses', as Rushdie himself put it—precisely a form of culture that is at home in or part of the modern world, in that it stages discursive plurality as its central function.

Religion takes it upon itself to impose meanings: of death, conception, gender, sexuality, marriage, property and value. It also claims the authority to draw the boundaries of acceptable and tolerated behaviour, speech and thought. Because of these things, religion, or at least fundamentalist religion, is undemocratic and is bound to be hostile to the project of radicalized democracy.

This is certainly how it has been seen by intellectuals in Algeria. It was the view, for example, of Tahar Djaout, a 39-year-old journalist, novelist and poet (founder and editor of the anti-Islamist weekly *Ruptures*) who was assassinated on 26 May 1993. He expressed surprise that people 'continue to believe that visions of society separated by ten centuries can coexist' and that they take seriously 'a party leader who proclaims that Algeria has no need for any law since the Quran already contains all that is needed'. In the last piece he wrote, arguing that dialogue is impossible, he maintained that there are only two families in Algeria, 'the family that is moving ahead and the family that is going backward'.[9]

The writer Karim Alrawi, deputy secretary of the Egyptian Organization for Human Rights, comments:

> It is hard to describe what it is like to be living in a society whose [secular, progressive] culture is dying . . . It is a little like watching a large and lumbering animal slowly being sucked into the mire; it is the knowledge that what was won by past generations so painstakingly is being lost, possibly forever . . . The cultural programme of the Muslim Brotherhood is a barely disguised attempt to turn the future into the past and the gains of 150 years of the Enlightenment into mass illiteracy . . . Culturally it will be as though time has stopped still and has begun to run backwards.[10]

Fundamentalist Islam is, in Rushdie's phrase, 'a revolution against history'.

But that confidence that religion is something essentially archaic and historically outdated and that its cultural presence always denotes the forces of nostalgia and reaction—a view that is supported by the evidence of Islamist politics in the examples mentioned above—is perhaps now not so easy to sustain as a general analysis. What if we reject that Enlightenment assumption, that narrative of the end of religion, which interprets cultural survivals from the past as annoying but temporary aberrations? We may have seen enough recent cultural survivals to suggest that the world will not be so easily cleansed of cultural forms that are at odds with democracy.

The French film-maker Chris Marker came across an astonishing spectacle while shooting a film about Medvedkin (a great Soviet film-maker) in Moscow in 1990. In the cemetery where he was filming Medvedkin's grave, Marker came across an old man dressed in the uniform of the White Guards of the pre-revolutionary tsarist state. His military insignia dated back some seventy years and had lain hidden away in some attic trunk or buried in a garden all those years, dangerous survivals, waiting for the moment when they could once again be worn as a declaration of identity and loyalty. We have all seen pre-First World War uniforms in Serbia, the extraordinary reemergence of religious life in Russia and the incredible tenacity of Tibetan Buddhism in Chinese-occupied Tibet. None of these things are mere survivals, kept alive in the befuddled heads of old folk. They are systems of meaning that can still find a place in the world, that can spring up again in answer to particular contemporary conditions of life. Why is that? And what needs do these things answer?

We really do not know what story we are in. Both the Marxist story and the more recent 'end-of-history' story allowed people to feel some confidence that the political and cultural options associated with fundamentalist religion were doomed to wither away, and were marginal historical phenomena, not in the main line of historical development. We no longer know that, however. The reason we do not know is that we do not know enough about human needs. We do not know what the *long-term* cultural conditions are for viable social life. What mechanisms of social cohesion, what sources of value, are necessary to the long-term reproduction of societies? Is it possible to sustain the trust and political goodwill that are the prerequisites for stable secular, pluralistic democracies? Perhaps this is where the incalculable nature of human needs exerts its force. We do not know whether cultural pluralism and a context of IT and communications are doomed to leave some ancient human cultural needs unsatisfied.

There are possibly dangerous and damaging paradoxes lurking within the apparently coherent ideals of cultural pluralism and radicalized democracy. Rather, it is precisely because these are not coherent, well-defined concepts whose coherence has been tested, but are open ideals that are as yet untested to the limit historically, that the possibility of incoherence and damaging contradictions could emerge.

The ideal of culturally pluralistic democracy is based on the gamble that it is possible for people with fundamentally different answers to the question 'What makes life worth living?' to invent and negotiate social and political frameworks that contain their different lives and cultures without a damaging mutual hostility and without coming to perceive each other as threats to their continued existence. But the truth is that we do not yet know whether such an ideal is viable in the long term, and if it is, then within what contexts and what limits. This is why it is a gamble, rather than a postulate which can be theorized. We do not know what the limits are to the coexistence of contending value-systems. We do not know whether pluralism and democracy are or could become universal values, or whether they are Western values that inevitably come into conflict with those of other cultures, and which can exist only in a state of more or less open warfare. In other words, we do not know how much of what we have inherited from Marx we will have to give up.

Notes

1. Introduction

1. There is a play on words here. For its article, *The Economist* borrowed the title of the work by the German pessimistic thinker Oswald Spingler, *The Decline of the West.*
2. I received the manuscript of Bekdashi's autobiography in 1994, a year before it was published in Damascus.

2. Marxism and the Arab World

1. Edward Said, *Orientalism: Western Conceptions of the Orient* (Routledge & Kegan Paul, London, 1978).
2. Samir Amin, *L'Egypte nassérienne* (Editions du Seuil, Paris, 1965); Anouar Abdel-Malek, *Egypt: Military Society* (Random House, New York, 1968); Mahmoud Hussein, 'Class Struggles in Egypt', *Monthly Review* (New York, 1968).
3. Simon Bromley, *Rethinking Middle East Politics* (Polity Press, Oxford, 1993).
4. Joel Beinin and Zachary Lockman, *Workers on the Nile* (Princeton University Press, Princeton, N.J., 1987).
5. Hanna Batatu, *The Old Social Classes and the Revolutionary Movements of Iraq* (Princeton University Press, Princeton, N.J., 1978).
6. Sami Zubaida, 'Community, Class and Minorities in Iraqi Politics', in Robert A. Fernea and W. Roger Louis (eds), *The Iraqi Revolution of 1958* (Tauris, London, 1991).
7. Ervand Abrahamian, *Iran Between Two Revolutions* (Princeton University Press, Princeton, N.J., 1982).

8. Assaf Bayat, *Workers and Revolution in Iran* (Zed, London, 1987).
9. Bill Warren, *Imperialism, Pioneer of Capitalism* (Verso, London, 1981).
10. Maxime Rodinson, *Israel and the Arabs* (Penguin, Hardmondsworth, 2nd edn, 1982); Isaac Deutscher, 'The Israeli-Arab War, June 1967', reprinted in *The Non-Jewish Jew and Other Essays* (Oxford University Press, London, 1968).
11. Ervand Abrahamian, *Khomeinism* (Tauris, London, 1993).
12. Sami Zubaida, *Islam, the People and the State* (Tauris, London, 1993).

3. The Demise of the Soviet Union and Eastern Europe

1. For a discussion of the vision of the 1980s in the 1961 party programme, see L. Schapiro, *The USSR and the Future* (Praeger, London, 1963), Ch. 3.
2. L. Brezhnev, Twenty-Sixth Party Congress, 1981. For a brief discussion, see G. Smith, *Soviet Politics: Struggling with Change* (Macmillan, London, 1992), pp. 54–8.
3. See S. White, G. Gill and D. Slider, *The Politics of Transition* (Cambridge University Press, Cambridge, 1993), Ch. 1, for a discussion of the loss of optimism and the search for new ideas.
4. D. Bell, 'Ideology and Soviet Politics', *Slavic Review*, Vol. 24, No. 4 (Dec. 1965); A. G. Meyer, 'The Functions of Ideology in the Soviet Political System', *Soviet Studies*, Vol. 17, Issue 3; and G. Lichtheim, 'The Transmutations of a Doctrine', *Problems of Communism*, Vol. 15 (July–Aug. 1966).
5. For a discussion of the forced programmes of industrialization, see T. H. Von Laue, *S. Witte and the Industrialisation of Russia* (Columbia University Press, New York 1963); H. Kuromiya, *Stalin's Industrial Revolution, 1928–31* (Cambridge University Press, Cambridge, 1988); and Timothy Luke, *Ideology and Soviet Industrialization* (Greenwood Press, Westport, Conn., 1985).
6. A. G. Aganbegyan, *The Economic Challenge of Perestroika* (Indiana University Press, Bloomington, Ind., 1988).
7. A. Nove, *An Economic History of the USSR*, 3rd edn (Penguin, Harmondsworth, 1992), Chs 11–13.
8. T. Zaslavskaia, *The Second Socialist Revolution: An Alternative Soviet Strategy* (Tauris, London, 1990).
9. G. White, *Riding the Tiger: The Politics of Economic Reform in China* (Macmillan, London, 1991).
10. See White, Gill and Slider, *Politics of Transition.*
11. G. Shakhnazarov, 'Governability of the World', *International Affairs* (March 1988).
12. For an excellent discussion of the de-ideologization of foreign affairs, see S. Kull, *Burying Lenin: The Revolution in Soviet Ideology and Foreign Policy* (Westview Press, Boulder, Colo., 1992).
13. A. Nove, *Glasnost in Action* (Unwin Hyman, London, 1989).

14. For a clear analysis of the dangers, see C. Shore, 'Lenin and the Crisis of Communism', *Government and Opposition*, Vol. 26, No. 1 (winter 1991).
15. M. Gorbachev, *Perestroika* (Collins, London, 1987).
16. Ibid.
17. M. McCauley, *Khrushchev and Khrushchevism* (Macmillan, London, 1987).
18. G. Schopflin, *Politics in Eastern Europe* (Blackwell, Oxford, 1993), Chs 6 and 7.
19. A. Aslund, 'Gorbachev, Perestroika and Economic Crisis', *Problems of Communism* (Jan.–Feb. 1991).
20. R. Hill, *Communism under the Knife* (Pinter, London, 1990).
21. M. Urban, *More Power to the Soviets: The Democratic Revolution in the USSR* (Elgar, Aldershot, 1990).
22. 'The First Congress of Peoples' Deputies, Moscow, 25 May–10 June 1989', in Oleg Glebov and John Crowfoot (eds), *The Soviet Empire: Its Nations Speak Out* (Harwood, Switzerland, 1989).
23. This defeat, though predictable, was not in fact widely predicted either in the Soviet-bloc countries themselves or in the West. See many of the first accounts of the revolution in Eastern Europe, e.g. Misha Glenny, *The Rebirth of History* (Penguin, Harmondsworth, 1990).
24. R. Hill, 'The CPSU: From Monolith to Pluralist', *Soviet Studies*, Vol. 43, No. 2 (1991).
25. See R. Pipes, *The Formation of the Soviet Union* (Harvard University Press, Cambridge, Mass., 1964).
26. For a discussion of the ethnic climate in the non-Russian republics, see Rasma Karklins, *Ethnic Relations in the USSR: The Perspective from Below* (Unwin Hyman, London, 1986).
27. See R. Hill, 'Managing Ethnic Conflicts', in S. White, R. di Leo and O. Cappelli, *The Soviet Transition* (Frank Cass, London, 1993).
28. For a discussion of the role of the RSFSR in the Union, see Aleksei M. Salmin, 'From Union to Commonwealth', in White, di Leo and Cappelli, *Soviet Transition*.
29. R. Sakwa, 'The August Coup and the Triumph of Perestroika', in White, di Leo and Cappelli, *Soviet Transition*.
30. The logic of monopoly power and its transposition into Eastern Europe is given a very coherent treatment in M. Waller, *The End of the Communist Power Monopoly* (Manchester University Press, Manchester, 1993).
31. A Yakovlev, *The Fate of Marxism in Russia* (Yale University Press, London, 1993).
32. See S. Farber, *Before Stalinism: The Rise and Fall of Soviet Democracy* (Polity Press, London, 1990).
33. An excellent account of the Lenin cult is to be found in N. Tumarkhin, *Lenin Lives* (Harvard University Press, Cambridge, Mass., 1983).
34. For a discussion of the debate concerning the relevance of Marxism to pre-revolutionary Russian conditions, see S. R. Saunders Vosper, 'Reflections

on a Great Debate', *Soviet Studies*, Vol. 34, No. 3 (July 1982).

35. See I. Lapenna, *The State and Law in Soviet and Yugoslav Theory* (Bodley Head, London, 1972).
36. A. J. Polan, *Lenin and the End of Politics* (Methuen, London, 1984).
37. John E. E. Dalberg Acton, first Baron, *Essays in the Liberal Interpretation of History*, Selected Papers edited and with an introduction by W. McNeill (Chicago University Press, Chicago, Ill., 1967); *The History of Freedom and Other Essays* (Macmillan, London, 1907); and *Essays on Freedom and Power* (World Publishing Co., Cleveland, Ohio, 1964).
38. See L. Schapiro, *The Origin of the Communist Autocracy* (G. Bell, London, 1955).
39. M. Waller, *The Language of Communism* (Bodley Head, London, 1972).
40. For a discussion of the analysis of the legal Marxists, see R. Kindersley, *The First Russian Revisionists* (Clarendon Press, Oxford, 1962).
41. H. Timmermann, 'Is Gorbachev a Bukharinist? Moscow's Reappraisal of the NEP Period', *Journal of Communist Studies*, Vol. 5, No. 2 (June 1989).
42. A point made by M. Matthew in his *Privilege in the Soviet Union* (Allen & Unwin, London, 1978).
43. The terms 'Atlanticists' and 'Eurasians' are common in post-communist Russia and refer respectively to those leaning towards the West and those wishing to follow a unique and different path of development, i.e. midway between Europe and Asia.

4. Can Marx Survive the Collapse of Communism or 'Real Socialism'?
This chapter was translated by Aisha Hall and edited by Kate Soper.

1. Karl Marx, *Misère de la philosophie* [1847] (Editions Sociales, Paris, 1977), p. 119.
2. Fernand Braudel, *Civilisation matérielle, économie, capitalisme XV–XVIII siècle* (A. Colin, Paris, 1979), 3 vols.
3. Karl Marx, *Das Kapital*, vol. 25 (Dietz Verlag, Berlin, 1964), p. 453.
4. Karl Marx, letters to Choukovski (1877) and Vera Zassoulitch (1881) in *Sur les sociétés précapitalistes. Textes choisis de Marx, Engels et Lénine*, Preface by Maurice Godelier (Editions Sociales, Paris, 1970).

5. From Marxism to Liberal Nationalism: A Transformation in Palestinian Marxism

1. G. Labica (ed.), *The Critical Dictionary of Marxism* (Presses Universitaires de France, Paris, 1982), pp. 561–4.
2. See Muhammad Kamil al-Khatib (ed.), *al-Ishtirakiya* [Socialism] (Ministry of Culture, Damascus, 1991).
3. [The original title of the Arabic translation was *al-Hukoma wal-Thawra* [The Government and the Revolution]. The translator failed to differentiate between state and government—Ed.] On the development of socialism in the Arab world, see al-Khatib (ed.), *al-Ishtirakiya*, p. 7. See also Dr A. Hanna,

'al-Marxiya fil-Mashriq' [Marxism in the Mashreq], *al-Hadaf* weekly, No. 676 (6 June 1983) and No. 677 (13 June 1983).

4. *Rules of Admission to the Communist International* [June 1934] (Maspero, Paris, 1972), pp. 39–41.
5. Mustafa Sa'di (Java), 'The National Question in the Seventh Congress of the PCP', *International Press Correspondence*, No. 5 (21 Jan. 1931), p. 83.
6. The Conference of the Delegates of the Palestinian Communist Party and the Syrian Communist Party, 'The Tasks of the Communist in the Arab National Movement', *International Press Correspondence*, No. 1 (4 Jan. 1933), pp. 8–10 and No. 3 (Jan. 1933), p. 32.
7. 'A Call by the PCP: The Uprising in Palestine', *International Press Correspondence* (4 July 1936), p. 822.
8. Musa al-Dajani (head of the League), internal circular entitled, 'Our National Movement is the Movement of the Arab Masses', Third Circular (23 Feb. 1944).
9. Hasan Itani, 'The Relation between the Workers' Movement and Our National Industry', *al-Ittihad* (Haifa) (19 Nov. 1944).
10. Khalil Shner, 'Our Workers' Movement's Attitude towards Our National Industry', *al-Ittihad* (30 Dec. 1945).
11. Resolution of the League, n.p., 1951.
12. See the PCP Programme, Documents of the First Congress, n.p., 1983.
13. Karl Marx, *Capital*, Vol. 1 (Progress Publishers, Moscow, 1985), p. 28.
14. The new party's internal rules represent the first attempt at restructuring the party organization on the basis of the concept of a wide democracy. This arrangement differs radically from the previous, heavily centralized structures.

7. The Arab Communist Parties in Search of an Identity

This chapter relies on a series of interviews, discussions and conversations with leading figures in the Arab communist parties. Some of these interviews were published in *an-Nahj*, a quarterly review issued for the Centre for Socialist Studies in the Arab World (Nicosia, Beirut, Damascus) between 1983 and 1995. Among the leading personalities interviewed were:

Mahmoud Amin al-'Alim (member of Central Committee, Egyptian Communist Party): Damascus, 1989; Cairo, 1989 and 1993.

Khaled Bekdash (general secretary, Syrian Communist Party): Damascus, 1983.

Bashir Barghouthi (general secretary, Palestinian Communist Party): London, 1992–93.

Yousif Faisal (general secretary, Syrian Communist Party–splinter group): Damascus, 1989 and 1990.

Muhammad Harmal (general secretary, Tunisian Communist Party): Tunis, 1987.

George Hawi (former general secretary, Lebanese Communist Party): Damascus, 1984.

Aziz Muhammad (former general secretary, Iraqi Communist Party): Damascus,

1983–84.

Karim Muruwa (Politbureau member, Lebanese Communist Party): London, 1993 and 1995.

Ibrahim Nugud (general secretary, Sudanese Communist Party): Khartoum, 1989.

Tawfiq Ziyadin (general secretary, Jordanian Communist Party): Damascus, 1989; Amman, 1995.

The chapter also relies on discussions and debates during the seminar on 'Perestroika and the Arab World' coordinated by the author in Damascus in 1989.

1. Khaled Bekdash, 'Memoirs', unpublished manuscript provided by the Centre for Socialist Studies in the Arab World, Damascus, 1993.
2. Author's interviews with Bashir Barghouthi, London, 1992–93.
3. Ibid.
4. Author's interviews with Karim Muruwa, London, 1993 and 1995.
5. The Iraqi Communist Party ladder was as follows: (i) nomination (6, 9 or 12 months); (ii) membership of a cell (1 year minimum); (iii) membership of a base committee; (iv) membership of the bureau of a base committee; (v) membership of a neighbourhood committee; (vi) membership of the bureau of a neighbourhood committee; (vii) alternate membership of a city committee; (viii) full membership of a city committee; (ix) membership of the bureau of a city committee; (x) membership of a district (or province) committee; (xi) full membership of a district (or province) committee; (xii) membership of the bureau of a district (or province) committee; (xiii) alternate membership of the Central Committee; (xiv) full membership of the Central Committee; (xv) alternate membership of the Political Bureau; (xvi) full membership of the Political Bureau. To be General Secretary, the member needed to pass through all these sixteen levels.
6. Author's interviews with Bashir Barghouthi, London, 1992–93.
7. Ibid.

8. Globalization in Question

1. De Anne Julius, *Global Companies and Public Policy* (RIIA/Pinter, London, 1990); and Kenichi Ohmae, *The Borderless World* (Collins, London, 1990).
2. Paul Hirst and Grahame Thompson, 'Globalization, Foreign Direct Investment, and International Economic Governance', *Organization*, Vol. 1, No. 2 (Oct. 1994), pp. 295–6.
3. Jim Tomlinson, *Can Governments Manage the Economy?*, Fabian Tract No. 524 (London, Jan. 1988).
4. James Tobin, 'Speculator's Tax', *New Economy* (IPPR), 1994, pp. 104–9.
5. Sylvia Ostry, 'The Domestic Domain: The New International Policy Arena', *Transnational Corporations*, Vol. 1, No. 1 (Feb. 1992), pp 7–26.
6. Paul Hirst and Grahame Thompson, *Globalization in Question: The International Economy and Possibilities for Governance* (Polity Press, Cambridge, 1996), Ch. 4.

7. Karel Williams, Colin Haslam, John Williams, Andy Adcroft and Sukhdev Johal, *Factories as Warehouses: Japanese Manufacturing Foreign Direct Investment in Britain and the United States*, Occasional Papers on Business, Economy and Society, No. 6 (Polytechnic of East London, 1992).
8. Hirst and Thompson, 'Globalization, Foreign Direct Investment, and International Economic Governance', pp. 295–6.
9. Hirst and Thompson, *Globalization in Question*, Chs 6 and 7.
10. Will Hutton, *The State We're In* (Cape, London, 1995).
11. Charles F. Sabel, 'Learning by Monitoring: The Institutions of Economic Development' in N. Smelser and R. Smedberg (eds), *Handbook of Economic Sociology* (Princeton/Sage, Princeton, N.J., 1994); Charles F. Sabel, 'Bootstrapping Reform: Rebuilding Firms, the Welfare State and Unions', *Politics and Society*, Vol. 23, No. 1 (March 1995).
12. Charles F. Sabel, 'Flexible Specialization and the Re-emergence of Regional Economies' in Paul Hirst and Jonathan Zeitlin (eds), *Reversing Industrial Decline?* (Berg, Oxford, 1989).
13. Michel Albert, *Capitalism vs Capitalism* (Whurr, London, 1993).
14. Sabel, 'Bootstrapping Reform'.
15. Michael Artis and Sylvia Ostry, *International Economic Policy Coordination*, Chatham House Papers No. 30 (RIIA/Routledge, London, 1986); Robert D. Putnam and Nicholas Bayne, *Hanging Together: Cooperation and Conflict in the Seven-Power Summits* (Sage, London, 1987); and Grahame F. Thompson, *The Political Economy of the New Right* (Pinter, London, 1990), Ch. 7.
16. Grahame F. Thompson, 'Economic Autonomy and the Advanced Industrial State' in Anthony G. McGrew, Paul G. Lewis et al., *Global Politics* (Polity Press, Cambridge, 1992), Fig. 2, p. 147.
17. OECD figures for 1990: see P. Hirst and G. Thompson, 'The Problem of Globalization . . .', *Economy and Society*, Vol. 21, No. 4 (Nov. 1992), Fig. 2, p. 376.
18. Grahame F. Thompson, 'The Evolution of the Managed Economy in Europe', *Economy and Society*, Vol. 21, No. 2 (May 1992), Fig. 1, p. 146.
19. Commission of the European Committees, 'One Market, One Money', *European Economy*, No. 44 (Brussels, Oct 1990), Table 7.5, p. 187.

9. Intentional Development and Marx

1. R. Walker, 'California Rages Against the Dying of the Light', *New Left Review*, No. 209 (1995), p. 42.
2. Ibid., p. 56.
3. For an elaboration of all that follows, see M. P. Cowen and R. W. Shenton, *Doctrines of Development* (Routledge, London, 1996).
4. A still useful account of the genesis of the idea of development is to be found in R. A. Nisbet, *Social Change and History: Aspects of the Western Theory of Development* (Oxford University Press, New York, 1969); and

History of the Idea of Progress (Basic Books, New York, 1980).

5. See G. Iggers (ed.), *The Doctrine of Saint-Simon: An Exposition, First Year 1828–29* (Beacon Books, Boston, Mass., 1958); and G. Lenzer (ed.), *Auguste Comte and Positivism: The Essential Writings* (University of Chicago Press, Chicago, Ill., 1983). Useful initial commentaries are: D. G. Charlton, *Positive Thought in France during the Second Empire 1852–1870* (Clarendon Press, Oxford, 1959); and T. R. Wright, *The Religion of Humanity: The Impact of Comtean Positivism on Victorian Britain* (Cambridge University Press, Cambridge, 1986). The Saint-Simonian influence on Mill is best seen in his *Spirit of the Age*, in *Collected Works of John Stuart Mill*, Vol. 22 (University of Toronto Press, Toronto, 1986).
6. There is a wealth of literature on Newman's notion of 'development', but see O. Chadwick, *From Bossuet to Newman: The Idea of Doctrinal Development* (Cambridge University Press, Cambridge, 1957); and N. Lash, *Newman on Development: The Search for an Explanation in History* (Sheed & Ward, London, 1975).
7. K. Marx, *The Holy Family, or Critique of Critical Criticism: Against Bruno Bauer and Company*, in *Collected Works*, Vol. 4 (Progress Publishers, Moscow, 1975); and *The German Ideology*, in *Collected Works*, Vol. 5 (Progress Publishers, Moscow, 1976).
8. For example, see G. W. F. Hegel, *Lectures on the Philosophy of World History: Introduction: Reason in History* (Cambridge University Press, Cambridge, 1975); *Philosophy of Right* (Clarendon Press, Oxford, 1952); and *Philosophy of Mind* (Clarendon Press, Oxford, 1971). Again, there is a voluminous literature, but for Hegel's triad in political theory, see, for example, Z. A. Pelczynski (ed.), *The State and Civil Society: Studies in Hegel's Political Philosophy* (Cambridge University Press, Cambridge, 1984); and for 'doubling', H. Uchida, *Marx's 'Grundisse' and Hegel's 'Logic'* (Routledge, London, 1988); and A. Shamsavari, *Dialectics and Social Theory: The Logic of Capital* (Merlin Books, Braunton, Devon, 1991).
9. A. G. Frank, *Capitalism and Underdevelopment in Latin America: Historical Case Studies of Chile and Brazil* (Penguin, Harmondsworth, 1967); and *Dependent Accumulation and Underdevelopment* (Macmillan, London, 1978); Mao Tse-tung, 'On Contradiction', in *Selected Works of Mao Tse-tung*, Vol. 1 (Lawrence & Wishart, London, 1955); and 'On the Mass Line', in *Selected Works of Mao Tse-tung*, Vol. 3 (Foreign Publishing House, Peking, 1965).
10. F. List, *The National System of Political Economy* (Augustus Kelly, New York, 1991). Marx's 1845 attack on List is in 'Draft of an Article on Friedrich List's Book', in *Collected Works*, Vol 4.
11. G. A. Cohen, *Karl Marx's Theory of History: A Defence* (Clarendon Press, Oxford, 1978); and *History, Labour and Freedom: Themes from Marx* (Clarendon Press, Oxford, 1988).

12. Shamsavari, *Dialectics*.
13. K. Marx, *Grundisse: Foundations of the Critique of Political Economy* (Penguin, Harmondsworth, 1973), pp. 278–9.
14. J. A. Schumpeter, *The Theory of Economic Development: An Enquiry into Profits, Capital, Credit, Interest and the Business Cycle* (Harvard University Press, Cambridge, Mass., 1934).

10. Planning and Markets

1. I am grateful to Paul Auerbach and Philip Arestis for their very useful comments.
2. F. A. Hayek, 'The Use of Knowledge in Society', *American Economic Review* (1945), reprinted in Townsend (ed.), *Price Theory*.
3. Ludwig von Mises, 'Economic Calculation in the Socialist Commonwealth' (English translation of a German article published in 1920), in F. Hayek (ed.), *Collectivist Economic Planning: Critical Studies on the Possibilities of Socialism* (Routledge, London, 1935); Oskar Lange, 'On the Economic Theory of Socialism', in B. E. Lippincott (ed.), *On the Economic Theory of Socialism* (University of Minnesota Press, 1938), excerpted in H. Townsend (ed.), *Price Theory* (Penguin, Harmondsworth Adapted from F. C. Fourie, 'In the Beginning There Were Markets', in C. Pitelis (ed.), *Transaction Costs, Markets and Hierarchies* (Blackwell, Oxford, 1993).
4. See R. H. Coase, 'The Nature of the Firm', *Economica* (1937).
5. See D. Lavoie, *Rivalry and Central Planning* (Cambridge University Press, Cambridge, 1985).
6. Karl Marx, *Capital*, Vol. 3, quoted in A. Nove, *The Economics of Feasible Socialism* (Allen & Unwin, London, 1983), p. 12.
7. See Nove, *Economics of Feasible Socialism*, Part 1.
8. Karl Marx, *Capital*, Vol. 1 (New Left Review/Pelican, Harmondsworth, 1976), p. 480.
9. See M. Dietrich, *Transaction Cost Economics and Beyond* (Routledge, London, 1994), p. 17.
10. Because Coase views the firm as an organization or multi-period agency, production does not always involve firms: see G. Hodgson, 'Transaction Costs and the Evolution of the Firm', in Pitelis (ed.), *Transaction Costs*. Dietrich's view (influenced by Fourie) includes one-person firms which are consistent with simple commodity production, whereas Coase has an employment relation in mind, more akin to a capitalist firm (although Coase's firm could also be organized on cooperative or participatory lines).
11. See Hodgson, 'Transaction Costs and the Evolution of the Firm'.
12. See P. Auerbach, 'On Socialist Optimism', *New Left Review*, No. 192 (1992).
13. P. Auerbach, M. Desai and A. Shamsavari, 'The Transition from Actually Existing Capitalism', *New Left Review*, No. 170 (1988), p. 76.
14. Nove, *Economics of Feasible Socialism*, p. 20.

15. The debate does not seem to have affected the theory and practice of planning in the Soviet Union at the time. See ibid., Part 1.
16. For a very interesting review of this debate which contrasts with mainstream accounts, see Lavoie, *Rivalry and Central Planning*.
17. See Hayek, 'The Use of Knowledge in Society'.
18. See the critical review of the debate by Lavoie, *Rivalry and Central Planning*.
19. Nove, *Economics of Feasible Socialism*, p. 179.
20. J. E. Roemer, 'An Anti-Hayekian Manifesto', *New Left Review*, No. 211 (May–June 1995), p. 120. For Stiglitz, see note 21.
21. J. E. Stiglitz, *Whither Socialism?* (MIT Press, Cambridge, Mass., 1994), p. 275.
22. Ibid., p. 277.
23. B. Coriat and P. Petit, 'Deindustrialization and Tertiarization: Towards a New Economic Regime', in A. Amin and M. Dietrich (eds), *Towards a New Europe? Structural Change in the European Economy* (Edward Elgar, Aldershot, 1991).
24. Cf. the view of M. Piore and C. F. Sabel, in their book *The Secret Industrial Divide: Possibilities for Posterity* (Basic Books, New York, 1984), that new flexibility will reduce the role of high-volume production.
25. R. Boyer, 'The Transformation of Modern Capitalism: By the Light of the "Regulation" Approach and Other Political Economy Theories', *CEPREMAP Occasional Paper*, No. 9,143 (Paris, 1991).
26. E. T. Penrose, *The Theory of the Growth of the Firm*, 2nd edn (Blackwell, Oxford, 1980).
27. G. B. Richardson, 'The Organisation of Industry', *Economic Journal* (1979).
28. M. H. Best, *The New Competition* (Polity Press, Cambridge, 1990), p. 131.
29. J. Bleeke and D. Ernst, 'Is Your Strategic Alliance Really a Sale?', *Harvard Business Review* (Jan.–Feb. 1995).
30. S. E. Sjostrand, 'The Many Faces of Capitalism', in S. E. Sjostrand (ed.), *Institutional Change: Theory and Empirical Findings* (M. E. Sharpe, Armonk, 1993).
31. Michel Albert, *Capitalisme contre capitalisme* (Seuil, Paris, 1991).
32. Alfred Chandler, *Scale and Scope* (Harvard University Press, Cambridge, Mass., 1990).
33. Best, *New Competition*.
34. This is in contrast to the hierarchical firm which forms the basis of the analysis used by Williamson and Chandler. See, for example, O. E. Williamson, *Markets and Hierarchies* (Free Press, New York, 1975); and A. D. Chandler, *The Visible Hand* (Belknap/Harvard University Press, Cambridge, Mass., 1977).
35. See Dietrich, *Transaction Cost Economics*, p. 181.
36. N. Rosenberg, *Exploring the Black Box: Technology, Economics, and History* (Cambridge University Press, Cambridge, 1994), pp. 87–108.

37. Ibid., p. 87.

11. Marxism and Deconstruction: The West Versus the Other

1. Jacques Derrida, *Specters of Marx*, trans. Peggy Kamuf (Routledge, New York and London, 1994).
2. A succinct illustration of the disputes generated around this issue is provided by an anecdote cited by Martha Nussbaum in her article, 'Human Functioning and Social Justice: In Defence of Aristotelian Essentialism', *Political Theory*, Vol. 20, No. 2 (May 1992). Nussbaum relates how, at an international conference on value and technology, a French anthropologist expressed regret that the introduction by the British of the smallpox vaccine to India had eradicated the cult of the goddess to whom the local community used to pray in order to ward off smallpox. When it was objected that it was surely better to be healthy than ill, the answer was given that Western medicine can only think in terms of binary oppositions of health and illness, life and death, and was hence blind to the radical otherness of other cultures.
3. Francis Fukuyama, *The End of History and the Last Man* (The Free Press, New York, 1992).
4. *Specters of Marx* plays at great length on the notion of the times being 'out of joint' (see, in particular, Ch. 1 and pp. 77–8). The reference is to Hamlet's speech in response to the visitation of his father's ghost at the beginning of the play: 'The time is out of joint. O cursed spite, that ever I was born to set it right.' (*Hamlet*, Act I, Scene V.)
5. Listed in summary form, the ten 'plagues' of the contemporary world order are: (1) the 'new unemployment'; (2) homelessness; (3) economic competition; (4) the contradictions of the 'free' market; (5) foreign debt; (6) the arms industry; (7) nuclear weapons; (8) inter-ethnic wars; (9) the capitalist 'phantom states' of the mafia and drug cartels; and (10) the West's hegemony over the interpretation and application of international law. See Derrida, *Specters*, pp. 81–6.
6. The longest section of *The German Ideology* is devoted to a discussion of Stirner's work even though Marx describes its author as having the 'shallowest brain' of the Young Hegelians. First published in German as *Der Einzige unde sein Eigentum*, Stirner's book appeared in English as *The Ego and His Own*, trans. Steven Byington (Benjamin Tucker, New York, 1907).
7. Derrida, *Specters*, p. 59.
8. Ernesto Laclau and Chantal Mouffe, *Hegemony and Socialist Strategy* (Verso, London, 1985); Ernesto Laclau, *New Reflections on the Revolution of our Time* (Verso, London, 1990); Chantal Mouffe, *The Return of the Political* (Verso, London, 1993).
9. Derrida, *Specters*, p. 66.
10. 'The Deconstruction of Actuality', interview with Jacques Derrida, trans. by Jonathan Ree, *Radical Philosophy*, No. 68 (autumn 1994), p. 32. The interview was originally published in the French monthly, *Passages*, in

August 1993.
11. See Steven Lukes, *Marxism and Morality* (Clarendon Press, Oxford, 1985), Chs 2, 4 and 5.
12. The phrase 'critical criticism' is used by Marx in *The German Philosophy* to describe the stance of those Young Hegelians (notably the Bauer brothers) who viewed the task of philosophy as that of a permanent contemplative critique.

12. Simplicity and Complexity: On the Foundations of Marx's Methodology

1. For a non-technical account of developments in complexity theory, see M. M. Waldrop, *Complexity* (Penguin, Harmondsworth, 1993); or R. Lewin, *Complexity* (Dent, London, 1993). For a technical discussion, see G. Nicolis and I. Prigogine, *Exploring Complexity* (W. H. Freeman, New York, 1989); and D. L. Stein, *Lectures in the Sciences of Complexity* (Addison-Wesley, New York, 1989). For an intermediate alternative, see the excellent work by J. Cohen and I. Stewart, *The Collapse of Chaos* (Penguin, Harmondsworth, 1994).
2. Cohen and Stewart, *Collapse of Chaos*, p. 2.
3. Ibid., p. 7.
4. On these points, see Nicolis and Prigogine, *Exploring Complexity*, pp. 1–3; I. Prigogine and I. Stengers, *Order Out of Chaos* (Harper Collins, London, 1985), Chs 1–3.
5. On Kant's life and work, see E. Cassirer, *Kant's Life and Thought* (Yale University Press, New Haven, Conn., 1981). Kantian views on knowledge are elaborated in his first critique, *The Critique of Pure Reason* (Macmillan, London, 1929). On Hegel's critique of Kant, see G. W. F. Hegel, *Logic* (Clarendon Press, Oxford, 1873), pp. 69–71. Kant's third critique, *The Critique of Judgement* (Oxford University Press, Oxford, 1952), goes some way to overcome the dualism of his first critique and is thus closer to Hegel's later criticism. For a detailed discussion of all these points, see A. Shamsavari, *Dialectics and Social Theory* (Merlin Books, Braunton, 1991), Ch. 4.
6. On this issue, see V. Gerratana, 'Marx and Darwin', *New Left Review*, No. 82 (Nov.–Dec. 1973). For *Capital II*, see K. Marx, *Capital*, Vol. 2 (Penguin, Harmondsworth, 1978).
7. Prigogine discusses his pioneering work and its philosophical implications in I. Prigogine, *From Being to Becoming* (W. H. Freeman, New York, 1980). See also Nicolis and Prigogine, *Exploring Complexity*.
8. In *Complexity*, Waldrop gives an elaborate history of the work of the scientists associated with the Santa Fe Institute, as well as an account of how the institute began and how it works.
9. See P. W. Anderson, K. J. Arrow and D. Pines (eds), *The Economy as an Evolving Complex System* (Addison-Wesley, Redwood City, Cal., 1988); W. B. Arthur, 'Self-Reinforcing Mechanisms in Economics', in Anderson,

Arrow and Pines (eds), *The Economy*; W. B. Arthur,'Competing Technologies, Increasing Returns and Lock-in by Historical Events', *Economic Journal*, Vol. 99, No. 394 (March 1989); W. B. Arthur, 'Positive Feedbacks in the Economy', *Scientific American* (Feb. 1990); and P. Ormerod, *The Death of Economics* (Faber, London, 1994).

10. See a detailed discussion of these concepts in Cohen and Stewart, *Collapse of Chaos*, Ch. 13.
11. Nicolis and Prigogine, *Exploring Complexity*, p. 5.
12. Prigogine and Stengers, *Order Out of Chaos*, p. 14.
13. The following two sections draw freely on Chs 2, 5, 6 and 9 in Shamsavari, *Dialectics and Social Theory*, but there are many fresh departures from those chapters, including a new analysis of the formal and substantial aspects of S-concepts.
14. The first historicist approach is due to Engels: see F. Engels and K. Marx, 'A Contribution to the Critique of Political Economy' [1859], in K. Marx, *A Contribution to the Critique of Political Economy* (Progress Publishers, Moscow, 1970). A good example of the structuralist approach is B. Fine and L. Harris, *Rereading Capital* (Macmillan, London, 1979). The rationalist approach is originally due to Schmidt, Sombart and Rubin (see note 21 below). For a modern rationalist approach, see M. Morishima and G. Catephores, *Value, Exploitation and Growth* (McGraw-Hill, London, 1978).
15. This work by Marx represents an introduction to *Grundrisse* (Penguin, Harmondsworth, 1973) and dates back to 1857; hence the now generally accepted title.
16. Marx, *Grundrisse*, p. 102.
17. For a discussion of the literature on this issue, see Shamsavari, *Dialectics and Social Theory*, Ch. 2, Section C.
18. Ibid., Ch. 2.
19. See G. W. F. Hegel, *Science of Logic* (Allen & Unwin, London, 1969), p. 830.
20. K. Marx, *Theories of Surplus-value*, Part III (Progress Publishers, Moscow, 1971), pp. 112–13.
21. For a discussion of Schmidt and Sombart's views, see Engels' Supplement to Marx, *Capital*, Vol. 3 (Penguin, Harmondsworth, 1981). For Rubin's views, see I. I. Rubin, *Essays on Marx's Theory of Value* (Black & Red, Detroit, 1972), p. 255.
22. See Hegel, *Logic*, p. 244; and Shamsavari, *Dialectics and Social Theory*, Chs 2 and 4.
23. Marx, *Capital*, Vol. 3, pp. 445–6.
24. Hegel, *Science of Logic*, pp. 601–2.
25. Marx, *Grundrisse*, p. 85.
26. Ibid., pp. 85–6.
27. Ibid., p. 86.
28. Ibid.

29. Ibid., p. 87.
30. Ibid.
31. Ibid., pp. 88–9.
32. Ibid., p. 89.
33. Jean-Baptiste Say (1767–1832) formulated Say's law, according to which every producer brings his demand for goods to the market along with his supply and thus supply creates its own demand.
34. Marx, *Grundrisse*, p. 94.
35. Ibid.
36. Ibid., p. 96.
37. Ibid., pp. 96–7.
38. Ibid., p. 97.
39. Ibid.
40. Ibid., p. 99.
41. Prominent examples of this interpretation are G. Plekhanov, *The Development of the Monist View of History* (Foreign Languages Publishing House, Moscow, 1956); N. Bukharin, *Historical Materialism: A System of Sociology* (University of Michigan Press, Ann Arbor, 1969); and G. A. Cohen, *Karl Marx's Theory of History: A Defence* (Oxford University Press, Oxford, 1979). For critiques of this interpretation, see G. Lukacs, *Political Writings* (New Left Books, London, 1972); R. W. Miller, *Analyzing Marx* (Princeton University Press, Princeton, 1984), Ch. 5; and Shamsavari, *Dialectics and Social Theory*, Introduction.
42. For a fuller discussion, see Shamsavari, *Dialectics and Social Theory*, Ch. 9.
43. For a more detailed analysis, see ibid., Ch. 6.
44. K. Marx, *Capital*, Vol. 1 (Penguin, Harmondsworth, 1976), p. 645.
45. Ibid.
46. A prominent example of Ricardian Marxism is I. Steedman, *Marx after Sraffa* (New Left Books, London, 1977). Examples of analytical Marxism (inspired by Cohen, *Marx's Theory of History*) include J. Elster, *Making Sense of Marx* (Cambridge University Press, Cambridge, 1985); and J. Roemer (ed.), *Analytical Marxism* (Cambridge University Press, Cambridge, 1986).

Additional References

P. Davies (ed.), *The New Physics* (Cambridge University Press, Cambridge, 1989)
J. Gleick, *Chaos* (Sphere, London, 1987)
G. W. F. Hegel, *Philosophy of Right* (Oxford University Press, Oxford, 1952)
K. Marx and F. Engels, *Selected Works* (Progress Publishers, Moscow, 1969)

13. Hegemony and Politics

1. Lyubov Isaakovna Axelrode (pseudonym 'Orthodox') (1868–1946) was a philosopher and literary critic, and a Social Democrat. After the Second Congress of the Russian Social Democratic Party in 1903, she joined the Mensheviks and opposed Lenin's philosophical views.

2. Georgi Valantinovich Plekhanov (1856–1918) was a philosopher and literary critic, and the founder of the Marxist organization in Russia. He joined the Mensheviks in 1903. A collection of his works was published posthumously in three volumes under the title, *Selected Philosophical Works* (Progress Publishers, Moscow, 1976).

14. Marxism and Hope

1. Karl Marx and Friedrich Engels, *Manifesto of the Communist Party* (1848), trans. Samuel Moore, in Karl Marx, *Political Writings*, Vol. 1: *The Revolutions of 1848*, ed. by David Fernbach (Penguin, Harmondsworth, 1973), p. 79.
2. Karl Marx, 'Economic and Philosophical Manuscripts of 1844', in Karl Marx, *Early Writings*, trans. Rodney Livingstone and Gregor Benton, ed. by Lucio Colletti (Penguin, Harmondsworth, 1975), p. 348.
3. Karl Marx, *Grundrisse: Foundations of the Critique of Political Economy (draft)*, trans. Martin Nicolaus (Penguin, Harmondsworth, 1973), p. 105.
4. See, for example, W. G. Runciman, 'The "Triumph" of Capitalism as a Topic in the Theory of Social Selection', *New Left Review*, No. 210 (March/April 1995), pp. 33–47.
5. Jean-Paul Sartre, *Critique of Dialectical Reason*, Vol. 1 (1960), trans. Alan Sheridan-Smith, ed. by Jonathan Rée (New Left Books, London, 1976).
6. Immanuel Kant, 'An Old Question Raised Again: Is the Human Race Continually Progressing?' (1798), trans. Robert E. Anchor, in Immanuel Kant, *On History*, ed. by Lewis White Beck (Bobbs-Merrill, Indianapolis, 1963), p. 147. See also Larry Krasnoff, 'The Fact of Politics: History and Teleology in Kant', *European Journal of Philosophy*, Vol. 2, No. 1 (April 1994), pp. 22–40).

15. Fewer Illusions, More Humility: Marxism, Culture and Politics

1. *New York Review*, 24 March 1994, p. 26 (my italics).
2. *Guardian*, 1 Feb. 1995 (my italics).
3. Ernesto Laclau in Stuart Wilks (ed.), *Talking About Tomorrow: A New Radical Politics* (Pluto Press, London, 1993).
4. *Guardian*, 25 May 1995.
5. *Cabling London* (Greater London Council, London, 1982).
6. Raymond Williams, *Television: Technology and Cultural Form* (Fontana, London, 1974).
7. *Cabling London*, p. 7.
8. Abdullahi an-Na'im, 'What Do We Mean by Universal?', *Index on Censorship*, Vol. 23 (Sept./Oct. 1994), p. 126.
9. See 'File on Algeria', *Index on Censorship*, Vol. 23 (Sept./Oct. 1994), pp. 135–70.
10. Karim Alrawi, 'Goodbye to the Enlightenment', *Index on Censorship*, Vol. 23 (May/June 1994), pp. 112ff.

Abbreviations

CCP	Chinese Communist Party
CPSU	Communist Party of the Soviet Union
DFLP	Democratic Front for the Liberation of Palestine
EC	European Community
EMS	European Monetary System
ERM	Exchange Rate Mechanism
EU	European Union
FDI	Foreign Direct Investment
G5	Group of 5 [countries]
G7	Group of 7 [countries]
GATT	General Agreement on Tariffs and Trade
GCC	Gulf Cooperation Council
GDP	Gross domestic product
GDR	German Democratic Republic
GNP	Gross national product
GS	Gold Standard
ICP	Iraqi Communist Party
ILE	Inter-Linked Economy
IMF	International Monetary Fund
IT	Information technology
JCP	Jordanian Communist Party
LDC	Less Developed Country
MDC	More Developed Country
MNC	Multinational Corporation
NAFTA	North American Free Trade Area

NEP	New Economic Policy [USSR]
NIC	Newly Industrializing Country
OECD	Organisation of Economic Cooperation and Development
OPEC	Organization of Petroleum Exporting Countries
PCP	Palestinian Communist Party
PDRY	People's Democratic Republic of Yemen [South Yemen]
PFLP	Popular Front for the Liberation of Palestine
PPP	Palestinian People's [Sha'b] Party
RSFSR	Russian Soviet Federated Socialist Republic
SOAS	School of Oriental and African Studies, University of London
TNC	Transnational Corporation
UK	United Kingdom
US	United States
USSR	Union of Soviet Socialist Republics

Contributors

'AMIR ABDULLAH has been a leading Marxist politician and theoretician of the Iraqi Communist Party, and has held leading positions in the ICP Politbureau and Central Committee. He was Iraqi Minister of State from 1972 to 1978. Abdullah is the author of several works on Marxist politics and the new world economic order.

M. P. COWEN is Reader in Economics at London's Guildhall University. His books include *Doctrines of Development* (with R. W. Shenton); and *Indigenous Capital in Kenya* (with Scott MacWilliam).

SAMI DANIEL is Associate Dean of the Faculty of Human Sciences at Kingston University, UK. He specializes in the economics of organization and the economics of strategy.

MAURICE GODELIER is Director of Studies in Anthropology at the Ecole des Hautes Etudes en Sciences Sociales, Paris. Among his numerous publications are *Transitions et Subordinations au Capitalisme*; *The Mental and the Material*; and *Rationalité et Irrationalité en Economie*.

FRED HALLIDAY is Professor of International Relations at the London School of Economics. His books include *Arabia without Sultans*; *Iran: Dictatorship and Development*; and *Islam and the myth of Confrontation*. Several of his books have been published in Arabic.

PAUL HIRST is Professor of Politics at Birkbeck College, University of London. He is the author of *Durkheim, Bernard and Epistemology*; *Pre-Capitalist Modes of Production* (with Barry Hindess); and a forthcoming book on globalization.

FALEH A. JABAR is a London-based Iraqi author and researcher. His works in Arabic include *Religious Thought in Iraq*; *Hypothesis on Socialism*; *The Structure of Islamic Thought* (essays); *The Classical Roots of the Theory of Alienation*; and *State and Civil Society in Iraq*. He has also translated *Das Kapital* into Arabic.

ERNESTO LACLAU is a political theorist and Director of the Centre for Theoretical Studies in the Humanities and Social Sciences, University of Essex, UK. He is the author of *Politics and Ideology in Marxist Theory* (with Chantal Mouffe); *Hegemony and Socialist Strategy*; and numerous essays on political theory and socialist politics.

JOHN MEPHAM is Reader in English at Kingston University, UK. He has been a member of the national Committee for European Nuclear Disarmament and of the Radical Philosophy Group. In the 1970s he co-edited the 4-volume *Issues in Marxist Philosophy*.

JOHNATHAN RÉE teaches Philosophy at Middlesex University, UK. He was actively involved with the magazine *Radical Philosophy* from its foundation in 1972 until 1994. His publications include *Proletarian Philosophers*; and *Philosophical Tales*. He is currently working on a book entitled *Subjectivity and the Human Voice*.

ALI SHAMSAVARI is Senior Lecturer in Economics at Kingston University, UK. He is the author of *Dialectics and Social Theory: The Logic of Capital*.

MAHIR SHARIF is a leading Palestinian historian and activist, now based in Damascus. His numerous works in Arabic include: *The Communist International and the National Problem in Palestine, 1919–1948*; *On Communist Thought in Palestine*; and *A Search for an Entity: Palestinian Political Thought, 1908–1993*.

R. W. SHENTON is Associate Professor in the Department of History, Queen's University, Canada. He is the author of *Development of Capitalism in Northern Nigeria*; and *Doctrines of Development* (with M. P. Cowen).

KATE SOPER is a Senior Lecturer in Philosophy at the University of North London. Her publications include: *On Human Needs*; *Humanism and Anti-Humanism*; *Troubled Pleasures*; and *What is Nature? Culture, Politics and the Non-Human*. Soper has been associated with the *New Left Review* and is a longstanding member of the Editorial Collective of *Radical Philosophy*.

SUSAN SAUNDERS VOSPER is a Lecturer in Politics at Birkbeck College, University of London. She has contributed to *Questions in Soviet Government and Politics*; *Defending Politics—Bernard Crick and Pluralism*; and articles and reviews in *The Journal of Communist Studies* [now *Communist and Transition Studies*], *Soviet Studies* [now *Europe and Asia Studies*], *Political Quarterly* and *Political Studies*.

Index

Note: Page number followed by 'n' indicates a footnote.